W9-DJI-771

TROJAN HORSE

This book is dedicated in loving memory
of my father Ivor James

Other books by Barrie G. James:

The Future of the Multinational Pharmaceutical Industry to 1990

The Marketing of Generic Drugs

Business Wargames

TROJAN HORSE

The Ultimate Japanese Challenge
to Western Industry

Barrie G. James

MERCURY BOOKS
Published by W.H. Allen & Co. Plc

Copyright © 1989 Barrie G. James

All rights reserved. No part of this publication may be reproduced, stored in a retrieval system, or transmitted in any form or by any means, electronic, mechanical, photocopying, recording, or otherwise without the prior permission of the publishers.

First published in 1989
by the Mercury Books Division of
W.H. Allen & Co. Plc
Sekforde House,
175–9 St. John Street,
London EC1V 4LL

Set in Meridien by Phoenix Photosetting, Chatham, Kent
**Printed and bound in Great Britain by
Anchor Press Ltd, Tiptree, Essex**

This book is sold subject to the condition that it shall not, by way of trade or otherwise, be lent, re-sold, hired out or otherwise circulated without the publisher's prior consent in any form of binding or cover other than that in which it is published and without a similar condition including this condition being imposed upon the subsequent purchaser.

British Library Cataloguing in Publication Data

James, Barrie G.
    Trojan horse : the ultimate Japanese
    challenge to western industry.
    1. Western Europe. Manufacturing
    industries.
    Foreign investment by Japanese
    companies
    I. Title
    332.6'7352'04

    ISBN 1–85251–091–9

ACKNOWLEDGEMENTS

I am extremely grateful for the assistance of a number of people in Europe and the United States who have contributed a great deal of time and effort to help make *Trojan Horse* a reality.

Akio Tanaka, Deputy Director-General of Jetro in London, and Philippa Thorne and Kathryn Brennan of Jetro's Research Department provided much of the background information on Japanese manufacturing investments in Europe. On the other side of the Atlantic, Susan McKnight of the Japan Economic Institute in Washington D.C. provided similar data for the US. These two contributions were of great value in helping to produce a balanced view of the overall size, direction and depth of Japanese investments in the West.

A debt of gratitude is due to William Lyons in Washington D.C., and especially to John Lock and Cheryl Hetrick of Georgetown University's School of Business. John and Cheryl's patience and skills in obtaining data from the labyrinthine US government sources in Washington were essential contributions.

Edward Lincoln of the Foreign Policy Studies Program at the Brookings Institution, also in Washington D.C., shared with me his thoughts on the long-term implications of Japanese manufacturing investments in the US. Malcolm Trevor, Director of the Japan Industrial Studies Programme at the Policy Studies Institute in London and Chairman of the Euro-Japanese Management Studies Association, generously shared his time and knowledge enlightening me on current European concerns and Japanese investment policies. Ed and Malcolm's insightful comments were invaluable in helping me to broaden the scope of the project and identify new areas for research.

At the European Community in Brussels a number of people made valuable contributions to *Trojan Horse*. Brendon Cardiff discussed with

v

me his ideas on the broad issues facing the EEC in terms of competitiveness and technology and their relationship with Japanese manufacturing investments, while Monika Frisken kindly supplied me with detailed historical data on the EEC–Japan trade balance. Alaistair Stewart of the Trade Policy section of the Directorate-General for External Relations made a vital contribution by outlining the development and application of European Community policies and practices on Japanese assembly operations and briefed me on the key findings of the major Community actions on 'screwdriver' plants in 1988.

In Paris, François Pham of the OECD's Scientific, Technological and Industrial Indicators Division kindly gave me new and unpublished information on world trends in R & D investment and trade which updated earlier OECD reports.

In Switzerland, Kevin Kearney and Alan Mortby at the Bank of International Settlements in Basle generously provided me with detailed information from the BIS's formidable data bank on currency performance, and Michael Finger of GATT in Geneva brought me up to date with statistical data on world trade.

I am also indebted to Jonathan Morris of the Cardiff Business School at UWIST and Peter Dicken of Manchester University who gave me access to their research on Japanese manufacturing investments and to Barry Wilkinson and Nick Oliver, also at UWIST, whose insightful comments were invaluable.

Since I have entered the information age firmly clutching a hand-powered pencil it was left to Regina Djabarzadegan, who, with continued good humour, deciphered my hieroglyphics and turned them into a readable draft. Jo Münch and Yvonne Irmak burnt the midnight oil and did a splendid job putting together the final manuscript.

Last but by no means least my wife Mary gave an irritable author the encouragement and support necessary to develop, research and write *Trojan Horse*.

While all of these people were instrumental in helping me to complete *Trojan Horse*, I have the sole responsibility for its content and views.

BARRIE G. JAMES

Basle, Switzerland

INTRODUCTION

'Most Japanese products are distributed through companies with such proud names as Thomson-Brandt, Telefunken, Saba, Blaupunkt, to name just a few. They are the Trojan Horses of the Japanese industry. – *Dr. Max Grundig, 1984*

Twelve years from now it is quite possible that the world's fourth and fifth largest industrial powers behind the US, Japan and the EEC will not be Russia and China, but Japanese industry in the US and in the EEC.

Déjà vu? The similarity with Jean-Jacques Servan-Schreiber's opening sentence in his best-seller *The American Challenge* is deliberate. Exactly twenty years ago Servan-Schreiber warned that the growing US industrial presence in Europe was a major threat to the social, economic, political and technological future of Europe.

Europe was 'colonized' by US multinationals, but the effect of US manufacturing investments over the last twenty years has been more positive than negative. US firms came to terms with European sensitivities, not least as a result of the controversy created by *The American Challenge* and adopted a responsive attitude to their investments, business policies and practices. They were also quick to spot the advantages of 'Europeanizing' their presence. By creating fully integrated manufacturing, developing local suppliers, building R&D facilities, using Europe as an export base for Africa, Eastern Europe and the Middle East and by transferring both managerial skills and technology, they helped to accelerate the post-war development of European industry and made a net contribution to Europe's economy.

Twenty years later Europe and the US face a similar challenge:

Japanese manufacturing investments in both continents. Ironically those very conditions which provided the US with its comparative advantage making it such a formidable competitor to Europe in the 1960s – access to large amounts of low-cost capital, a strong currency, new technology and the ability to transform raw science into low-cost and high-quality marketable products through superior managerial and organizational skills – have been, or are in the process of being, transferred to Japan. Today the prime movers in global business are Japan's financial, technological and managerial muscle and the US and the EEC are wallowing in the wake of Japan's industrial slipstream.

Japanese investments in the West have been growing through the last decade. Initially much of this was in real estate and government and corporate bonds and buying into banking, insurance and other financial services. In a volte-face Japanese investment in the mid-1980s shifted rapidly towards building up productive capacity in the form of assembly plants in the US and in the EEC.

Trojan Horse focuses on the many problems created by these assembly plants and on ways that the West can channel these investments into more productive contributions to its reindustrialization.

The book is divided into seven parts. Parts 1 and 2 identify the decline in the value of the dollar and increasing protectionism in the West as the key forces driving Japan's move away from exporting finished products to 'localizing' imports through assembly plants in the West.

Part 3 shows how these driving forces fit into Japan's shift in industrial strategy as it moves to become *the* globalized player in the world economy. It examines the changing role of manufacturing investments, the emphasis on technology, the development of global supply networks and the changes going on in managerial style as Japan moves downstream from an export to a global manufacturing economy.

Part 4 examines the many and complex implications of Japanese assembly plants in the West from the Japanese and Western perspectives. It looks at their effects on the transfer of managerial and labour skills and technology, at the quality and quantity of employment that they create, and their effects on the trade balance and on Western economic structures and competitiveness.

Part 5 focuses attention on the crisis in Western competitiveness. It shows not only how government policy, or non-policy, has contributed to the decline but also the seminal effect of mediocre management on the erosion of Western competitiveness.

Part 6 builds on the previous chapters, identifies the convenient excuses being used to avoid confronting the issue and presents a series of approaches which can be used to channel Japanese investments into patterns which make real economic and social contributions to the West.

Part 7 concludes *Trojan Horse*. It describes why forceful approaches are not being taken and raises issues which go far beyond the short term and question the very future of an industrialized West, which continues to ignore the Trojan Horse effect of Japanese low value-added assembly plants.

Trojan Horse is not written as a stereotype exercise in Japan 'bashing' but to place Japanese inward investments in assembly plants in perspective and identify the few benefits and many problems they create. *Trojan Horse* is designed to sensitize decision-makers in the West to the risks of ignoring the threats of unconditionally embracing the current low-value-added content of Japanese assembly plants and to stimulate a new dialogue both within the West and with Japan to improve the quality of inward investment.

CONTENTS

PART 1

THE PRICE OF SUCCESS

1

THE PHOENIX FACTOR

In forty years Japan has developed the world's most dynamic economy. Japan's rise from the ashes of defeat in 1945 to its position second only to the US as an economic superpower within four decades has been spectacular.

With little usable land, high population density, limited natural resources, virtually no proprietary technology and a devastated industrial base Japan had only one option in the late 1940s: to pursue a deliberate economic policy of self-interest to survive and grow[1]. Given Japan's circumstances, the only viable policy was to import essential raw materials, add value and export finished product while limiting other imports. By continuously reinvesting the proceeds of this export-driven system Japan could rapidly develop the infrastructure necessary to create and sustain a modern industrial society essential to maintain headway in a world dominated by the industrialized resource-rich Western nations.

Japan's economic policy was successful not due to its inherent pragmatism but rather because it was supported by a set of well integrated and superbly implemented trade, industrial and business strategies. These not only reinforced each other but also supported the thrust of Japan's economic drive to export and to develop its industrial base to compete effectively on a global scale.

Japan's trade strategies were carefully designed to produce a positive net economic effect. On the export side of the equation the policy was *expansionist* – the strategy was designed to take full advantage of the opportunities presented by a world trade system led by the US which was dedicated to the principles of free trade. The export strategy was supported by a set of long-term government programmes. For example, maintaining an artificially low yen value against the major

3

Western currencies, providing liberal credit and tax incentives for exporters and, through diplomatic initiatives, securing and maintaining access to Western markets by diffusing objections to its aggressive export practices. There were all instrumental in furthering Japan's expansionist trade strategy.

On the import side of the trade equation the policy was *exclusionary*. Apart from essential raw materials, food and technology few other imports were permitted. A network of controls limiting access to foreign exchange together with tariff and non-tariff barriers effectively stifled volume imports. Those few foreign capital investments which were allowed were strictly controlled through limits on the repatriation of profits, minority holdings and enforced technology transfer to Japanese firms. These restrictive import policies protected Japanese firms from foreign competition in Japan and gave them the time to develop the critical mass necessary to compete on a world scale.

The restrictions on imports and on inward capital investment in Japan forced foreign firms to license or at best form joint ventures with Japanese firms to get limited access to the Japanese market. As a result Japanese firms were able to obtain the latest Western technology at minimal cost. This provided the push to modernize Japan's industrial base and the pull to adapt continuously to new technology to move up the value-added chain.

However, Japan's economic policy was far more structured than a set of coordinated export–import strategies suggest. Capital controls were used to prevent Japanese money from leaving Japan and to help fund domestic industrial development. This avoided heavy borrowing on international capital markets and the resulting interest penalties. Long-term tax incentives were used to promote continuous industrial reinvestment to upgrade plant and equipment and to develop high levels of consumer saving. This resulted in a very large proportion of GNP devoted to industrial investment and a low proportion spent on high-value consumer purchase. To depress domestic consumption in favour of exports consumer products were highly priced and taxed and credit was both limited and expensive.

Literally Japan's expansionist and exclusionary trade strategies enabled Japan simultaneously to 'eat' and 'have' its economic cake – at the expense of the rest of the world's trading nations.

Japan's industrial strategies were designed to ensure that Japanese industry continuously moved up the value-added chain to maximise the national return on investment.

The success of Japan's industrial strategies was based on creating a mutuality of interest among the key players. Government, industry and labour in Japan developed a tightly knit relationship spearheaded by MITI, the Ministry of Finance and the Economic Planning Agency. These government agencies used 'administrative guidance' – powers of persuasion backed by financial (taxes, guarantees and subsidies) and legislative (cartels, import restrictions and technology acquisition) muscle to ensure that industrial strengths were matched to opportunities created by technology change and customer needs on a global scale. This helped move Japanese firms in sequence into investment patterns in plant, equipment and technology to meet changing market demands and to improve the value-added component of Japan's industrial output.

In the early 1950s the focus was on labour-intensive industries like cutlery, textiles and toys. In the 1960s the spotlight changed to accumulating competence in the heavy industries – chemicals, coal, shipbuilding and steel – to develop the key building blocks for a modern industrial infrastructure and to mass-producing simple consumer products. By the 1970s the target moved to achieving strong capabilities in precision instrumentation such as cameras and machine tools and in complex consumer products like cars, electronics and pharmaceuticals. In the 1980s the emphasis shifted again – to developing world-class leadership positions in advanced electronics, aerospace, biotechnology, computers and other knowledge-intensive industries (see Figure 1.1).

This continuous change in industrial emphasis moved Japanese companies out of decaying businesses *before* their competitive advantage eroded. By funding disinvestment, by underwriting the search for new technologies to develop new industries, by creating cartels to gain expertise and the scale of production necessary to compete effectively in world markets the Japanese government acted as both an industrial paymaster and as a competitive arbitrator. Invariably the Japanese government initiated restructuring while the business was still growing, which reduced the economic and social impact of running down industries.

The cumulative effect of these long-term government policies was an unprecedented level of cohesiveness in industrial development which helped to adapt continuously Japan's industrial base to improve its competitive profile.

Most evaluations of Japan's industrial success focus on the use of

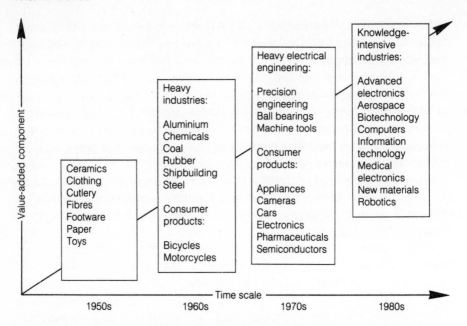

Figure 1.1. Japan's integrated industrial policy was designed to move companies in a timed sequence to meet national goals of improving the value-added component of Japanese industrial output.

efficient industrial policies and miss the valuable contribution made by Japanese companies. Japanese firms were quick to grasp the fact that national economic goals designed to continuously improve Japan's competitiveness were largely the same as their own interests and objectives – securing and maintaining profitable positions in world markets.

The logic of Japan's economic policy underpinned by effective trade and industrial strategies and supported by administrative guidance persuaded most Japanese firms to follow national goals of maximising exports and continuously upgrading the economy to a higher value-added profile.

Japanese companies, although helped by favourable government policies, were also supported by a responsive labour environment. Weak unions and a highly educated and disciplined work force which accepted the necessity of long periods of austerity in the national interest helped companies to implement government industrial policies[2]. Companies built on these advantages by using effective labour practices and by creating efficient management techniques

6

such as inventory and quality control procedures to improve productivity and quality and by focusing their organizations on better meeting customer needs.

Japan's 40-year phoenix-like rise from the ashes of defeat to industrial superpower status was less of a miracle and more the result of single-mindedness, long-term vision, effective cooperation between government, industry and labour and efficient implementation. Binding this together was a strong sense of national purpose and the ability of the bureaucracy to mobilise a relatively disinterested consensus around a view of what is in the national interest[3]. By leveraging a favourable set of circumstances to the hilt Japan built both an economy and an industrial base which by the mid-1980s was second only to that of the US.

2

THE GAME PLAN

In the early post-war period Japanese companies quickly picked up the fact that the cornerstones of successful business strategies were effective product and market policies – essentially selling the right product to the right people. Almost without exception, Japanese firms have used a strategy based on a formula of high-volume, low-price, high-quality products with mass customer appeal to successfully penetrate world markets[4].

Low prices require low-cost manufacturing capability. To achieve penetration prices Japanese firms concentrated on developing volume and cost leadership positions by centralizing production in large, highly automated continuous process plants built well beyond domestic needs to service world-wide demand. By continuously upgrading their manufacturing plants Japanese firms were able to develop steep cost curves for their products. To reduce costs further, product designs and components were standardized and model proliferation limited. As Japanese labour costs began to rise in the mid-1970s the abandonment in 1971 of fixed exchange rates began to rob Japan of its artificially low yen value. This, together with the high cost of imported oil caused by the twin OPEC price increases, forced many firms to switch the production of labour-intensive low-value-added components and assembly to affiliates and contractors in the newly industrialized countries (NICs).

Low costs and low prices were only one facet of product policy. Japanese companies developed a leadership position in quality control world-wide. High quality was built in to products to reduce the need for after-sale service and to create customer satisfaction. Since the initial strategy was to penetrate the low end of the market and then move up-market with more expensive products to capture higher margins, the focus on

8

quality helped to create and develop a sustainable customer franchise.

Obviously identifying the right markets and maintaining access to them was central to the success of the game plan. Given a strategy based on continually moving up-market with more expensive products, the only viable targets for Japanese companies were the OECD nations – a group of countries with developed economies, stable politics and sophisticated customers with high levels of disposable income. Consequently Japanese firms shifted their emphasis away from the less developed countries (LDCs) and increasingly concentrated their efforts on OECD countries, focusing mainly on the US and the EEC.

This targetting proved to be highly successful. By 1986 Japan was responsible for 60 per cent of all OECD exports of telecommunications equipment, 25 per cent of all car exports and 24 per cent of all office and data processing equipment – the majority of which were destined for the OECD nations[5].

The commitment of the West to free trade and a general reluctance to react forcefully to Japan's expansionist and exclusionary trade practices provided Japan with a unique opportunity to pursue a mercantilist economic policy with little fear of retaliation.

Western trade policies were governed by the attitudes of the US and the Europeans. The US believed that to develop a peaceful political order it was essential to build a stable and prosperous economic order. Give Japan's proximity to the USSR and to China, US political policy was designed to ensure that Japan had a flourishing economy. Since the European countries were economically more dependent on foreign trade than the US they were conscious of the need to avoid sanctions which could damage their income from trade. This attitude still prevails in Europe. Although the German market was suffering from the diversion of Japanese car exports from the US in 1985 and 1986, the German government was reluctant to impose protectionism since it exported more than half of its total output and stood to lose more than it would gain in a trade war. In 1985 German car exports were worth $28 billion while imports accounted for only $6 billion[6].

The general lack of retaliatory duties, tariffs and volume limitations by the West created very little pressure on Japanese companies to invest in manufacturing plants in their major export markets. Diplomatic pressures on Japan to reciprocate and open up its home market were poorly coordinated and weakly applied by Japan's key Western trade partners. This virtually assured Japan free access to Western markets and largely limited competition in Japan to Japanese firms

9

who, through fierce competition, were able to eliminate marginal performers and develop the critical mass necessary to compete on a global scale.

To resource-poor Japanese firms emerging from the painful post-war reconstruction programme viable business strategies meant approaches which minimised risk. Traditional market entry strategies included building manufacturing plants, entering into joint ventures with local partners, licensing out products and exporting finished products. Japanese firms used all of these approaches to varying degrees to build strong market positions in the West. However, due to a general aversion to risk Japanese firms largely avoided direct investment in manufacturing facilities outside Japan. Exceptions to the rule were few and were mainly responses to specific acts of protectionism and, in a few cases, to market development strategies pursued by a small number of Japanese companies.

The UK's Voluntary Restraint Agreement (VRA) on colour television imports in 1973, for example, was the trigger for a number of Japanese assembly plants. Sony in 1974 was followed by Matsushita and Mitsubishi in 1979 and by Sharp in 1985. Similarly, the US Orderly Marketing Agreement (OMA) on colour televisions in 1977 was anticipated by Sony in 1974 and followed by Toshiba (1978) and Sharp (1979). Matsushita and Sanyo made acquisitions of Quasar (1975) and Warwick (1976), respectively, as alternative forms of direct investment to preserve market access.

In contrast, direct investment as a deliberate market development strategy was pursued by few firms. YKKs' policy to build wholly owned manufacturing plants in almost all markets in which it operated was designed to provide the flexibility to adapt its zipper and fastener products to local customer needs[7]. YKKs' first plant was built in the US in 1974 and in Europe, in the Netherlands, in 1964. European plants followed in West Germany (1967), the UK and Italy (1970), Belgium and Spain (1971), France (1972), Austria (1977), Denmark (1982) and Greece (1984)[8]. Similarly, Honda's first motorcycle assembly plants outside Japan were built in Belgium in 1967 and in the US in 1973. By 1984 Honda had 44 motorcycle assembly plants in 30 countries[9].

While joint ventures with local companies reduced the financial risk their main attraction to Japanese firms in the 1960s and 1970s was a reduction in the level of *market* risk: that is, using the joint venture partner to transfer its down-market skills – knowledge of the market, distribution system and customers – to provide a firm base for future direct manufacturing investment.

However, few joint ventures were created in the West because of Japanese and Western perceptions that the other partner had relatively little to offer. Among those few joint ventures created most were not lasting successes as the Japanese quickly came to the conclusion that they could do far better on their own. For example, the joint ventures between Hitachi and GEC and Toshiba with Rank to assemble colour televisions in the UK in the late 1970s failed in both cases largely due to differences in objectives between the partners[10]. Kawasaki's sixteen-year association with Unimation in robotics in the US is one of the rare exceptions to the rule[11].

Licensing-out strategies were not widely pursued by Japanese companies through the late 1970s for the simple reason that Japan's stock of innovation was relatively low and its companies had developed few innovative products and processes. As Japan's technology base expanded the level of licensing out to Western firms increased. However, the number of agreements were limited for several reasons. If the market opportunity existed or could be created Japanese firms obviously preferred to market the finished product themselves and technology transfer agreements were perceived by the Japanese as tantamount to mortgaging their future. Those licences that were granted fell into two categories: first those where the Japanese company licensed its product on a quid pro quo basis for the rights to a Western product in Japan; and second those where the Japanese partner decided that the investment was too high and the Market too complex – for example, prescription drugs – and was not in a position to exploit market opportunities fully.

Almost all Japanese companies used exports of finished product sourced in Japan as the cornerstone of their strategy to build strong market positions in major Western markets. Exports offered the best of all worlds to Japanese companies. By centralizing production in Japan they were able to concentrate on economies of scale in production to leverage costs and quality to maximise customer satisfaction – the key elements in their competitive strategy. This approach avoided the risks of penetrating new markets – high entry costs in fixed local investment, unfamiliar market conditions and the transfer of valuable production and process technology and know-how.

Japanese firms used two routes to develop their finished product export business: Original Equipment Manufacture (OEM) and branded products.

OEM strategies were widely used to penetrate both the US and the European markets. The major benefits of OEM strategies are the concentration on volume, essential to pursue cost leadership, and the opportunity to gain valuable market experience with very limited exposure to market risk. For example, Japanese computer firms lacked the direct sales and service operations vital to sell large mainframe computers in competition with the world leader, IBM. OEM strategies by Fujitsu, Hitachi, Mitsubishi and NEC were designed to use third-party Western firms with established sales and service networks as surrogates to compete more effectively against IBM[12]. The main OEM attraction for Western firms was low-cost, high-quality products from reliable suppliers which helped to fill gaps in their product line.

While early OEM deals were often centred on component supply Japanese firms quickly moved up the value-added chain from simple bicycles and transistor radios to more complex and sophisticated products such as cars, computers and machine tools. Table 1.1 illustrates some of the OEM arrangements between leading Japanese and Western companies.

Table 1.1. Selected Western OEM Agreements with Japanese Suppliers

Product	Japanese supplier	Western recipient
Camcorders	Matsushita	Kodak (US)
Cash registers	Omron	Sweda (Sweden)
Computers (portable)	Kyocera	Tandy (US)
	Mitsui	Kaypro (US)
(mainframe)	Fujitsu	Amdahl (US), ICL (UK), Siemens (BRD)
	Hitachi	BASF (BRD), National Advanced Systems (US), Olivetti (Italy)
	Mitsubishi	Sperry (US)
	NEC	Bull (France), Honeywell (US)
Copiers	Canon	Olivetti (Italy)
	Fuji	Rank Xerox (UK)
	Minolta	IBM (US)
	Mita	Develop (BRD), Gestetner (US)
	Ricoh	Nashua (Europe), Savin (US)
	Konica	Olivetti (Italy)
Diesel engines	Shibaura	Perkins (UK)

Product	Japanese supplier	Western recipient
Farm and construction machinery	Kawasaki	Aveling Barford (UK)
	Komatsu	Int. Harvester & Bucyrus Erie (US) and Lancer Boss (UK)
	Hitachi	Fiatallis (Italy)
Film	Konica	Fotomat (US)
	Fuji	Migros (CH)
Cars	Mazda	Ford (Australia, US)
	Mitsubishi	Chrysler (US)
	Toyota	General Motors (US)
Machine tools	Murata	Bendix (US)
	Okuma	Houdaille (US)
	Yasuda	Bridgeport (UK)
Switchgear	Mitsubishi	Northern Engineering (UK)
Televisions	NEC	Magnavox (US)
	Sanyo	Sears, Roebuck (US)
	Sharp	Montgomery Ward (US)
	Toshiba	Sears, Roebuck (US)
VCRs	Matsushita	GE, Magnavox, RCA, Sears, Roebuck & J.C. Penny (US), EMI/Thorn (UK), Telefunken (BRD), Thomson (France), Saba (Norway) & Granada (Spain)

Significantly, with the exception of retailers, most of the Western firms marketing Japanese OEM products 'rebadged' under their own brand names were high-technology companies with extensive R&D facilities and not small local firms. While many of the OEM arrangements were originally designed to plug holes in product lines, others covered huge gaps in the basic product range of Western firms and appeared to be more the product of desperation than of careful attention to tactical weaknesses[13].

Branded product strategies, where the Japanese company's products were sold under its own brand name, were widely used to penetrate Western markets. The main advantage of branding was to establish a franchise direct with the end customer and to capture the higher margins available to branded products. Initially local marketing was often handled by one of the Japanese *sogo shosha* (trading houses)

13

or by independent distributors. Later, as the business developed, the Japanese firms' wholly owned marketing and distribution organizations took over these tasks to increase downstream control. By 1984 Japanese investments in wholesaling alone in the US exceeded the entire value of all US investments in Japan and managed at least 70 per cent of all Japanese exports to the US. This vertical integration, combining manufacturing, distribution and selling activities, provided a very high degree of control over the marketing of Japanese products and complemented Japanese finished product export strategies.

The decision for OEM or branded product strategies depended largely on the policies of individual Japanese firms. Honda and Sony, technology leaders, have steadfastly refused OEM business while Matsushita, Mitsubishi and Nissan had policies incorporating both OEM and branded sales. Other companies who initially entered the market as OEM suppliers, such as Sanyo and Sharp in the US, later moved into branded sales. In most cases initial OEM strategies which let Western firms assume early market risks provided Japanese companies with the opportunity to build their own brand entries from a secure OEM base. By the mid-1970s Japanese products were widely perceived by Western consumers as being more durable, of higher quality and greater value for money than those of many Western companies. By 1980 almost all Japanese producers of finished products were obtaining the bulk of their business in the West from branded rather than OEM sales.

3

WINNING WAYS

By any measure Japan's post-war economic policy has been remarkably successful. Japanese companies achieved leadership positions in many industries, and by the early 1980s Japanese firms dominated the world market for a wide range of industrial and consumer products (Figure 3.1).

These successes in world markets have transformed Japan's economic position. In 30 years Japan's exports grew twice as fast as industrial production – from 9 per cent in 1955 to 19 per cent in 1981 – and tripled in the same period as a percentage of GNP from 7 to 20.2 per cent[14]. As a result Japan increased its share of world trade largely at the expense of the US and, if intra-EEC trade is excluded, also the EEC (Figure 3.2).

Japan's increasing share of world trade, together with its exclusionary import policies, translated into growing trade surpluses in the 1980s while the US and the EEC began to record growing trade deficits with Japan (Figure 3.3).

The power of business support for Japan's economic policy based heavily on export-driven development strategies, backed up by effective product and market policies, provided Japan with a continuous strong economic growth from the mid-1960s. Between 1967 and 1971 Japan's exports increased from $10 to $24 billion – an average annual increase of more than 20 per cent. Exports increased steeply for high value-added products: cars from 370,000 to 2.4 million units, television sets from 2.7 to 6.3 million and tape recorders from 8 to 22 million units. As a consequence Japan's GNP growth significantly outpaced those of the EEC and, with the exception of 1983 and 1984, the US (Figure 3.4).

This continuous, strong growth coupled to favourable currency

15

Market segments   World market share (%) 1984

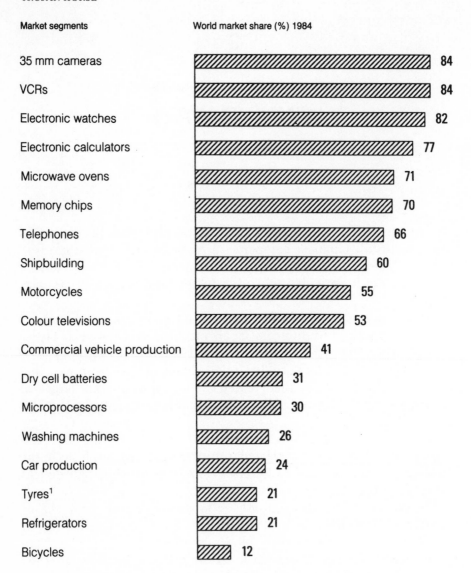

Market segments	World market share (%) 1984
35 mm cameras	84
VCRs	84
Electronic watches	82
Electronic calculators	77
Microwave ovens	71
Memory chips	70
Telephones	66
Shipbuilding	60
Motorcycles	55
Colour televisions	53
Commercial vehicle production	41
Dry cell batteries	31
Microprocessors	30
Washing machines	26
Car production	24
Tyres[1]	21
Refrigerators	21
Bicycles	12

Figure 3.1. Japan's highly effective export-based marketing strategies, coupled to high-quality, low-cost products, rapidly secured significant market shares in many product categories on a world basis.

[1] Includes Dunlop

Source: *Financial Times* and *Fortune* (various issues).

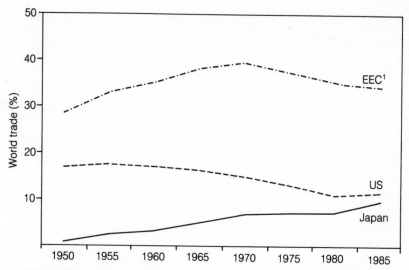

Figure 3.2. Japan's increase in its share of world trade was made at the expense of both the US and the EEC.

[1] Includes intra-EEC trade.

Source: International Financial Statistics, *IMF Yearbook 1985*, International Monetary Fund, Washington, D.C., 1986.

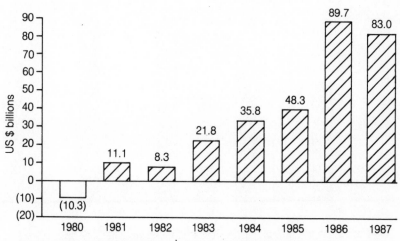

Figure 3.3. The increase in Japan's share of world trade and a restrictive import policy directly translated into growing trade surpluses in the 1980s.

Source: GATT, Geneva, September 1988

17

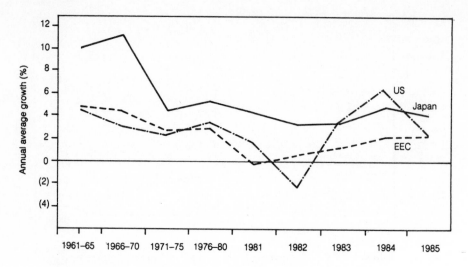

Figure 3.4. Japan's growth rate in real gross national product has consistently outpaced that of the US and the EEC.

Source: Economic Report of the President, Government Printing Office, Washington, D.C., 1986.

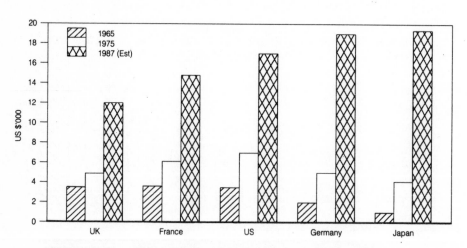

Figure 3.5. As a result of Japan's continual increase in GNP and favourable currency swings Japan now enjoys the highest gross domestic product on a per capita basis of the leading industrial nations (current prices and exchange rates).

Source: IMF, Eurostat (*Financial Times*, 13 May 1987).

swings in 1985–1987 enabled Japan to attain the highest per capita level of GNP in both growth and absolute terms among the leading industrial nations in 1987 (Figure 3.5).

While Japan had largely achieved its economic policy goals of creating higher standards of living by expanding its economy through the development of its industry to world standards of competitiveness, this success has produced a growing level of criticism from its main trading partners. The inability of the Western companies to counter the loss of their export markets in Africa, Asia and Latin America, to contain the erosion of their domestic markets by Japanese firms and to penetrate the Japanese domestic market began to create major problems in Japanese–Western trade relations during the late 1970s and early 1980s.

4

TRADE FRICTION

In market after market and country after country Japanese firms have out-produced, out-marketed and out-serviced their Western competitors – and brought new meaning to the words 'customer satisfaction'. However, the unbroken growth of Japan's business successes in the West, together with the inability of Western companies to penetrate the Japanese market, inevitably created a backlash of protectionism.

Trade friction has been a feature of Japanese–Western trade relations as far back as the first trade treaties in 1866[15]. The post-war success of Japan's trade strategies and the inability of Western nations to hold their own has been a growing thorn in the side of bilateral trade relations.

Japan's trade successes were acceptable in the West as long as Western trade grew and the US and the EEC had bilateral trade balances which were more or less in line with Japan. In the late 1970s the West experienced a slow-down in economic growth while that of Japan accelerated. This helped Japan rapidly to pile up trade surpluses with the US and the EEC and increased Japan's export-to-import ratio (Figure 4.1).

Since the West's economic slow-down resulted in high levels of unemployment the trade issue began to assume a high political profile on both sides of the Atlantic.

The driving forces behind trade friction in the West were the lack of success in penetrating the Japanese market and the inability of the West to stem the flow of Japanese imports into its markets. Penetrating the Japanese market has proved to be a frustrating experience for companies importing into Japan as well as for those establishing local manufacturing operations.

Since 1964 Japan has gradually removed many of the quantitative

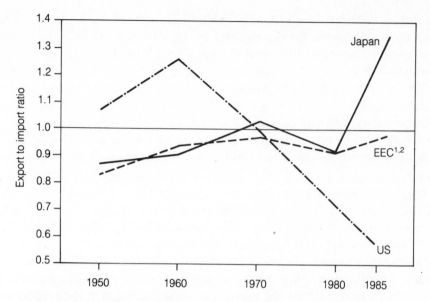

Figure 4.1. Japan's expansionist export and exclusionary import policies have enabled Japan to achieve a significant overall trade advantage over the US and the EEC in the 1980s.

[1] Includes intra-EEC trade
[2] Nine countries.

Source: International Financial Statistics, *IMF Yearbook 1985*, Washington D.C., 1986.

restrictions on imports and the 1985 three-year action plan, fully implemented in 1988, reduced or eliminated tariffs on 1860 industrial and agricultural items as well as eased certification and technical standards for imports[16].

Despite this liberalization many powerful lobbies are still able to exert a major influence on government policies and practices. As a result many opportunities in agriculture and in the banking, communications, construction, defence and insurance industries are effectively closed to foreign firms. The strong agricultural lobby, for example, has been able to get the Japanese government to pay its inefficient farmers $2,000 a tonne for rice, six to eight times the world retail price. When infrequent imports are allowed US wheat landed at $310 a tonne is sold to Japanese millers at $525 a tonne[17].

Added to formal restrictions are informal non-tariff barriers which have been very effective in limiting Western imports. While the con-

21

voluted distribution system is frequently blamed as a major trade problem this must be discounted as Japanese firms face the same problem. The real non-tariff barriers faced by Western firms are embedded in the firm Japanese belief that they and Japan are different. Consequently Western firms are faced with standards in Japan completely different from those in the West and designed to protect some form of presumed uniqueness. Western cars are subject to individual testing; new standards for skis have been developed since Japan's snow is believed to be 'different'; special grades are assigned to imported whisky and wine, which means higher duties pricing them out of the mass market; and Japanese stomachs are 'too small' and have room only for small locally produced tangerines[18]. These and other absurdities are typical of the industrial and cultural non-tariff barriers used to protect Japanese producers.

Against both tariff and non-tariff barriers Western firms have largely been unable to develop any meaningful volume of finished-product exports to Japan. Given the strength of Japanese firms in their domestic market, even if full liberalization occurs future opportunities for Western manufactured imports are slim. Viewed against the success of Japanese companies in exporting to the US and the EEC, Western governments and firms have become frustrated and believe that the opportunity for exporting to Japan in volume on a continuous basis is largely a myth.

Up to the mid-1970s investing in Japan was deliberately made unattractive for foreign firms. Forced partnerships with Japanese companies were the rule. These helped to transfer technology and process management techniques to Japanese partners and limit Western firms' managerial control. Added to these problems were exchange controls and limits to the remittance of dividends, which made investing in local production in Japan a marginal activity.

Compounding the whole issue was the attitude of management in US and, to a lesser extent, in European firms and the type of skills they possessed. Given the problems of producing in Japan, investments were high-risk, low-profit and involved long-term commitments. This was diametrically opposed to standard Western managerial practice, where the level of attraction tends to increase as the level of commitment and risk decrease. Marketing experience in the West differs from conditions in Japan where quality, reliability and after-sales service matter more than low prices[19]. Consequently Western firms frequently lacked the flexibility to handle new situations where past experience and skills were not directly transferable.

22

Despite these problems a number of Western companies have been able to develop a position in the Japanese domestic market with their own production facilities. US companies like Coca-Cola, Digital Equipment, IBM and Texas Instruments managed to secure high market shares[20]. For example, Coca-Cola holds 60 per cent of the soft drinks market and IBM has 30 per cent of the Japanese computer business[21]. While some companies like Braun (electric razors), Nestlé (instant coffee) and Wella (haircare products) have built a strong local franchise, European firms in general lagged far behind US firms in penetrating the Japanese market[22].

Some observers suggest that Western firms manufacturing in Japan have done so well that their performance offsets the trade surplus. The Japanese spend nearly three times as much per capita on foreign, particularly US, branded products as US consumers spend on Japanese imports[23]. However, since prices in Japan are 30 to 50 per cent higher than in the US the price comparisons are inflated by the high yen value vis-à-vis the dollar; high value masks low-volume consumption. More significant is the fact that foreign products sold in volume in Japan are almost always manufactured locally using Japanese labour. In contrast, Western consumers purchase Japanese products almost entirely made in Japan employing Japanese labour. As a result the value-added component in both scenarios is firmly in favour of Japan.

Whatever the reality of the situation, the firm perception in the West is that most US and European firms have had a much tougher time developing meaningful businesses in Japan than Japanese companies have had in the West. This has fuelled both government and business criticism in the West and has led to the belief that even when allowed local manufacturing in Japan is a marginal activity.

While Japan had a weak economy and was rebuilding its war shattered industrial base the West largely turned a blind eye to the fact that not only was the Japanese market effectively closed to foreign imports and investments but that Japan was using aggressive trading tactics. Despite a number of trade skirmishes in the early 1960s Japan was able to join the OECD in 1964 and the US and most European countries agreed to drop GATT Article XXXV which had excluded Japan from 'most favoured nation' treatment; OECD member countries quickly began to dismantle their discriminatory trade practices against Japan. This provided Japan with the opportunity to refocus its trade strategy away from the developing markets to the high-value OECD countries and to target specific industries with little fear of retaliation. While

23

Japan was committed to dismantle its own restrictive import practices to meet its OECD obligations these proceeded at a snail's pace. The result was that Japan enjoyed a significant competitive advantage over its trade rivals in having considerably earlier access to Western markets than either the US or the EEC had to Japan's domestic market.

Japan's government played a masterly game of securing and maintaining access to Western markets while procrastinating and delaying the opening of its own market. Japan's brinkmanship tactics of delay followed by nominal agreements to stave off retaliation contributed to a rising impatience in the West. Inevitably this led to a situation where Western governments became increasingly reluctant to give Japan the benefit of the doubt.

Apologists suggested that cultural differences and Japan's insular view of the world had made Japan unaware of the problems that it had created and that there was a lack of understanding on both sides as to what motivated the other. However, the view prevalent in the West was that Japan was both devious and duplicitous and did not follow the accepted rules of the international trade game. In the face of a steady stream of trade disputes the US and the EEC independently concluded by the late 1970s that actions spoke louder than words and increasing pressure was applied to Japan to both open up its domestic market and to restrict its exports to the West.

Japan responded by partially liberalizing its market restrictions in 1971–72 and again in 1981–82; however, this was only after intense diplomatic pressures. By skilful diplomacy and bureaucratic foot-dragging Japan was able to diffuse the situation temporarily and contain the full threat of Western competition in its domestic market.

Western companies found it difficult to play the import game when obscure or deliberately vague rules were applied, and, when these were lifted under pressure, new rules were found which continued to restrict imports. The results of Japan's liberalization measures were not immediately apparent on imports and, together with delay and confusion tactics, sent negative signals to the West. Again this helped to reinforce mistrust and resentment against Japan's perceived one-sided trade policy.

When these general market-opening measures failed to liberalize trade as fast and as comprehensively as expected the US took the lead and tried another tactic – Market-Oriented Sector Specific (MOSS) agreements. These were designed to push trade in specific areas to avoid getting bogged down in trying to get the recalcitrant Japanese to adopt widespread measures. The results were mixed. While the MOSS talks were successful in eliminating tariff and non-tariff barriers in some areas (medical equipment, pharmaceuticals and telecommunications), they were only partially successful in electronics and got nowhere in agriculture. This led some observers to conclude that nothing had been achieved that the Japanese had not already been willing to concede[24]. Overall general and sector-specific market-opening measures that were achieved through Western pressure largely failed to make a real impact on the flow of imports into Japan.

The reaction to Japan's growing exports to the US and the EEC was generally too late and poorly conducted. Western bureaucracy moved so slowly that in many instances firms were destroyed and whole industries decimated through selective targetting by Japanese companies before suitable restrictions were applied. When restrictions or anti-dumping tariffs were imposed the managements of Western companies failed to use the breathing space generated by the restrictions to restructure to meet the competitive challenge from more efficient Japanese firms.

When new legislation in the West appeared to be a significant threat Japanese companies were quick to react by either going along with the restrictions or converting their export business into local assembly plants. For example, the Voluntary Restraint Agreement on Japanese car exports to the US (1981–85) resulted in local assembly plants from Honda (1984), Mazda (1986), Mitsubishi (1989) and Nissan (1987) and a Toyota/GM joint venture. By quickly establishing local assembly operations Japanese firms were largely able to overcome protectionist legislation before the restrictions had a significant impact on their businesses.

Two key trade issues for the West have been volume and price competition from Japanese firms. The US and the EEC have tried unsuccessfully to control both the volume of Japanese imports and to ensure that Japanese firms did not use pricing tactics designed to put Western firms out of business – particularly 'dumping', where the in-market price of imported Japanese products was below that of the like product in Japan.

Volume restraints, variously known as OMAs and VRAs, designed to limit Japanese market penetration as a means to aid Western domestic industry have largely backfired. In practice they have allowed Japanese firms to form cartels with monopoly profits which are extremely attractive since they are protected by law. Inevitably they have led to higher consumer prices.

Import restraints encouraged Japanese firms to adopt a dual market strategy. They switched the mix of imports from low-priced to high-priced models, allowing them the freedom to trade up to higher-priced, higher-margin models sourced in Japan and build local assembly plants using components sourced in Japan to circumvent quotas on lower-priced models. The 1981–85 VRA in the US limited imports of fully assembled cars and light trucks to a fixed quota within which the share of individual Japanese firms was fixed at the annual average level prevailing during the previous three years[25]. This not only virtually guaranteed a share of 4 to 6 per cent of the US market but also encouraged Honda, Nissan and Toyota to move up-market with $20,000+ imported cars. Since the VRA excluded the sales of cars from Japanese assembly plants in the USA which relied on imported components and knockdown kits sourced in Japan, they were able to maintain manufacturing economies of scale and transfer variable labour expenses to the lower-cost US. The initial VRA limited Japanese imports to 1.8 million cars a year. As demand expanded the US market from 7.8 million in 1982 to more than 10 million cars in 1987, Japan's share increased to 2.3 million imported cars a year – *excluding* cars locally assembled from components imported from Japan.

The overall value of the 1981–85 VRA was also questionable in its effects on protecting consumers, employment and in helping to restructure the US car industry. By rationing the sale of Japanese cars the US consumers were reckoned to have paid an average of $1,300 more per car than if the market had been free[26]. Between 1981 and 1985 the import quotas were believed to have added $460 million to US car industry profits[27]. Depending on the interest group making the estimate, the number of jobs at risk in the US car and component industry by terminating the VRA varied by a factor of 50 (Table 4.1).

Table 4.1. Estimates of the Number of Jobs at Risk in the US Auto Industry if the VRA on Japanese Cars was Lifted in 1985.

	Number of jobs at risk
Federal Trade Commission	15,000
Merrill Lynch	50,000
Chase Econometrics	150,000
United Autoworkers Union	200,000
Chrysler	750,000

Source: *Business Week*, 18 March 1985.

While export restraints have proved to be of dubious value in protecting domestic industry both the US and the EEC have continued to rely on these measures to limit the volume of Japanese exports. For example, while the UK has a gentleman's agreement restricting Japanese imports to 10 to 12 per cent of its car market, France has a limit of 3 per cent, while Italy allows 2750 cars and 750 four-wheel-drive vehicles to be imported annually. All of these bilateral deals are of dubious legality under both GATT and the EEC competitive legislation. With some satisfaction Japan can point to the fact that, in 1986 the US had 27 and the EEC 53 export restraints compared to Japan's 23[28].

Unfair price competition from Japanese companies has been a major concern in the West since Japanese companies have consistently used predatory pricing to buy market share and consolidate market position. Dumping – selling product below cost or below fair home market price – has been a consistent issue with Western governments. While this has been regarded as an initial market penetration tactic there is considerable evidence to suggest that dumping continues to be a major Japanese strategy. Between 1983 and 1986, for example, the EEC imposed punitive anti-dumping duties against Japanese firms in ten major product categories (Table 4.2).

Table 4.2. EEC Anti-Dumping Actions Against Japanese Companies 1983–1986.

Product	Year	Duty (%) levied
Outboard motors	1983	22
Miniature ball-bearings	1984	4–15
Ball-bearings	1985	1–22
Tapered roller bearings	1985	2–45
Hydraulic excavators	1985	3–32
Electronic typewriters	1985	21–35
Glycine	1985	15
Electronic scales	1986	1–27
Housed bearings	1986	1–18
Photocopiers	1986	1–15.8

Source: *The Financial Times*, 27 August 1986.

27

The US has suffered from similar problems. Between 1970 and 1987 the US instituted a large number of anti-dumping actions against Japanese firms of which 36 were still in force in mid-1987.

However, as with export restraints anti-dumping duties have had a limited effect on halting the flow of Japanese exports. Following the punitive duties levied on the $1 billion imports of Japanese photo-copiers to the EEC in 1986 Canon, Konica, Matsushita, Minolta and Ricoh either began local assembly of components sourced in Japan or boosted production in existing European assembly plants to circumvent duties[29].

Adding to the problems created by volume and price restraints is the fact that Western governments have limited manpower resources available to investigate and initiate protective measures and even fewer resources to monitor compliance. The EEC's 25-person anti-dumping unit is unable to keep up with the number of complaints[30]. The understaffed and overworked US Customs Service, charged with enforcing more than 1,000 trade laws, duties and quotas, reduced its staff slightly between 1980 and 1986 when the value of US merchandise imports rose 50 per cent from $250 billion to $368 billion[31].

Compounding these problems are measures designed to sidestep anti-dumping restrictions. The most favoured is transhipment to a third country where enough 'value' is added to qualify as that country's product. Japanese steel companies faced with anti-dumping duties in the US ship to Canada where value is added. This can range from using the steel in Canadian-built cars to putting a bend in galvanized sheet steel in products destined for the US. Similarly, Japanese pipe manufacturers ship pipe to Thailand where it is threaded and then shipped to the US free of the import quotas imposed in 1985 on pipe shipped from Japan[32]. In many cases the transhipment is designed merely to change customs documents to mask origin. In Europe, for example, Belgium has become the second largest importer of some types of Japanese machine tools which are then re-exported to other European countries, confusing voluntary restraint agreements.

Japanese companies can get an exemption from an anti-dumping order from the US Department of Commerce if the firm sells at fair market value for two years and by pledging not to dump in the future. With an agency as overworked and understaffed as the US Customs Service there is little monitoring of future activities. At the same time bureaucracy has prevented the West from making effective new trade legislation and implementing these laws quickly. The new 1,000-page

US Omnibus Trade and Competitiveness Act of 1988 took three years to finalize and involved 23 committees and subcommittees. The key committee responsible for resolving differences between the House of Representatives and the Senate Trade bills had 199 members[33].

Overall the protective measures taken by Western governments to control the volume and price of Japanese imports have been too late and have largely failed to protect the consumer, industry or labour and increased rather than reduced the economic impact of Japanese imports.

5

THE KATAKANA ON THE WALL

Japan seriously underestimated political attitudes in the West and misread the growing tensions on bilateral trade in the early 1980s. Conversely the West lacked an appreciation of the motivations behind Japan's economic policy and of the domestic political realities in Japan.

With continuing high levels of unemployment and low levels of economic growth in the West both the US and EEC conveniently identified that the cause of their persistent industrial problems was Japan's mercantilist policy dedicated to success at any price. This added a high level of emotional hostility to the whole issue of Japan–Western trade.

Japan was seen to require and expect a profit from an international trade system which it consistently failed to respect: its success was largely due to a one-way trade policy – a voracious appetite for export at any cost. By 1986 the trade surpluses in Japan's favour had reached a level where it began to be believed that unless checked this would dislocate the post-war multilateral free trade system which had brought an unprecedented degree of wealth to the world. Since representations over trade issues with Japan had traditionally been met with soothing words and little action anger built up over the vast differences between the continuous pledges of the Japanese government to reform its role in world trade, which proceeded at a snail's pace, and the failure of Western governments and companies to make headway.

The West's reaction to Japan's success was part ego and part misjudgement. Loss of place and pride figure heavily in contemporary Western trade attitudes to Japan. When Japan began to displace Western firms in the 1960s in Africa, Latin America and the Middle East this was widely regarded as part of the game and volatile, low-priced, high-risk markets were not considered a major loss. However, when Japanese firms began to displace Western firms in their home markets, sandwiching local companies between lower-priced and higher-quality products, pride surfaced. The ego issue swelled as the Japanese moved into higher value-added and high-technology products. The US had become so used to being the world leader in high technology that it came as a rude shock to find that the high-technology industries which the US had virtually created were no longer competitive with those of Japan. Imports of high-technology products by the US grew six times faster than exports from 1980, turning a trade surplus of $26.6 billion into a deficit of $22.6 billion by 1986[34].

Loss of primacy in high technology led to the abortive 1986 US–Japan agreement on semiconductors, which was designed to be a landmark in both opening the Japanese market and protecting the US domestic market. The pact set minimum prices for D-ram chips produced in Japan and sold in any country and committed the Japanese government to help US firms to increase sales in Japan to 20 per cent of the market in 1991. This was above the 15 per cent that Japanese firms held in the US in 1986[35]. The pact was much too successful in increasing US prices, which pushed up the costs to end users who began to complain. As the Japanese began to lose their overseas markets to producers from the NICs, who were not covered by the pact, the chips began to pile up in Japan, pushing down local prices to make it even harder for US firms to compete in Japan. The EEC, left out of the agreement, appealed to GATT to investigate the fairness of third country price-fixing bilaterally between the US and Japan – particularly as the EEC imported 59 per cent of its semiconductors, mostly from the US and Japan[36]. The pact was both unworkable and unenforceable since it was designed to fix the world price of a commodity in excess supply and contributed to increasing trade friction between the US and Japan; it brought the EEC into conflict with the US over discriminatory trade practices created by the bilateral agreement.

Misjudgement has been a major contributor to trade friction. Passions were aroused in the EEC, where it was realized that the composition of trade with Japan had changed radically. In 1970, 43.2 per cent of EEC exports to Japan consisted of high-value-added machine tools and machinery. By 1985 this had shrunk to 26.2 per cent and the EEC's exports to Japan were dominated by low-value processed and semi-processed goods[37]. Japan's economic strategy had changed its industrial base in two decades from making low-value-added labour-intensive goods to producing high-value knowledge-intensive products. Japan had also concentrated from early 1960s on building up import substitution industries. The result was that by the 1980s Japan had a highly integrated, self-sufficient industrial base and its economy had more need for raw materials and luxury consumer goods than it had for high-value manufactured imports. As a consequence of ego and misjudgement the West found itself trying to sell products to Japan which Japanese firms and consumers did not want.

Tensions grew in the US in 1986 as a result of its largest ever trade deficit of $170 billion, aggravated by the $200 billion budget deficit, which transformed the US from a leading creditor to a leading debtor. Pressures from anti-trade groups, organized labour and industry lobbyists increased in 1986 and 1987. The use of the trade deficit by several Democratic candidates for the Presidential nomination in 1988 as a major campaign issue gave the US trade deficit high visibility. New trade legislation was inevitable as a result of these pressures and a number of bills were proposed. These bills requested the toughest protectionist measures since 1945 and contained a wide range of controversial clauses, all of which had strong reciprocity and retaliatory components. Not to be outdone, the EEC, which had suffered a trade deficit growth with Japan in 1985 and 1986 that increased much faster and in absolute terms by a higher amount than the US, began to increase pressure on Japan[38]. In mid-1987 the EEC refused to agree to existing tariffs on six key Japanese imports unless Japan offered measures to open up its market, and emergency tariffs were approved on other products if evidence arose of export diversion from the US[39]. Later the EEC approached Japan for compensation for the admission of Spain and Portugal to the EEC since it was estimated that Japan would gain $1.2 billion in lower import tariffs[40].

These new trade initiatives placed considerable pressure on Japan. Both the US and the EEC stepped up demands in the belief that their bilateral trade balances were going from bad to worse and that past experience showed that the Japanese had a strong tendency to respond with concessions only to those that it respected. Confrontation and tough tactics were felt to be the only way to show Japan that it was no longer acceptable to maintain double standards to sustain its mercantilist approach to trade at the expense of the rest of the world.

Japan's attitude to trade and to its relationships with the West are conditioned by both national self-perceptions and trade realities. Firmly planted in the Japanese psyche is the mind-set that Japan is a small, vulnerable island nation with few natural resources and Japan and the Japanese are fundamentally different. Consequently it is very difficult for the Japanese to accept that Japan is no longer a fragile and poor nation but rather an industrial superstar with a world-wide economic impact. The geographic isolation, emotional insulation and ethnic distinctiveness of the Japanese has led to a xenophobia which perpetuates a national self-perception that no longer fits with reality. This insecurity and an inward-looking value system contribute to outdated domestic views of Japan as a nation solely reliant on foreign trade for survival.

Displaying the attitude of 'poor little Japan' to Western nations suffering from high unemployment, partially as a result of Japan's trade success, is not calculated to win sympathy in either Washington or Brussels. Rather it reinforces the view that Japan has no intention of becoming a responsive and responsible partner in the world economy – unless it is forced to reciprocate.

From a trade perspective the Japanese see themselves as free traders and have considerable pride in their industrial success. As a result they are unhappy about being persecuted for their success and there is considerable resentment and frustration with the US and the EEC. Both are seen to be cornering Japan and using it as a scapegoat for competitive problems, overvalued currencies and inefficiency largely of their own making which they cannot or will not fix. Japan is unsympathetic to what it views as hypocritical claims that the Western markets are freer than those in Japan. Japan can point to the fact that by 1987 its average tariff rates at 2.1 per cent were lower than those of both the US, at 4.3 per cent, and the EEC at 4.8 per cent and that none of its import restrictions were incompatible with those of GATT[41]. In terms of trade surplus it is convenient to forget that the US ran trade surpluses continuously for 80 years between 1891 and 1971 and in 1975 had the biggest current account surplus ($18 billion) of any OECD country[42].

Increasingly overt attempts to open up the Japanese market and to force Japan to change its economic focus to domestic growth through fundamental changes in taxation, the use of land, housing and the distribution system and to deregulate industries to suit the West are widely seen as lacking in understanding of Japan's political realities and as reverse imperialism. As such they are considered abusive, selfish and unreasonable. As a demonstration of its economic responsibility Japan can point to the fact that it uses much of its annual capital outflow to finance the US budget deficit. In 1986 Japan purchased US bonds, notes and treasury bills to the value of $64 billion[43], which Japan maintains kept the US afloat.

Japan's ingrained approach to shifting the blame to the West, while partially true, portrays a continuing inflexible attitude to trade, particularly when compared to other nations reliant on exports. Taiwan and South Korea, for example, with 44 and 39 per cent of their 1987 exports going to the US, rapidly offered marketing opening measures and concessions to maintain access to the US market. Major tariff reductions, pledges to boost imports and trim exports were made both to placate the US and to distance them from an intransigent Japan. These measures served to further isolate Japan and reinforce the belief that Japan is an uncooperative player in world trade.

The search for right and wrong in the trade disputes between Japan and the West is futile. Depending on perspective, both sides are guilty and innocent. Right and wrong matter less than perception and the issue boils down to an incompatibility of interests and values. While Japan believes that multilateral not bilateral trade balances are significant, the Western nations have an opposing view and the problem is seen as insensitivity on the part of the West and inefficiency by Japan. Despite the widespread acknowledgement that many Japanese products have a greater degree of technical sophistication, better quality and superior after sales service than their Western counterparts there is an underlying belief that Japan's continuing success has been largely achieved through selfish manipulation and unfair trade practices. Given Japan's intransigence in resolving numerous trade issues, protectionism became a growing reality in the mid-1980s.

6

VULNERABILITY

The phenomenal success of Japan's trade and industrial policies and increasing resentment in the West increased protectionism in the mid-1980s. By single-mindedly focusing on the US and the EEC and progressively targetting higher-value-added industries any form of restriction limiting access or increasing the costs of doing business would have a significant impact on Japanese firms using exports as their major business strategy. Since Japan concentrates heavily on exporting high-value-added manufactured goods and the US and the EEC absorb 63 per cent and 23 per cent, respectively, of the world's exports of these products more protectionism would devastate many Japanese firms[44].

The free trade system and the lack of forceful retaliation against Japanese exports worked so well that most major Japanese exporters never bothered to invest in production facilities in the West. Through the late 1970s a large part of Japanese offshore investments was made in the Asian NICs to shift low-value-added labour-intensive activities to low-cost countries to maintain overall cost advantages. Consequently few Japanese exporters had any appreciable productive capacity in the West. Those companies that did build productive capacity were largely involved in assembling Japanese-produced components.

In 1983 only 2 per cent of Japan's manufacturing output was sourced outside Japan, and as late as 1986 Japan's offshore production was limited to 5 per cent, albeit of a much higher value, of total manufacturing output. In comparison US manufacturing firms had around 20 per cent of capital investment in production located outside the US[45]. This low ratio of overseas production to export sales made Japanese firms very vulnerable to any increase in protectionism (Figure 6.1).

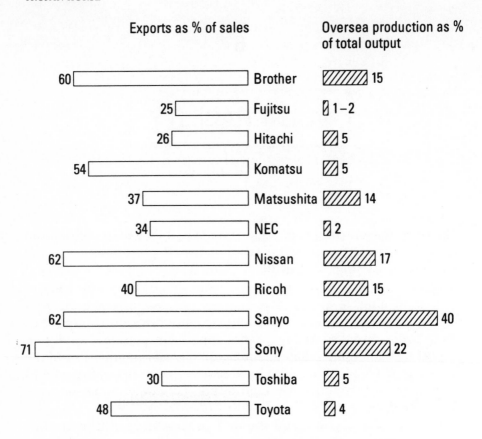

Figure 6.1. The low ratio of overseas production to exports in major Japanese companies makes them highly vulnerable to increased protectionism (1986).

Sources: *Business Week, The Economist, Financial Times, Forbes, Fortune* and company annual reports.

   With an investment gap between producing and consuming countries, a reliance on shipping finished product halfway around the world and a government becoming more limited in its ability to diffuse and deflect mounting criticisms over its trade practices, Japanese companies were placed in an increasingly vulnerable position as protectionism increased in the West. At the same time the Asian NICs, with relatively fixed exchange rates against the dollar, began to improve their cost advantage over Japan every time the dollar parity fell against the yen. As a result Japan got caught in a sandwich between protectionism which began to limit her access to those markets with a volume of sophisticated consumers with a high level of disposable income – the US and the EEC – and the Asian NICs, whose cost advantage began to exclude Japanese companies from the lower end of world markets (Figure 6.2).

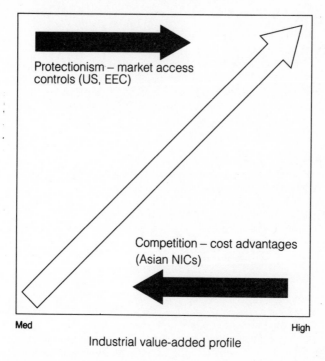

Protectionism – market access controls (US, EEC)

Competition – cost advantages (Asian NICs)

Med   High

Industrial value-added profile

Figure 6.2. Japan's industrial policy of moving its industry up the value chain is vulnerable to both increased protection in its major markets – the US and EEC – and to competition from the Asian NICs, who now have considerable cost advantages.

Japanese companies are faced with the most protectionist atmosphere since the 1930s, a fundamental restructuring of trade laws in the West together with a loss of the low-end markets and to severe cost competition from the Asian NICs. Japanese firms have no option but to rapidly develop local assembly operations in the West in order to maintain market access and circumvent increased protectionism.

SUMMARY

While Japan has developed the world's most dynamic economy and Japanese companies have had unparalleled success in attaining strong market positions for a wide range of products in the West these successes are threatened by the spectre of increased protectionism.

There is considerable evidence to suggest that the fault lies largely with Japan's exclusionary import policies, aggressive trade practices and procrastination rather than with conspiracy and cooperation between Japanese companies to achieve world market domination. However, blame also lies with the West for failing to enter the Japanese market aggressively and for not responding effectively both politically and economically to the competitive challenge posed by more efficient Japanese companies.

While it is convenient for the Japanese to blame trade disputes on misunderstandings and on the West for creating its own problems, neither holds water. Both the US and the EEC hold similar views about their trade disputes with Japan and have been able to penetrate each other's markets fairly freely. Japan's self-centred, narrowly focused view of world trade has ignored the mutuality of interest necessary in a global economy based on interdependence.

Whatever the rights and wrongs of individual trade disputes with Japan a widespread belief has developed that Japan observes only the letter and not the spirit of an interdependent global economy. Since perception is reality the West has begun to question its fundamental trade relationships and is set on a course of increased protectionism.

By playing the tariff game better than the West, Japan was able to avoid building any appreciable manufacturing capacity in the West. In the short and mid-term this provided Japan with phenomenal cost and quality advantages over its Western competitors. However, when the trade climate began to change to a more protectionist environment Japanese exporters found themselves increasingly vulnerable. The US alone absorbed 38.5 per cent of Japanese exports in 1986 and any significant restriction of Japan's access to the US market would have a devastating effect on Japan's economy[46].

In its most difficult economic period since 1950 Japan is being confronted with a number of new challenges. It is being forced on the one hand towards stimulating domestic demand to absorb an increasing level of imports from the West while on the other reducing its exports to decrease the imbalance with its major Western trade partners.

For Japanese companies to continue to grow under these new political imperatives there is only one option – offshore production in both the US and the EEC. By building up local assembly capacity within the markets of their major trading partners Japanese firms can ensure a freedom of market access which is becoming increasingly untenable in the face of trade imbalances created by growing Japanese imports of finished products.

PART 2

RED INK ON THE SUN

7

THE FAILURE OF ENDAKA

Mounting Western trade imbalances with Japan and slow progress in opening up Japan's domestic market increased the possibility of a trade war. Market intervention appeared to be the only way to diffuse the tense situation between Japan and its Western trade partners.

The governments of Japan, the US, France, Great Britain and West Germany met at the Plaza Hotel in New York on 21st and 22nd September 1985 and agreed to drive down the value of the dollar by appreciating the yen. By manipulating exchange rates the Group of Five planned to reduce the growing US trade deficit and stoke up domestic demand in Japan to relieve growing pressures on the international trade system.

The plan was completely successful in appreciating the value of the yen against the dollar – by a staggering 85 per cent in the 39 months between June 1985 and September 1988 (Figure 7.1). However, the

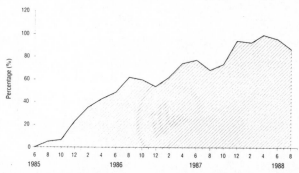

Figure 7.1. In the 39 months from June 1985 to September 1988 the Japanese yen appreciated by a phenomenal 85 per cent against the US dollar.

Source: Bank of International Settlements, Basle, October 1988.

multiple short-term effects of the appreciating value of the yen, or *endaka*, were very different from those anticipated by the Group of Five on the US and EEC trade deficits with Japan, on stimulating the Japanese market and on boosting world demand and supply, and created a new set of major problems for the West.

The J-curve, the economic theory describing the effects of currency devaluations, did not have an immediate effect on the US balance of trade following the dollar's massive devaluation. According to the theory the US trade deficit should have increased slightly as the lower-valued dollar created higher prices for imports, which should have started to fall as consumers began to shun the higher prices. At the same time exporters, blessed with a lower-valued dollar, should have been able to sell more overseas, which would cause an upswing in exports. The decline in imports and the increase in exports created by the devaluation of the dollar in turn should have produced a strong movement towards a balance in US trade.

In reality the adverse trade position of the US got steadily worse. The US merchandise trade deficit actually increased in 1986 over 1985 by almost 20 per cent to $147.7 billion. Japan's share increased by some 17.6 per cent to a record of $58.6 billion, almost 40 per cent of the overall US trade deficit. Adding insult to injury the US negative trade balance with Japan continued to grow in absolute terms and reached $59.8 billion in 1987 (Figure 7.2).

The reasons for the sustained growth in US imports and in Japan's share of the import surplus in the face of the dollar devaluation are complex.

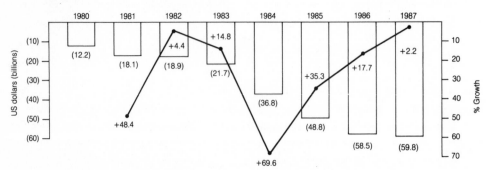

Figure 7.2. US merchandise trade deficits with Japan have grown progressively worse since 1980.

Source: US Department of Commerce.

44

First, US consumers defied the logic of the J-curve and continued to favour higher-priced Japanese over lower-priced US-made products. Japanese firms with well accepted brand leaders were able to make significant price increases, reducing some of the impact of *endaka* on profits without appreciably losing customers. Honda, for example, with the highest car quality rating in the US was able to sustain a 14.1 per cent price increase in September 1986 with no impact on sales volume[47]. Most Japanese companies, however, decided to absorb much of the appreciation of the yen by maintaining prices to preserve hard-won market share at the expense of reduced margins. For example Sharp's margins on its video products fell from 6.3 per cent in 1983 to 2.1 per cent in 1986[48]. By increasing prices with no corresponding fall in demand or by maintaining prices and absorbing currency losses, Japanese firms were able to sustain a flow of imports which significantly reduced the immediate impact of *endaka*.

Second, US firms adopted a policy of maintaining offshore prices by increasing export prices to both Japan and Europe even though the dollar had lost value against both the yen and EEC currencies. As a result the dollar devaluation had its greatest effect on the profit and loss statements of major US exporters. These firms were able to pick up windfall profits created by the continuously declining dollar with fixed local and increased export prices – at the expense of an increase in the share of exports. Domestic producers also seized the opportunity and rapidly followed the price increases of Japanese products in the US to improve their margins. The behaviour of US companies – short-term profit-taking rather than building market share with lower prices – helped to contain the effect of the dollar devaluation at the expense of higher prices for consumers.

Endaka also had the effect of increasing Japan's trade surplus with the EEC. While the yen fell significantly against the dollar from June 1985 to 1987, it fell (with the exception of the pound) only marginally against the major EEC currencies (Figure 7.3).

Sensing the opportunity, many Japanese companies switched their export emphasis from the US to the EEC. By taking advantage of the stronger EEC currencies Japanese exporters could still sell at competitive prices and not be forced to absorb the effects of the yen appreciation. As a result of this refocusing of exports the EEC's trade deficit with Japan mushroomed in 1986 to $21.5 billion – an increase of 46.3 per cent over 1985, and increased again marginally in 1987 (Figure 7.4).

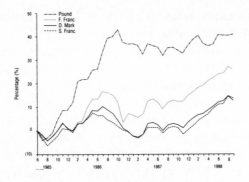

Figure 7.3. The major European currencies, with the exception of the pound, remained relatively stable against the yen from mid-1985 through 1987. This encouraged Japanese firms to switch export emphasis from the US to Europe to pick up windfall profits.

Sources: Bank of International Settlements, Basle, October 1988.

The European car market was a prime recipient of this massive diversion of exports. In 1986 Japanese car exports to the EEC increased by 19 per cent over 1985 compared to an increase in car exports to the US of only 1.5 per cent[49]. To West Germany alone, Europe's largest car market, Japanese car imports increased by 30 per cent in 1986 to take almost 15 per cent of the market[50]. To put this into perspective, by 1986 the Japanese were selling as many cars in Germany as were British, French and Italian manufacturers *combined*.

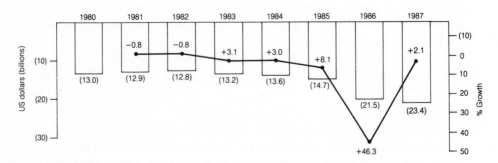

Figure 7.4. The EEC maintained a fairly stable trade deficit with Japan (1980–84); the sharp growth from 1985 reflects the switch in export emphasis from the US as Japanese firms took advantage of stronger European currencies.

Sources: UN Data Bank 'Comtrade', 1980 to 1985, and Eurostat 'Comext', 1986 to 1988.

The switch in export emphasis into stronger currencies helped to cushion the effects of *endaka* on Japanese firms. However, this increase in exports to the EEC heightened the already poor trade relationships between the EEC and Japan and triggered calls for new limits on Japanese imports to Europe[51].

Endaka had little effect on stoking up Japanese domestic demand for lower-cost imports. Despite the steep rise in the value of the yen, Japan's current account surplus actually widened from $49 billion in 1985 to $85.8 billion in 1986 – and again to $87.7 billion in 1987. This growth in exports and the limited impact of lower-cost imports on Japan's trade surplus were due to a combination of factors.

First, depending on the currency used to measure Japan's export and import performance, there can be a growth or a decline. For example, Japan's trade surplus with the US in 1986 either increased by 30.1 per cent to $51.4 billion or decreased by 7.6 per cent to 8.7 trillion yen. Similarly, while the yen value of Japanese imports fell by 30.7 per cent the volume of imports rose by 12.5 per cent[52].

Second, there was a coincidental fall in world energy and raw material prices. Since around 70 per cent of Japan's imports are fuel and raw materials a major price decline, for products which are largely denominated in dollars, had a considerable dampening effect on the value of imports. For example, when measured in yen Japan's 1986 oil bill alone fell by 60 per cent. If the dollar-denominated oil is stripped out, Japan's imports are estimated to have actually risen in dollar terms by 12.6 per cent in value and by 13.8 per cent in volume[53]. Figure 7.5 illustrates the various ways in which Japan's 1986 trade surplus and import performance can be viewed.

Third, the multilayered Japanese distribution system, together with controls by government agencies, was probably able to hold back at least one half of the benefits from lower-cost dollar imports. Despite the drop in the value of the dollar and much cheaper energy and raw material costs Japanese consumer prices actually increased by 0.5 per cent between September 1985 and September 1986[54].

Finally, Japanese consumers still instinctively buy Japanese or at best buy foreign products produced in Japan. Japanese industrial purchasing is largely concentrated among Japanese companies through obligations as a result of financial connections through *keiretsu* (groups of financially integrated firms), or long-term experience.

Overall the lower value of the dollar was not the immediate incen-

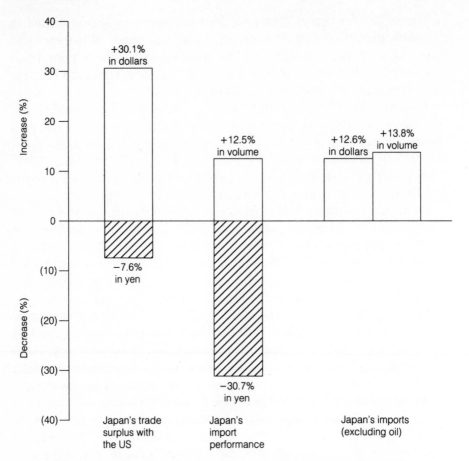

Figure 7.5. Japan's trade performance in 1986 depends largely on how trade surpluses and imports are measured.

Source: *The Economist*, 4 April 1987.

tive that it was planned to be in order to open up the Japanese domestic market to US imports. Compounding the problem was a simultaneous worldwide slowdown in customer demand and industrial over-supply occurring across industries from computers and consumer electronics to shipping and textiles. This was due partly to low economic growth in the US and the EEC, the debt mountains of Latin America, political instability in much of Africa and the Middle East and the lethargic economies of China and Eastern Europe.

The effect of this sluggish demand was heightened by widespread industrial overcapacity. The combined effects of poor investment decisions in the late 1970s, miscalculations of demand, the impact of technology change and increased automation and plentiful supplies of low-cost raw materials and energy, which encouraged newcomers and marginal producers, all came home to roost (Table 7.1).

Table 7.1. The slowdown in consumer demand and over-investment in production facilities on a world scale led to significant overcapacity in many industries in 1986–87.

	Estimated productive overcapacity (%)
Cars	30
Heavy equipment	40
Semiconductors	70
Steel	30–40

Source: *Wall Street Journal*, 10 March 1987

The slowdown in customer demand, coupled to high levels of over-capacity, helped to depress international trade, which offset the benefits of the higher valuation of the yen against the dollar.

Overall the appreciation of the yen in the short term failed to meet the Group of Five's objectives of reducing the US trade deficit and in stoking up Japan's domestic demand. In fact, the US and the EEC trade deficit with Japan *increased* while the growth in the value of Japanese imports was relatively modest. This increased pressures on the world trade system and reinforced the Western view that Japan's domestic market was largely closed and gave more credence to the belief that Japan is nothing more than a trade predator. As a result the US and the EEC in early 1987 began to increase political pressure on Japan to open up its domestic market and to reduce exports.

Hidden beneath the rhetoric of the Japanese, who protest good faith, and the West, who believe the opposite, four new factors have emerged about international trade.

● Trade theory is based on the free play of market forces responding to changes in comparative advantage. Unfortunately, comparative advantage is transitory and elusive since exchange rates are volatile, technology changes are rapid and few markets are really free. Consequently classical theories about free trade are based on outmoded and impractical ideas which are incompatible with reality.

- Intervention by central banks may no longer be powerful enough by itself to stabilize exchange rates or manipulate the economies of several large trading nations.

- Major companies now operate totally in the context of a global economy rather than within national boundaries. If they choose to pursue policies of narrow self-interest rather than broader national and international interests they can effectively undermine the priorities of the central banks and the policies of their own governments.

- Given the failure of *endaka* to achieve its predicted effects in the short term many observers began to question whether bilateral trade balances were still meaningful guides to industrial competitiveness. One school of thought, for example, suggested that local production by foreign firms replaced exports in the balance of trade equation. For example, in 1984 the sales of the 300 largest US firms in Japan totalled $43.9 billion while Japanese firms manufacturing in the US had sales of only $12.6 billion. The difference of $31.1 billion was almost identical to the $31.2 billion trade surplus in Japan's favour[55]. Others have taken this argument even further and suggest that Japan could be importing 51 per cent more if foreign companies had not built local manufacturing plants. If those firms had remained offshore it was estimated that the US would be exporting 174 per cent more to Japan and European exports to Japan would be 201 per cent higher[56].

Whether or not a new set of theories about international trade is emerging is academic. The fact is that *endaka*, despite its massive effect on the dollar–yen exchange rate, did not have a material impact on the US trade deficit in the short term. Rather it changed the nature of the game for Japan and placed the West in a potentially much more dangerous position.

8

COPING WITH ENDAKAFUKYO

Although *endaka* had limited short-term impact on international trade, it did have an immediate impact on Japanese competitiveness. Rather than *endaka*, a high yen value, Japanese industry saw the problem as *endakafukyo*, a high yen recession.

The hallmark of Japan's export success has been highly efficient low-cost production emphasizing high product quality at very competitive prices. *Endaka* effectively put paid to both low costs and competitive prices and rapidly eroded Japan's competitiveness by turning its export-based companies into high-cost competitors.

The decline in Japan's cost advantage as a result of *endaka* is clearly seen in Figure 8.1 which shows the strong increase in Japan's exchange-rate-adjusted manufacturing costs since 1985. At the same time the manufacturing cost position of the US improved while that of the EEC, although favourable, declined on a relative basis. This change in competitive dynamics has had a major impact on the profitability of Japanese firms.

The progressive increase in the value of the yen began to show up quickly on the bottom line of Japanese companies with a heavy stake in exports. During the six months to September 1986, Nissan, Japan's second largest car firm, registered its first loss (of 19 billion yen) since becoming a public company in 1951[57]. Other major exporting companies registered falls in both sales and net income in the 1986 fiscal year as a direct result of *endaka* (Table 8.1).

By mid-1986 economic research surveys were predicting falls in sales and net income of all Japanese manufacturers of 8.3 per cent and 14.6 per cent, respectively, in the fiscal year ending March 1987[58], with steeper declines for companies reliant on exports.

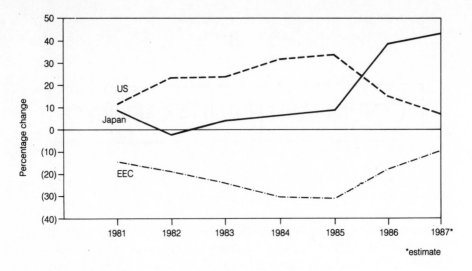

Figure 8.1 Japan's cost advantage over the West has steadily declined since 1984. (Percentage change in exchange rate-adjusted manufacturing costs in Japan, the US and the EEC: 1981–87)

Source: European Commission, Brussels, May 1987.

Table 8.1. The effects of *endaka* on sales and net income in 1986 compared with 1985 (year ending March 1986).

	Sales (%)	Income (%)
Ashai Chemical	− 7.3	−10.0
Casio Computer	−18.0	−69.0
Hino Motors	−16.0	−31.0
Honda	− 4.2	−48.0
Kawasaki	−20.0	(loss)
Komatsu	+ 3.3	−32.6
Nippon Mining	−38.0	−62.0
Sumitomo Metals	−22.0	−69.0
Toshiba	−10.0	−65.0

Source: Company reports

Table 8.2. The forecast decline in Japanese company performance as *endaka* cut into profits (year ending March 1987)

Company	Year end	Sales	Net income	Change in net income in fiscal year
		(billion yen)		(%)
Ashai Chemical	March 1986	1019	5.6	−39
Fujitsu	March 1986	1692	38.9	−12
Hitachi	March 1986	5010	150.2	−13
Honda	February 1986	2909	146.5	−41
Kobe Steel	March 1986	1171	10.5	−100
Mazda	October 1985	1669	39.5	−70
Matsushita Electrical	November 1985	5053	246.4	−30
Mitsubishi Electric	March 1986	2109	30.0	−20
Mitsubishi Heavy Industries	March 1986	3533	66.4	−25
Nissan	March 1986	4628	35.7	−72
Nippon Steel	March 1986	2685	36.6	−100
Sanyo	November 1985	1500	36.2	−59
Sharp	March 1986	1216	35.9	−11
Sony	October 1985	1421	73.0	−15
Sumitomo Metal	March 1986	1108	16.6	−100
Toshiba	March 1986	3373	59.4	−24
Toyota	June 1986	6305	255.2	−15

Source: Nomura Securities (*The Economist*, 6 September 1986)

By December 1986 the predictions had widened to a 13 per cent fall in sales and an 18 per cent decline in net income for all Japanese firms for fiscal 1986 ending in March 1987[59]. Whatever the predictions, the reality was that Japanese companies with a substantial stake in exports were witnessing a growing haemorrhage in profitability.

Faced with the rapid impact of *endaka* on profitability and sales, Japanese companies responded with a wide range of programmes to cut costs to halt the erosion of their competitiveness. While many companies adopted product redesign to simplify manufacturing to lower costs, the main push came in automation.

Japanese manufacturers have continuously and heavily invested in automation to lower production costs. For example, in 1986 Toyota was producing four times as many cars as in the late 1960s with the same amount of labour as a result of increased automation[60]. Most Japanese companies have continued to invest in automation through the *endaka* period, conscious of the fact that only minor productivity improvements are possible through increased capital investment in the short term with the major impact coming in the mid-term.

Much of Japanese industry is not vertically integrated and relies on outside component suppliers who are either part of *keiretsu* or independent manufacturers. An immediate reaction to *endaka* was pressure on outside suppliers to lower costs. For example, Mitsumi, a key component supplier to Matsushita, Sony and Toshiba, was forced to cut prices on average by 20 per cent. This brought a net operating loss of $1.1 million on revenues of $294 million in the first six months of 1986[61]. Other companies started to source an increasing amount of labour-intensive component supplies and assembly in lower-cost countries, particularly the newly industrialized countries (NICs) of Asia, to assist in reducing costs.

While oil and many other commodities declined in price due to over-supply, as well as a result of their denomination in dollars, primary producers in Japan also came under heavy pressure to reduce prices. With imported coal at $49 a ton and domestic coal at a government-set price of $150 a ton, major problems began to develop between the government and the mining companies on one hand and the users on the other[62]. Similarly, with Korean hot-rolled steel coil selling at 62,000 yen a ton against 72,000 yen a ton for the domestically produced equivalent Japanese companies began to make major changes to their procurement policies in favour of lower-cost imports[63].

Traditionally Japanese companies faced with adversity have managed to shed their temporary labour, which generally forms up to 30 per cent of the work force of most companies. If the company was part of *keiretsu* there were often opportunities for redeployment to other companies within the group – the traditional economic shock absorber.

As almost all major companies are also major exporters and were being squeezed by *endaka*, reassignment and retraining within *keiretsu* became a limited option. Consequently Japanese companies adopted a wide range of alternative strategies to reduce their labour costs.

Companies in relatively good shape were able to take a longer-term view. Toyota, for example, in 1986 announced that its 1987 hiring programme would be cut by 18 per cent[64]. Other companies were forced to take progressively firmer action to reduce labour costs. Nippon Steel, with 30 per cent of its sales in direct exports and another 30 per cent in supplies to the equally hard hit export-based car and electronics industries, first sharply reduced working hours, then reduced its labour force and finally introduced lay-offs in rotation to spread the economic hardship[65]. Labour cost-reduction programmes in other firms took the form of direct lay-offs in shipbuilders like Ishikawajima-Harima Heavy Industries and Hitachi Zosen[66]; incentives for early retirement in consumer electronic firms such as Aiwa and Sansui[67]; subcontracting labour to other companies and transferring part of the work force in Isuzu to newly created subsidiaries or to its dealerships as in the case of Nissan[68]. While some companies brought more of work previously subcontracted in-house to make use of idle labour protected under lifetime employment guarantees, other firms like Kobe Steel closed down whole plants[69].

While the effect of the different approaches to cutting labour costs varied widely some companies managed to obtain significant cost reductions. Nissan, for example, managed to cut costs by $360 million, or 20 per cent, which helped to move the company into the black in the second half of fiscal 1986 after an operating loss of $122 million in the first half of 1986. Nissan again cut costs in 1987 by $1.08 billion after a $1.54 billion reduction in 1986. Lower costs of materials and components by squeezing suppliers provided $690 million in savings with the rest coming from streamlining production and shedding workers[70]. Other companies have had similar cost reduction successes in 1986 and planned further cuts in 1987. Mitsubishi cut its costs by 15 per cent and planned a further 15 per cent reduction. Honda reduced costs by 10 per cent in 1986 with a further 20 per cent set as a target for 1987. Toyota, already very efficient, cut its costs by 5 per cent with a similar percentage planned for 1987[71].

Endaka also forced a reappraisal of product mix strategies. Traditionally Japanese companies started in a niche at the low end of the product line. After establishing a reputation for reliability and quality the company moved up the product value-added chain with new and more expensive models. *Endaka* has had a significant impact on the degree and direction of product mix changes. Japanese companies began to concentrate their efforts on higher value-added products to add more margin per unit sold. For example, Sansui, a maker of audio products, increased its production and promotion focus on products costing $1000 and over and Mitsubishi Electric concentrated its efforts on higher-value large-screen stereo-equipped televisions[72]. Similarly, car companies such as Mazda, Mitsubishi, Nissan and Toyota moved rapidly up-market with high performance, increased luxury and new technology to increase margins. Honda even created a new image for luxury and sports cars and built a separate US dealer network to handle products under the Integra and Acura brands[73].

Companies also began to diversify into new technologies in an effort to distance themselves from declining industries and move into higher value-added opportunities. Kirin, a major brewer, and Hitachi, a significant force in electronics, moved into biotechnology while steel makers like Nippon Steel and Nippon Kokan respectively bought into advanced computer-aided design systems and silicon wafer technology[74].

The standard business approach of increasing prices to offset cost escalation presented Japanese firms with a dilemma: to compensate for the massive rise in the value of the yen required major price increases. However, increases in prices on the scale necessary to compensate for the rise in the yen would lose hard-won market share.

No Japanese company in the US increased prices in line with the yen and most firms adopted policies of absorbing the loss with minimal price increases to cushion some of the impact on profitability while remaining competitive. In the US from September 1985 to September 1986, compared with a yen increase of 50 per cent, Japanese prices for binoculars increased 10 per cent, cars 15 per cent and computer peripherals 6 per cent, while photographic film prices remained unchanged[75].

In the US market Japanese car sales were so strong between 1980 and 1985 that few companies offered dealer or customer incentives. This led several Japanese car firms to misjudge their 1986 price increases. Nissan increased its list prices by 20 per cent in total from October 1985 – and its market share fell from 5.3 per cent in 1985 to 4.8 per cent in 1986[76]. Similarly, Komatsu increased its prices for construction equipment in a flat North American market by an average of 18 per cent in 1986. Despite offering substantial dealer discounts Komatsu saw its market share fall from 11 per cent in 1985 to 9 per cent in 1986[77].

The relatively modest price increases in comparison to the high value of the yen, in addition to failing to bridge the exchange gap, also created a problem for Japanese management. By absorbing the losses and accepting lower or no margins to maintain a competitive price, Japanese firms were in fact practising dumping – selling a product below fair market value or below cost – opening up the possibility of competitive claims for the imposition of anti-dumping duties. In

August 1987 the US Commerce Department ruled that Japanese companies were illegally dumping roller bearings in the US by failing to increase prices as the yen strengthened against the dollar. The ruling was likely to be used as a precedent by other US companies that did not regain domestic sales despite the 85 per cent rise in the yen against the dollar between June 1985 and September 1988[78].

Many companies were able to register gains from the combination of cost reduction, product mix changes and price increases. For example, effective price increases of 10 per cent in both the US and the UK and 5 per cent in Germany, coupled to cost-reduction measures, enabled Japanese car manufacturers to break even at about 122 yen to the dollar, 185 yen to the pound and 65 yen to the deutsche mark when the yen rate stood at 150, 240 and 81, respectively[79].

While all these responses to *endakafukyo* helped to blunt much of the erosion of Japan's cost competitiveness, no amount of short-term savings were able to fully accommodate the yen's fall against the dollar to 130 in December 1987. This spurred major Japanese exporters to shift a growing amount of their final assembly operations into their Western markets both to capture lower labour costs and to reduce transportation charges.

9

THE COMPETITIVE SQUEEZE

Endaka, by changing the cost structure of Japanese industry, sand-wiched Japanese companies between increasing competition from the newly industrialized countries of Asia on one hand and from revitalized competitors in the West on the other.

The NICs – particularly Hong Kong, Korea, Singapore and Taiwan – were able to significantly increase their competitive position as a result of *endaka*. Two factors worked to the advantage of the Asian NICs. First, their currencies were virtually pegged to the US dollar throughout 1986 – the year of highest yen appreciation. The Korean won and the New Taiwan dollar increased by only 7 per cent and 5 per cent respectively against the dollar in 1986, while the yen appreciated against the dollar by approximately 25 per cent in 1986 alone[80]. Each increase of the yen value against the dollar lifted the price gap between the NICs and Japan and improved their competitive position. Second, the NICs enjoyed relatively low labour costs compared to Japan. In 1986 the average hourly labour cost in Taiwan was $3.50 compared to $14.00 in Japan[81] and Korea's labour cost for steel of $23 per metric tonne provided a major competitive advantage over Japan's cost of $132 per metric tonne[82].

With relatively fixed currencies and low labour costs the NICs were able to make considerable inroads into Western markets, picking up previously secure Japanese business. For example, Goldstar of Korea picked up Matsushita's OEM colour television business with General Electric in the US when GE refused to accept Matsushita's claim for increased costs. Matsushita assembled the colour televisions in its US plant with 50 per cent of the value imported in component form from Japan[83]. Similarly the OEM business in K-Mart and Sears, Roebuck's retail outlets in the US, once solidly supplied by Japanese firms, moved to Goldstar.

The NICs began to invade the low end of the market which the Japanese were beginning to vacate as they moved upmarket to secure bigger margins to compensate for *endaka*. By mid-1986 Hyundai, after less than 18 months in the market, was the leading car importer in Canada with an 8 per cent market share. Hyundai passed Volkswagen, Subaru and Mazda to become the number four imported car in the US in 1986 after Honda, Toyota and Nissan[84].

The NICs used a two-pronged attack to cement these gains. The first was centred on a push with consumer advertising to establish brand name recognition in the US and Europe, and the second was building plants to avoid possible future protectionist moves. Hyundai started building a Can$325 million car assembly plant in Canada and Samsung established colour television, video recorder and microwave assembly plants in Europe. By the end of 1986 Korean firms alone had invested $200 million in US assembly plants[85].

The effects of *endaka* and the increased competition from the Asian NICs were quickly reflected in their economic performance. In the first six months of 1986 the economies of Hong Kong, Korea and Taiwan registered gains of 5, 11.1 and 8.1 per cent at the expense of Japan, which grew at less than 3 per cent[86]. To put this performance into perspective, the combined US trade surplus in favour of the four Asian NICs at the end of 1986 at $30 billion was about equal to the US *combined* imports from France, Germany and the UK and just over one half of the trade surplus run up by Japan with the US in 1986[87].

For the first time Japan was facing severe competition in its major export markets from countries using its own past formula of success – highly efficient low-cost production emphasizing high product quality at very competitive prices. At the same time Japan faced another challenge . . . from a revitalized West.

First, *endaka* lost Japanese companies their formidable cost edge over their Western rivals in most industries. At best, Western products cost the same and as the yen appreciated against the dollar many US companies actually became lower-cost producers than their Japanese competitors. Second, through a combination of restructuring, deregulation, privatization and strategic alliances Western companies held the promise of becoming more efficient and more competitive.

In the 1980s well over half of the major corporations in the US had undergone some form of restructuring. Companies as diverse as AT&T, Chrysler, Exxon, Ford, General Electric, General Motors, IBM, ITT, Kodak and Union Carbide closed operations, reduced work forces and spun off subsidiaries to streamline their operations to make them more competitive. Thousands of other companies in fear of and as a result of being acquired or merged in the take-over boom of the early 1980s also restructured, resulting in the elimination of unprofitable operations and surplus manpower. In the US the restructuring had a major impact on productivity. Although manufacturing and mining represented only a quarter of US output they accounted for 50 to 65 per cent of all mergers and acquisitions between 1980 and 1986. In the same period the manufacturing and mining sector achieved productivity gains of 3.3 per cent – three times the 1.1 per cent increase registered by the non-agricultural sector of the US economy[88].

European firms like AEG-Telefunken, ASEA-Brown Boveri, Atlas Copco, Rolls-Royce, SKF, BSN, Ford (Europe), Citroën–Peugeot, Fiat, GM (Europe), Guinness, ICI, Jaguar, Olivetti, Philips and Thomson also went through major restructuring programmes to improve their competiveness. While mergers and acquisitions also increased in Europe with similar effects on competitiveness another change has occurred with the privatization of government-owned firms supporting the free market policies of European governments. In the UK, companies involved in air transport, aerospace, armaments, car manufacturing, banks, nuclear medicine, oil, telecommunications, trucking and utilities have been sold to the private sector. In France, banks, chemical firms, insurance companies and televisions stations, in Italy car firms, in Spain car and oil firms and in Sweden steel companies have been sold or are planned for sale to the public.

Added to the increases in Western productivity were two widely pursued business strategies complementing the drive for increased competitiveness. The first was based on customer demand for better product quality and service which was reflected in quality ratings. For example, Chrysler, Ford and GM in 1986 were making much better cars than they were in 1981 as a result of adopting Japanese zero-defect approaches in the mid-1970s[89]. Second, Western companies moved rapidly to form wide-ranging strategic alliances with other Western and, increasingly, Japanese firms to find, develop, produce and market new products and processes.

Japanese companies for the first time were facing growing competition from an increasing number of regenerated Western firms which were able to meet both Japanese costs and levels of productivity. Coupled with increased product quality and the opportunities provided by strategic alliances, Western firms were beginning to move towards a position where they could really begin to challenge Japan's competitiveness across a wide range of businesses.

10

BAD NEWS FOR THE WEST

While the rise in the value of the yen against the dollar had a major short-term impact on Japanese companies the mid-term outlook is a lot less bleak than is generally perceived. In fact, the effects of *endaka* on Japan's competitiveness and its economy are far more positive than has been credited and the West has *more* than less to fear from *endaka*.

Concern over the effects of *endaka* on Japanese business consistently fails to acknowledge that the impact has been largely on Japan's marginal firms and underestimates the financial strength of Japanese companies and the level of government support given to industry. As late as 1985 some 15 per cent of Japan's exports were produced by thousands of small companies focusing on low-cost, low-technology products such as cutlery and tools in almost 100 regional centres. More than 80 small low-technology exporters of metalware, porcelain and machine tools went bankrupt between November 1985 and March 1986 as a result of the effects of *endaka*[90]. The rise of the yen also sounded the death-knell of much of Japan's labour-intensive smokestack industry which began to give way to the Asian NICs in much the same way as the West's smokestack industries were forced to give way to those of Japan in the 1960s and 1970s.

Endaka has begun to force the mediocre and the marginal firms and activities out of Japan's economy and will encourage acquisitions and mergers to reduce the total number of companies and make the survivors much more competitive. Combined with major restructuring, improvements in production economics, low-cost raw materials, reductions in the labour force, product mix changes and selective price increases the survivors will be leaner and much more of a threat to the West. With a greater emphasis on a higher value-added product mix of high-technology products, Japanese firms will come into direct

conflict with the premium areas of the market where Western manufacturers retreated after losing their battle in the low-priced segments
against the Japanese in the 1970s. By wiping out a large portion of
Japan's marginal businesses and industrial activities, forcing a massive
concentration on productivity improvements and focusing on
advanced technology, higher-margin business, Japanese industry's
response to *endaka* may well come back to haunt the West.

Part of Japanese industry's strength has been its financial muscle
and most major Japanese companies have a lot of accumulated financial fat to burn through after record profits in 1983 and 1984. As a
result they have not been as hard hit as the financial reports for fiscal
years 1985 and 1986 and the projections for fiscal 1987 suggest.
Matsushita, for example, had an accumulated surplus of $13 billion in
its balance sheet at the end of fiscal 1986[91]. Many firms also have the
opportunity to sell marketable securities and realize foreign exchange
profits related to the payback of loans. Together with cash reserves
they provide a financial cushion against the effect of *endaka*.

Even more enterprising Japanese firms have used sophisticated fund
management, or *zaitech* (financial technology), to obtain a new earnings
stream from investing their surplus funds. Almost half the companies in
the non-financial sector of the Tokyo Stock Exchange made net profits on
financial items in fiscal 1986. These profits were enough to offset operating
losses in the mainstream businesses for major manufacturing companies
like Nissan, Sanyo and Sony[92] (Table 10.1).

Table 10.1. The leading proponents of alternative income strategies in Japan in fiscal
1986 (year to March 1987)

	Zaitech profit (billion yen)	Percentage change	Percentage of pre-tax profits
Toyota	159.0	+11.9	48
Nissan	127.0	+93.4	107
Matsushita	115.4	+11.4	61
Mitsubishi	46.3	+3378.1	58
Sony	39.1	+29.4	107
Sharp	30.9	−16.2	81
Toa Nenryo	23.0	+51.4	25
Sumitomo	21.6	(loss in 85)	46
Nippon Oil	21.0	+11.8	106
Sanyo	18.0	−44.3	118

Source: *The Financial Times*, 10 June 1987

This strong financial position is not only a result of strong export performance. The structure of Japanese industry and a combination of creative accounting and fiscal conservatism on the part of Japanese companies have helped to strengthen their financial base. The Japanese economy is dominated by *keiretsu*, which have the depth of resources to finance and the operations to redeploy labour to help to reduce the impact of cyclical downturns in the economy. Large accumulated profits and the ability to switch financial and human resources were major assets in combatting the full effects of *endaka*.

Japanese attitudes towards finance and the financial system also work in favour of Japanese firms. In fiscal 1985 ending on 31st March 1986 the average yen–dollar exchange rate was 221 – very close to the average level of 238 for the previous four years[93]. Fearing the worst, Japanese exporters rapidly depreciated stocks, plant and equipment, lowering reported profits. Since the tax system allows firms to switch special untaxed reserve funds into debt this depressed profits and helped to reduce taxable income in fiscal 1985. As profits in Japan are normally understated – the price/earnings ratios on the Tokyo Stock Exchange are on average four times higher than those on the London or New York Exchanges – the measures taken to reduce profits even further suggest that most Japanese firms are still relatively strong and can ride out the estimated two to three years necessary to fully restructure their businesses to combat the effects of *endaka*. This is borne out by two facts. First, despite the 61 per cent rise in the value of the yen against the dollar between September 1985 and February 1987 there were remarkably few corpses of medium and large-sized Japanese firms. Second, corporate bankruptcies actually fell for the 26th consecutive month in February 1987, by 14.9 per cent from a year earlier. While 769 companies between October 1985 and February 1987 went out of business as a result of *endaka*, none were major firms and the total direct job losses totalled only 18,156[94].

The fact is that there are large numbers of Japanese companies with the financial muscle to ride out the effects of *endaka* while they restructure to regain their competitiveness. Those that disappear will be the marginal firms who do not have the cash or the technology to create and maintain sound businesses. Those that remain will be even more formidable competitors.

Japanese government has a long and complex relationship with industry and has traditionally adopted programmes designed to support business. The government's domestic spending pulled Japan out of its industrial slumps in 1971, 1975 and in 1977. *Endaka* has proved to be no exception to this policy and has triggered a number of government actions to assist business in overcoming the impact of *endaka*.

Early in 1986 new legislation gave tax relief to exporters to keep changing their product lines, and lobbying from small firms produced low-interest loans for exporters in financial difficulties[95]. The Japanese government's accommodating monetary policy included reducing the discount rate five times from the beginning of 1986 – to 2.5 per cent, the lowest in the post-war period. This helped to ease credit conditions and beef up cash flows, so reducing financial pressures on many companies[96].

In specific industries the government provided the initiative for restructuring. For example, government plans in the hard-hit shipbuilding industry which faced a cost disadvantage of 35 per cent from Korea were wide-ranging. To help the industry shed a 20 per cent excess capacity the Japanese government allowed mergers, regroupings and a cartel and absorbed the repayment of liabilities incurred in job losses, losses on the sale of excess capacity and bought unneeded land and equipment. Finally, to ease national unemployment the 1987 budget included a one-year plan of $737 million designed to create 300,000 new jobs through employee subsidies and retraining programmes. Overall the government spending package launched in mid-1987 totalled 600 billion yen[97].

With an impact largely confined to marginal businesses, restructuring, supported by strong internal cash reserves and government policies of intervention and support, *endaka* had a relatively short-term effect on Japan's industrial competitiveness. More important for the West was the fact that the survivors would emerge leaner and more competitive than ever before.

The key concern in Japan following *endaka* is a 'hollowing out' of Japan's industrial base and the problems this will create through unprecedented unemployment in the late 1980s. However, it is wishful thinking to assume that Japan will follow the same route and suffer the same traumas as the US and the EEC as their industries attempted restructuring in the late 1970s and early 1980s in response to Japanese competition.

Japan's real economic problem lies in the growing uncompetitiveness of its labour-intensive heavy industries. However, restructuring began in Japan's smokestack or heavy industries in the late 1970s when aluminium, coal, shipbuilding, steel and even the textile industries began to reduce employment ahead of predictable declines in output and competitiveness. These industries were allowed to set up cartels, coordinate capacity cuts, close uneconomic plants and diversify out of their core businesses[98]. Much of the surplus labour in Japan's heavy industries through reassignment within *keiretsu* was successfully redeployed ahead of *endaka* since the annual economic growth in the early 1980s of 4 to 5 per cent per annum created more new jobs than were lost. While it is recognized that most smokestack industries in Japan will never be able to adjust to the full effects of *endaka*, the overall economic impact will be limited since much of the slack has already been taken up.

For over a decade Japan has had a policy of moving out of labour-intensive smokestack industries into clean, knowledge-intensive higher value-added industries strongly supported by government incentives. Many Japanese companies have already made significant strides to diversify outside their businesses to make them less vulnerable to *endaka*. For example, Kawasaki Steel expects that 40 per cent of its business will come from outside the steel industry by the year 2000, compared with only 20 per cent in 1987, and Nippon Steel plans to double its sales by 1995 to $31.4 billion with half its sales coming from new ventures like theme parks and computers[99]. Kubota, the largest Japanese producer of agricultural equipment, spent $75 million largely on buying minority status in five leading-edge California computer component manufacturers starting in October 1986. Kubota unveiled its first state-of-the-art mini-super computer in record time in August 1988.

Japan is becoming a more mature and diversified economy. Jobs in the service sector including finance, wholesaling, retailing and restaurants are beginning to grow rapidly and provide new employment opportunities. While manufacturing jobs declined by 380,000 in January 1987, over the same period in 1986 employment increased in the service sector by 610,000[100]. MITI estimates that the service industries created 4.8 million new jobs in Japan from 1970 to 1980 and will keep creating new employment in the service sector at the same pace for at least the next decade[101].

Unemployment, however, is a major concern. While unemployment among Japanese male workers registered 3.1 per cent in July 1986 (the highest on record since employment statistics were first collected in 1953), these levels would be welcomed in Brussels or Washington, as would the forecast increases in unemployment compared with those in the US or the EEC[102] (Table 10.2).

Table 10.2. The increase in Japan's unemployment as a percentage of the labour force as a result of *endaka* compared to the US and the EEC.

	1983 (%)	1984 (%)	1985 (%)	1986 (%)	1987 (%)	1988 (%)
Japan	2.7	2.7	2.6	2.75	3.0	3.25
US	9.6	7.5	7.2	7.0	6.75	6.5
EEC	10.2	10.8	11.5	11.5	11.5	11.5

Source: *OECD Economic Outlook*, No. 39, OECD Paris, September 1986, and OECD estimates (*Wall Street Journal*, 6 January 1987)

In fairness, Japan's unemployment figures are grossly undercast. Excluded are school-leavers and graduates looking for jobs, thousands of part-time workers who make up a substantial part of the labour force, the self-employed, who account for 10 per cent of the workforce, and heavy overmanning in the service industries[103]. When these are included in the labour statistics Japan's unemployment level is roughly comparable to that of the US.

The underlying employment issue in Japan in the mid-term is developing new jobs, while phasing out the marginal firms and the 'padding' which occurs throughout Japanese industry, without creating and maintaining high unemployment levels. While *endaka* will certainly have an effect on employment, particularly among new job seekers, part-time and self-employed workers, the predicted growth in service industry jobs as Japan moves towards a more mature economy will overcome much if not all of this unemployment. MITI estimates, for example, that while Japan will lose approximately 560,000 manufacturing jobs by the year 2000 this will be more than offset by the creation of 1,170,000 new jobs in the service and high-technology industries[104].

The good news for Japan is that *endaka* has helped to purge the Japanese economy of the mediocre companies and the marginal industries with little real impact on economic development or unemployment. The bad news for the West is that the revitalized Japanese survivor is a much leaner and meaner competitor than before.

SUMMARY

Japan has been hard hit by *endaka*. However, it was far from a fatal body blow. Japan's economic position, accounting for some 10 per cent of the world GNP, is strong enough for Japan to withstand the immediate effects of *endaka*.

Endaka is forcing a cure for some of the long-term economic problems by helping to move Japan away from protected marginal businesses and smokestack industries towards a more competitive high-technology industrial base and a broader service sector.

Accumulated cash, the benefits of a favourable financial system and government assistance will enable most Japanese firms to ride out the two to three years needed to restructure. As the economy matures and the service sector increases, enough new jobs will be provided to mop up much of the unemployment created by *endaka*. Although Japan has suffered job losses this has been confined mainly to a few coal, shipbuilding and steel towns.

To their credit, Japanese firms have rapidly come to terms with a number of new business realities:

- The artificially undervalued yen has gone for good.

- Japan no longer has a significant production cost advantage over its international trade rivals.

- A restructuring of Japanese industry was both overdue and inevitable.

- The unavoidable price of restructuring will be a decline in manufacturing and in lifetime employment conditions.

- The politics and the economics of exporting favour increased offshore assembly in their major markets.

While restructured Japanese companies emerging from *endaka* will be far more competitive and a much stronger challenge to the West the real issue will be *how* they will compete in an increasingly cost competitive West.

For Japanese companies to continue to grow under these new cost conditions there is only one option: offshore production in both the US and the EEC. Japanese firms can maintain their cost competitiveness by building up local assembly capacity *within* the markets of their major trading partners, using highly sophisticated logistics systems and sourcing high value-added components in Japan to maximise the economies of scale and using low-cost local labour and services.

Endaka has in fact created two new spectres for the West: a much more efficient Japanese industrial structure bolted on to a rapid increase in Japanese productive capacity in the US and the EEC. Compounding the problem is a growing competitive challenge from the Asian NICs who are also emulating assembly plant operations in the West.

PART 3

PLAYING TO WIN

11

A NEW SET OF RULES

The curse of Japan's export-driven success has been a rapid increase in Western challenges to traditional export strategies. The Japanese response to these multiple challenges has been a major change in their strategic approach to business. At the heart of these second-wave business strategies is the drive to build up appreciable levels of manufacturing capacity in the West through direct investments, acquisitions and joint ventures to deflect the impact of growing protectionism and the high yen value.

Japanese overseas investment strategy is now concentrated on the wholly-owned manufacturing subsidiary. By starting up in a new purpose-built facility, using state-of-the-art production and process technology and machinery with selectively hired non-unionized labour on a greenfield site located in an economically depressed area Japanese firms can maximize investment grants and loans and deferred tax opportunities. By coupling this to a limited amount of local component sourcing Japanese companies can also minimize import duty and tax penalties:

- Komatsu's £12.5 million assembly plant in the UK will avoid 26.6 per cent EEC anti-dumping duties levied on imported excavators[105].

- Toshiba's $1.2 million video recorder production line at its existing US facility was developed with the objective of avoiding the future possibility of import surcharges[106].

- Matsushita's £6 million investment in an electronic typewriter and printer assembly plant in the UK was primarily motivated by the EEC's imposition of 21–23 per cent import duties in 1985 on Japanese electronic typewriters[107].

- Konica's DM20 million assembly plant for photocopiers in West Germany was built explicitly in response to the EEC's 15.8 per cent anti-dumping duties imposed in August 1986.

These tactics can leverage production costs to similar and even lower levels than those of local competitors saddled with old plant and a static work force. Ford UK, for example, estimates that Nissan's plant in the north of England has a unit cost advantage of $500 to $800 over Ford's UK-produced cars[108].

In the US, the UK, the Netherlands and West Germany wholly-owned manufacturing subsidiaries are the preferred Japanese approach to convert export supply into local production[109].

On a much smaller scale Japanese companies are using selective acquisitions of existing firms to provide a local production base. With the increasing value of the yen this provides the opportunity to buy high-value assets at low cost and low risk together with brand names and their distribution and customer franchises, which normally require considerable amounts of time and cash to develop independently.

Typically the companies acquired are in mature industries and have large fixed capital investments. Frequently the existing managements have run into severe problems but the Japanese saw opportunities for innovative business development. Asahi Glass' acquisition of Glaverbel in Belgium and de Maas in the Netherlands in 1981 for $40 million and Sumitomo Rubber's purchase of Dunlop's manufacturing assets in France, the UK and West Germany in 1984 for $450 million (and the independently owned US unit for $93.5 million in late 1986) are typical examples. Asahi Glass utilized its energy-saving production technology to lower costs and Sumitomo introduced its process technology and management skills to reduce costs and increase plant efficiency.

In other cases these acquisitions have been a formalization of existing informal links. Dainippon Ink and Chemicals, a major producer of printing inks, synthetic resins and specialty chemicals, strengthened its US position by first purchasing Kohl and Madden and Polychrome (1976) before acquiring the graphic arts unit of Sun Chemical in 1986 for $500 million, with whom it had had licensing links for printing ink technology for 30 years[110].

The Japanese interest in acquisitions has begun to accelerate. Japanese acquisitions of US companies in the first seven months of 1988 increased to 95 totalling $9 billion. This compares with 146 acquisitions totalling $6.4 billion in all of 1987, which was double the 1986 figure[111]. Japanese companies are also pursuing acquisitions in other countries with the same vigour. Publicly disclosed Japanese foreign acquisitions more than doubled in 1986 to 78, up from only 31 in 1985[112]. During 1987 and 1988 there was a significant change in acquisition policy and several Japanese companies made large-scale acquisitions of major US manufacturers, taking advantage of the low dollar-yen parity (Table 11.1).

Table 11.1. Major Japanese manufacturing acquisitions in the US (1987 and 1988)

Acquiror	Acquired	Cost (US$ billion)
Bridgestone	Firestone (tyres)	2.6
Sony	CBS (records)	2.0
Nippon Mining	Gould	1.1
Paloma	Rheem Mfg.	1.0
Dainippon Ink	Reichold Chemical	0.54
Ryobi	Motor Products	0.325

Acquiring rather than building plants has also enabled Japanese companies to buy market share rather than cause trade friction by taking sales away from existing producers. Asahi Glass' acquisitions of Glaverbel and de Maas, for example, gave Asahi a 10 per cent share of the EEC flat glass market without displacing existing competition[113]. Equity holdings and joint ventures are also increasing. However, there is a major shift in emphasis away from the first-wave objectives of establishing market presence to achieving linkages with other Japanese companies and to circumvent entry barriers created by political and competitive conditions:

- Increasing numbers of Japanese car assembly plants in the West have encouraged Japanese auto supply firms to follow suit and build up business to service the car manufacturers. Substantial equity holdings have been acquired in ailing US steel companies

75

– Kawasaki Steel purchased 50 per cent of California Steel, Nippon Kokan secured a 50 per cent holding in Wheeling, Pittsburgh and Sumitomo Metals acquired 40 per cent of LTV – all to supply Japanese car manufacturers in the USA[114]. Joint ventures in the component market have also increased. In the US Asahi Glass has a joint venture with PPG Industries to supply auto glass to Honda and Akebano is negotiating a joint venture with GM's Delco Moraine to produce brake components[115]. Similarly in the UK, Nihon has linked up with TI to produce exhaust systems, Ikeda Bussan with Hoover Universal to manufacture seats and headliners and Nippon Antenna with UTC International to produce aerials – all to supply Nissan's UK plant[116].

- In the US supercomputer market the larget customer, the US Government, prefers to purchase from US manufacturers for national security reasons. NEC's joint venture with Honeywell in 1986 was designed to use Honeywell's US sales network, which it already used to market its DPS-90 mainframe computer under the Honeywell label, to market its supercomputers[117]. Later in 1986 NEC formed a joint company with Honeywell and Cie. des Machines Bull in France to market NEC's Acos large main frame computers in the US and Europe.

In the first wave of competition Japanese companies were frequently the junior partners and even with a 50 per cent share generally left their Western partners to manage the business. In the second wave Japanese companies have reversed this position and are firmly in control of most of their manufacturing investments. For, example, in the auto supply and component business the Japanese partner's knowledge of his Japanese customers' needs and operating practices and the trust and loyalty built up over long-term relationships in Japan are more valuable than their Western partners' local marketing and distribution skills. In over 85 per cent of all equity holdings made in Europe after 1984 Japanese firms hold 50 per cent or more of the joint venture equity[118].

These equity arrangements are also moving away from agreements with local industrial partners to arrangements with consortia of development agencies such as the Irish Development Agency, North

Netherlands Development Corporation, Société Régionale d'Investissement de Wallon and the Instituto Nacional de Industria – and local banks and private individuals. This helps to create strong local community ties and political support and avoids the most frequent source of friction in joint ventures – other industrial partners.

By changing emphasis from finished-product exports to a mix of direct investments in assembly plants, acquisitions of companies and joint ventures with Western partners Japanese firms have essentially changed the nature of competition. Their Western rivals are now faced with a growing competitive challenge from Japanese firms operating *inside* their own markets which are almost immune to protective measures and the effects of *endaka*.

12

FROM FOLLOWER TO LEADER

To move up the industrial value-added chain to build secure competitive positions for the future, Japanese companies adopted a strong push for technology leadership. This required accelerating the process of acquiring, developing and introducing new technology.

To improve the strategic value of their research and development Japanese companies focused on increasing expenditure on R&D while keeping a balance between intellectual and physical investments and maintaining an equilibrium between basic and applied research and development. These tactics were geared to one objective: improving the flow of new, high value-added products.

Research is a high-risk and long-term cycle which has major financial implications. R&D expenses suffer higher inflation rates than consumer prices and costs rise exponentially when moving up the knowledge chain to more complex scientific problems.

To address a wider spectrum of research interests and increase the probability of success Japanese companies rapidly increased their research spending. Japan still lags the West in terms of total R&D expenditure; however, it has doubled its commitment as a percentage of gross domestic product (GDP) since 1979 with a sustained growth rate of more than twice that of its Western competitors[119]. To put this expenditure into perspective Japan, with a growing economy, was increasing its research expenditure when the economies of the US and the EEC were essentially flat. Overall OECD countries increased their collective GDP by only 4 per cent between 1980 and 1983 and the EEC by only 1 per cent.

While Japan was steadily increasing its R&D efforts those of the USA and EEC levelled off. The result was that Japan emerged a close second to the US in funding R&D in spite of the fact that the US has increased its R&D expenditure by more than 85 per cent since 1981[120] (Figure 12.1). These high Japanese R&D investments are understated. They do not cover the effect of the low-interest loans available in Japan for R&D, government loans for specific industry research, tax incentives, R&D tax credits and liberal tax deductions for R&D expenditures.

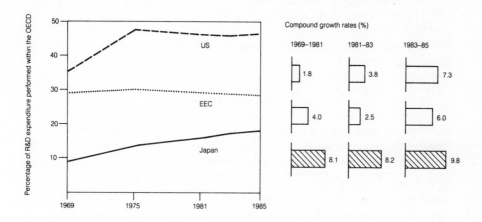

Figure 12.1. Japan's sustained commitment to improving its R&D (OECD = 100).

Source: OECD Science and Technology Indicators, No. 2 – R&D, Invention and Competitiveness, Paris 1986; updated 1988.

All of these have helped to offset increases and lower the effective cost of performing R&D and spurred greater levels of investment[121]. Japanese government agencies also act as catalysts to guide private sector R&D investment to focus on meeting national policy goals for technology development. These can be powerful stimulants for individual firms. Table 12.1 provides an overview of the key R&D projects funded by Japanese government agencies in 1987.

Since almost 70 per cent of Japanese industrial R&D is funded by companies (compared to around 50 per cent in the USA and the EEC) Japan's R&D is focused more closely on delivering customer-oriented products and processes. Compounding the problem for the West is the fact that the 50 per cent of industrial R&D sponsored by Western governments is largely devoted to military applications which have limited value in industrial products[122] (Figure 12.2).

Table 12.1. Japanese Government funding of advanced R&D projects: 1987.

Project	Sponsoring agency*	Fiscal year 1987 budget (yen billion)
Basic technologies for future industries (new materials, biotechnology, electronic devices)	AIST	6
Energy conservation technology (super heat pumps, energy accumulation systems)	AIST	11.5
New energy technology (coal, geothermal, hydrogen and solar energies)	AIST	44
Large-scale systems (advanced materials processing and machining systems)	AIST	15
Energy-related technologies (commercialization of fast breeder reactor and uranium enrichment)	ANRE	72
Fifth-generation computer project	MIIB	4
Free-flier system for unmanned space experiments	MIIB	1.7
Aerospace projects 7J7 with Boeing, V2500 with others	MIIB	4.7

* AIST: Agency for Industrial Science and Technology
  ANRE: Agency for Natural Resources and Energy
  MIIB: Machinery and Information Industry Bureau

Source: MITI

Despite the strong appreciation of the yen in 1986 and 1987 and its impact on export-based business, Japanese companies maintained a strong commitment to R&D. Honda's profits dropped by nearly one third in the first quarter of 1986 but its R&D spend went up by 25 per cent. Similarly, Konica with 50 per cent of its sales in exports recorded a pre-tax fall in profits of 20 per cent in 1985. Although profits were forecast to fall by up to a further 50 per cent in 1986 Konica was planning an 11 per cent increase in its R&D expenditure[123].

Companies have two basic investment decisions: physical (equipment, machinery, plant and buildings) and intellectual (research and development). Physical investments were cut back or dropped in the recession of the late 1970s and early 1980s by most Western companies to help maximize short-term returns. As a result their ratio of intellectual to physical investments increased. Japanese companies poured cash into new equipment, machinery and construction while increasing their R&D spend. By maintaining a balance between physical and intellectual investments Japanese companies were able to maintain their lead in production efficiency to maintain their compe-

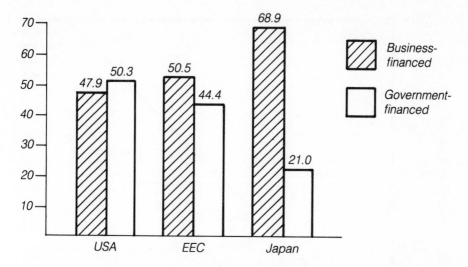

Figure 12.2. With industry providing over two thirds of the expenditure on R&D, Japan's R&D is more focused on industrial applications (percentage of R&D financed by business and government – 1985).

Source: OECD Science and Technology Indicators, No. 2 – *R&D, Invention and Competitiveness*, Paris 1986; updated 1988.

titive manufacturing advantage as well as renew plant and equipment. This helped them to absorb new technology faster and diffuse this technology through new products and processes more rapidly into global markets. The cash generated by these new products and processes was reinvested to continue the research, development, production and marketing of new products in a self-reinforcing cycle. While the data in Figure 12.3 cover the facility and R&D expenditures for only one fiscal year (1985) for twenty leading Japanese companies, they show the strong balance between physical and intellectual investments made by Japanese firms.

R&D expenditure levels suggest that the US remains strong in experimental development and the EEC in basic research, while Japan has maintained an equilibrium in the types of research activity funded (Figure 12.4). This is deceptive since it masks Japan's real strength in the innovative process as well as what Japan is doing to overcome its inherent weaknesses in technology.

Innovation usually consists of small increments and rarely of major breakthroughs. The Japanese, with limited experience in basic research, have concentrated on adding a large number of incremental

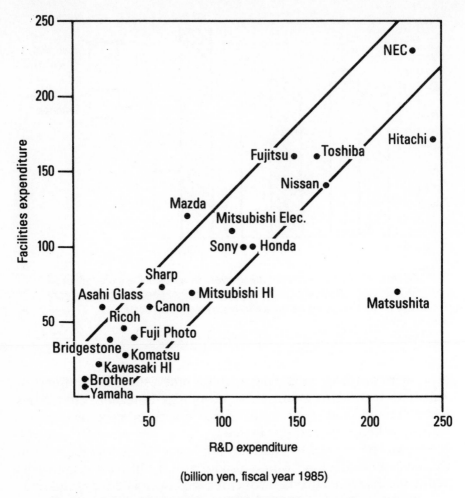

Figure 12.3. The balance between R&D and facility expenditures in leading Japanese companies assists moving products rapidly from conception through introduction in world markets.

Source: Japanese Company Handbook, Toyo Keizai, Shinposha, Tokyo, 1986.

improvements to products and production processes by investing heavily in building on previous and predictable knowledge rather than pioneering unproven technology. Since Japanese industrial R&D is geared to creating products for world markets, the development of mass-production systems and highly developed manufacturing and process technology skills to produce high-volume, high-quality products at low cost is the real strength of the Japanese R&D system[124]. As

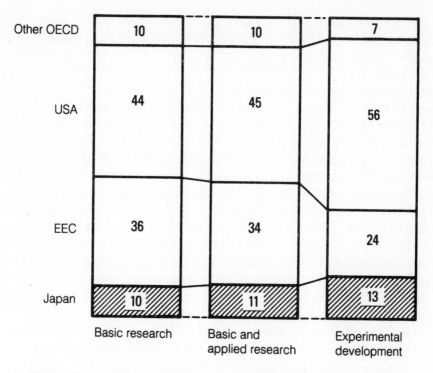

Figure 12.4. Japan's maintenance of a balance in research activity supports the rapid commercialization of new products. (Estimated R&D expenditure by activity – OECD countries 1985.)

Source: OECD Science and Technology Indicators, No. 2 – *R&D, Invention and Competitiveness*, Paris, 1986; updated 1988.

a very high percentage of industrial R&D is funded by companies in Japan the level of organizational integration of the innovative cycle, from conception through to mass production, is far higher than in Western companies. With a strong focus on delivering finished products, Japanese companies have developed advanced manufacturing techniques which have provided them with significant competitive advantages[125]. While Western companies concentrated on developing new products the Japanese focused on the nuts and bolts of basic manufacturing and found innovative ways of reducing machine set-up times, improving machine utilization, developing multi-machine handling, small-lot production and mixed production techniques, improving materials handling, perfecting continuous production systems and developing innovative inventory systems.

To go beyond improving on the technology of others meant that Japan had to overcome its limited experience in basic research and obtain access to leading-edge technologies. Many leading Japanese companies began funding basic research at US universities, coupling their investments to the presence of Japanese researchers on-site to obtain hands-on experience at the cutting edge of new technologies. For example, at the National Institute of Health in the US, one of the world's premier biomedical research centres, three quarters of the 311 Japanese researchers are on US-funded NIH fellowships and the rest are supported by Japanese institutions. Hitachi Chemicals' $12 million donation to the University of California at Irvine has secured the use of two thirds of its new biotechnology laboratory for 40 years, and at the Massachusetts Institute of Technology 42 Japanese companies have donated money and endowed 16 chairs at approximately $1.5 million each and spend some $4 million a year for access to MIT's research[126]. To add to the acquisition of basic knowledge many Japanese companies also established laboratories to obtain expertise in established US R&D excellence centres, particularly in California[127].

The combination of a knack of identifying growth opportunities, popularizing advanced technology with a market-oriented innovative system largely under the control of companies helped the Japanese to target selected industries and strengthen their R&D position relative to both the USA and the EEC. With the exception of aerospace, Japan has become a technological superpower second only to the USA and now equals and even surpasses the R&D efforts of the EEC in a number of industries (Figure 12.5).

The intensity of Japan's R&D focus is striking when the growth rates of Japanese R&D funding over time are compared to those of the USA, the engine driving world R&D. Japan's drive to increase its technology ran at up to five times the rate of the USA and the EEC across a wide range of industries between 1979 and 1983 (Figure 12.6). The results of Japan's push to achieve technology leadership through increased R&D expenditure, balancing capital investments and research activities and industrial focusing, have been spectacular.

Japan has become less dependent on imported technology to fuel its move into the leading-edge technologies which provide high value-added business opportunities. By 1985, Japan had moved towards closing the deficit in its technology balance of payments, tripling its receipts and reducing its net payments on patents and licences for imported technology, while the EEC's deficit widened by a factor of

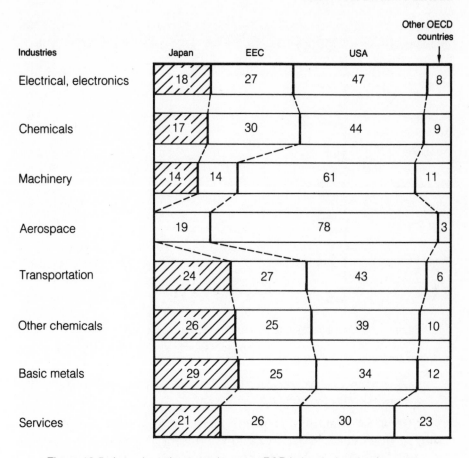

Figure 12.5. Japan's major commitment to R&D in key industries (percentage of R&D spent by key industry – 1983).

Electrical, electronics Electrical machinery, equipment and components	**Chemicals** Chemicals, drugs, and petrol refineries
Basic metals Ferrous and non-ferrous metals and fabricated metal production	**Machinery** Instruments, office machinery, computers and NC machines

Electrical, electronics
Electrical machinery, equipment and components

Basic metals
Ferrous and non-ferrous metals and fabricated metal production

Chemicals
Chemicals, drugs, and petrol refineries

Machinery
Instruments, office machinery, computers and NC machines

Aerospace
Aircraft and missiles

Other chemicals
Food, drink, tobacco, textiles, clothing, rubber and plastics

Transportation
Vehicles, ships

Services
Utilities, construction transport, storage and commercial and engineering services

Source: OECD Science and Technology Indicators, No. 2 – *R&D, Invention and Competitiveness*, Paris 1986; Updated 1988.

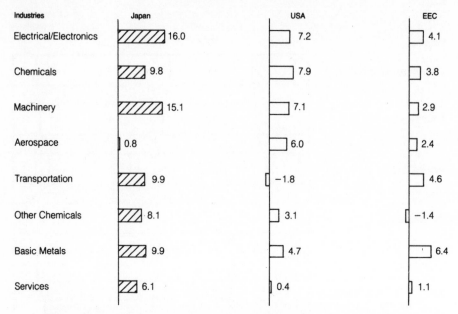

Industries	Japan	USA	EEC
Electrical/Electronics	16.0	7.2	4.1
Chemicals	9.8	7.9	3.8
Machinery	15.1	7.1	2.9
Aerospace	0.8	6.0	2.4
Transportation	9.9	−1.8	4.6
Other Chemicals	8.1	3.1	−1.4
Basic Metals	9.9	4.7	6.4
Services	6.1	0.4	1.1

Figure 12.6. Japan's drive to increase its technology runs at up to 5 times that of the USA and the EEC. (Compound growth rates 1979–83, percentage.)

Source: OECD Science and Technology Indicators, No. 2 – *R&D, Invention and Competitiveness*, Paris, 1986; Updated 1988.

four. The USA remains the prime source world-wide of new technology; however, Japan is rapidly eroding the USA's traditional scientific lead. By 1983 Japan earned approximately the same as the UK and twice as much as West Germany from the sale of its technology and probably had closed its technology balance of payments gap by 1987[128] (Figure 12.7).

This strong increase in technology capability made Japan a principal source of new technology. The increased availability of new technology to Japanese companies also provided strategic opportunities for cross-licensing technology to Western firms. Many companies in the West became less willing to license their proprietary technology to Japanese companies without a quid pro quo through fear that they would be mortgaging their own future by cloning competition. For example, Hitachi tried unsuccessfully to obtain licences from Motorola to make the complex advanced 68020 microprocessor[129].

The dramatic increase in Japan's technological capability helped to dispel the widely held myth that the Japanese, through education and

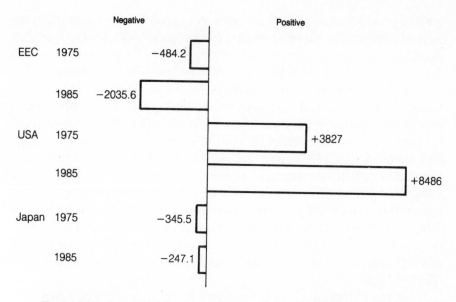

Figure 12.7. Japan's technology drive has reduced its dependence on foreign technology and improved Japan's balance in technology trade (US $ million).

Source: OECD Science and Technology Indicators, No. 2 – *R&D, Invention and Competitiveness*, Paris, 1986, Updated 1988.

culture, are copiers and modifiers of the ideas of others rather than innovators in their own right. Japan does have a number of problems with its drive for technology leadership. Much in Japanese society supresses creativity, bureaucracy is rife in research and conformity and good group dynamics are more valued in Japan than in Western research, where individuality is more prized[130].

While Japan does lack a surfeit of Nobel prizes in science – 4 compared to the American 139 – it does lead the world in a number of key technologies. In computer peripherals such as disk drives and printers, fibre optics, gallium arsenide memory chips, magnetic storage tape, numerically controlled machine tools and robotics, Japan has reached current levels of knowledge[131].

Where Japanese companies score heavily over their Western competitors is their ability to identify market applications for emerging technologies; to acquire and develop these technologies; and translate these ideas rapidly by concentrating resources into low-cost, high-quality products. Given Japan's selective capability to reach the frontiers of science in a number of advanced technologies and to translate these into successful new products there is every reason to believe that Japanese companies will increase their technological leverage.

Japan's industrial competitiveness has been improved as a direct result of its accelerated emphasis on technology. It is the only trading bloc with a positive balance of trade in all types of industrial technology, with absolute values two to three times those of the US in high and medium R&D-intensive industries. The EEC as a whole has a significant positive balance mainly in medium R&D-intensive industries. The EEC's surplus in high R&D-intensive industries has grown only marginally and it maintains its position in the low R&D-intensive 'smokestack' industries. Unfortunately the latter produce only low value-added opportunities and are unlikely to benefit from any upsurge in world economic growth or create new employment (Figure 12.8).

Japanese companies' long-term emphasis on technology has enabled Japan virtually to double its comparative advantage in high-technology trade in the 22 years from 1963 to 1985. In contrast, the comparative advantage of the US was virtually unchanged, while that of the EEC fell by almost 20 per cent. This helped to shift the centre of gravity for high technology in the 1980s from the North Atlantic to the North Pacific[132] (Table 12.2).

Table 12.2. The rise of Japan and the decline of the West in the development of comparative advantage in high-technology trade (Index of Comparative Advantage in High Technology Trade 1963–1985)

	1963	1970	1978	1983	1985
USA	1.27	1.18	1.27	1.26	1.25
EEC	1.01	0.94	0.88	0.82	0.80*
Japan	0.72	1.07	1.27	1.36	1.42
OECD	1.00	1.00	1.00	1.00	1.00

* Includes Portugal and Spain

Source: *Community Competitiveness in High Technology – the United States, the European Community and Japan: Trade and the World Economy*, B. Cardiff, Reading University, September 1986

Japan has been able to increase its overall export market shares and has doubled its share in the high and medium-intensive industries

	High	Medium	Low
USA	Positive (84)*	Positive (82, 83, 84)	Negative
EEC	Positive	Positive	Positive (79, 80, 83, 84)
Japan	Positive	Positive	Positive

R&D Intensity
*(negative years)

High
- Aerospace
- Office machines, computers
- Electronics and components
- Drugs
- Instruments
- Electrical machinery

Medium
- Automobiles
- Chemicals
- Non-electrical machinery
- Rubber, plastics
- Non-ferrous metals
- Other MFG industry

Low
- Stone, clay, glass
- Food, beverages, tobacco
- Shipbuilding
- Petrol refining
- Ferrous metals
- Fabricated metal products
- Paper, printing
- Wood, cork, furniture
- Textiles, footwear, leather

Figure 12.8. Japan's technology drive has produced a positive trade balance in all areas of R&D intensity – while that of its trade competitors has eroded (1970–84).

while those in the West have fallen as a result of Japan's increased competitiveness. Japan has lost market share marginally in the low R&D-intensive industries, which reflects its drive to higher value-added business and its gradual withdrawal from the low value-added smokestack industries which have a low level of R&D intensity (Figure 12.9). However, even in the smokestack industries Japanese

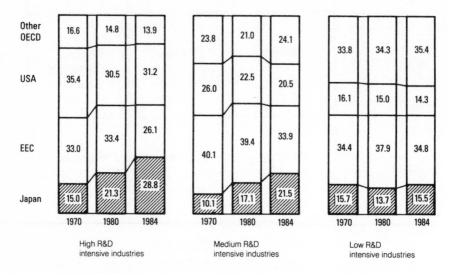

Figure 12.9. Japan's technology drive has progressively increased its export market share in the higher value-added industries – at the expense of its western competitors. (Intra EEC flows adjusted.)

Source: OECD Science and Technology Indicators, No. 2 – *R&D, Invention and Competitiveness*, Paris, 1986.

companies have selectively invested in R&D to maintain a profitable position. In steel, continuous R&D placed Japanese companies ahead of international competitors by eliminating impurities through improvements in steelmaking chemistry. This provided higher quality in full-scale production and, coupled with new state-of-the-art fuel-efficient continuous-casting techniques and fully computerized operations, offered integrated production control from the unloading of raw material to the shipping of finished product, improving efficiency[133]. Ironically, Japanese companies have developed the technological capability selectively to resurrect profitable niche areas in smokestack industries while their Western competitors, who created these industries, have been unable to run them competitively and have either let them die a slow death or have propped them up with massive government subsidies.

By bolting a capacity to invent – to discover and create new ideas – on to its proven capability to innovate – to convert knowledge into wealth – Japan will be in a far stronger position to improve its economic added value.

Through this major commitment to improving the quality and quantity of its R&D Japan has transferred itself within a decade from a follower to a leader in several areas of advanced technology.

Since these advances have been accomplished at the expense of a complacent West they have served to reinforce the fact that Japan is changing the nature of the game and playing it to win.

13

THE QUANTUM LEAP

Through the 1970s Japanese companies used strategies based on concentrating as many activities and resources as possible in Japan to develop cost leadership positions with high-volume, high-quality standardized products for export. At the same time their Western competitors were busy multinationalizing their businesses. This involved dispersing resources to build competitive advantages on a country basis by meeting local preferences with highly differentiated products (Figure 13.1).

With little protectionist pressure and an undervalued yen the centralized strategies of Japanese companies produced massive economies of scale, helping them to secure strong market positions in industries like cars, consumer electronics and machine tools. Western firms who decoupled their resources to build a competitive advantage based on meeting local market needs were extremely successful in industries like consumer package goods and services such as banking, insurance and retailing.

Even before the growth in protectionism and the increase in the value of the yen in the mid-1980s major Japanese exporters had begun to shift their emphasis subtly away from their centralized strategy. Although their strategy was highly successful they recognized that a number of emerging trends had the collective power seriously to affect their competitive cost advantage.

First, Japanese competitiveness was invariably focused on cost leadership based on continuous massive investments in new plant, machinery and processes concentrated in Japan to drive down costs. When labour costs began to rise substantially in the late 1970s many companies started to source low value-added components, sub-assemblies and even products in turn to South Korea, Hong Kong,

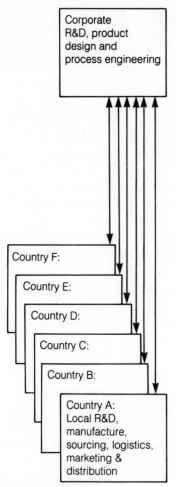

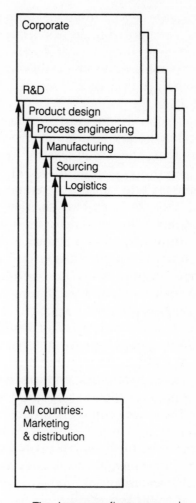

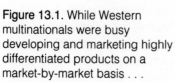

Figure 13.1. While Western multinationals were busy developing and marketing highly differentiated products on a market-by-market basis . . .

. . . The Japanese firms were using bi-dimensional strategies emphasizing high-volume, high-quality, low-priced standardized products.

Singapore and Taiwan, which offered natural cost advantages in labour. Japan, however, was able to continue to manufacture high and medium value-added products in Japan as a result of its strong focus on developing advanced production processes and techniques and the application of automated production, computer control and robotics to

93

leverage down the labour component in its costs. With an undervalued yen and growing domestic labour costs it became apparent to many Japanese companies in the early 1980s that their margins were highly vulnerable to unpredictable swings in yen values which could not be contained entirely by high levels of productivity and automated production.

Second, despite containerization, purpose-built bulk and car carriers and airfreighting for higher value-added products, which lowered shipping and handling costs, freight was still a major cost in an export-based strategy. In addition, long supply lines, which required extended delivery schedules, were vulnerable to interruptions in the continuity of shipments and to changes in consumer demand, which compounded the freight cost problem.

Third, Japan is a resource-poor country importing almost all its energy and natural resource requirements. The vulnerability to long lines of supply – oil from the Middle East and iron ore from Australia, for example – and fluctuating raw material and energy costs focused attention on both the need to secure dependable access through long-term supply contracts and to build or buy from value-added processing facilities near the raw material sources.

Fourth, Japan was moving towards eliminating its balance of trade deficit in technology and was beginning to export its rapidly expanding proprietary knowledge in product, process and production technology.

The increasing costs of technology and the rapid diffusion of this knowledge and the weak laws protecting proprietary technology increased business risk. This meant that new products and processes had to be introduced globally as rapidly as possible to obtain a competitive advantage and return a profit on the R&D investment.

Finally, as a result of focusing on a limited number of products to maximize volumes and offering low-cost high-quality products which created heavy consumer push allied to the pull of powerful distribution networks, many Japanese companies had created strong brand franchises among consumers on a world-wide scale.

The first three factors were instrumental in Japanese companies developing integrated sourcing, manufacturing and shipping strategies to leverage their costs and lower vulnerability across countries and regional boundaries to serve their business more efficiently (Figure 13.2).

The fourth and fifth factors focused Japanese attention on the increasing world-wide interdependence on technology. This led to

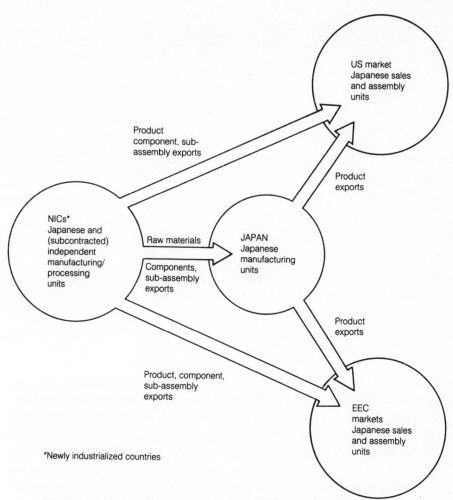

Figure 13.2. Japan has moved rapidly into integrated and co-ordinated sourcing, shipping and manufacturing strategies. These will leverage costs and lower vulnerability across countries and regional boundaries serving companies more efficiently.

building strong technology exchange agreements with Western companies and highlighted the need rapidly to spread R&D risk and return globally. As a result it fostered the development of Japanese-owned sales and distribution networks essential to support rapid product diffusion and build on global customer franchises (Figure 13.3).

The by-product of Japanese cost-leadership strategies – which required significant capital investment to achieve economies of scale

95

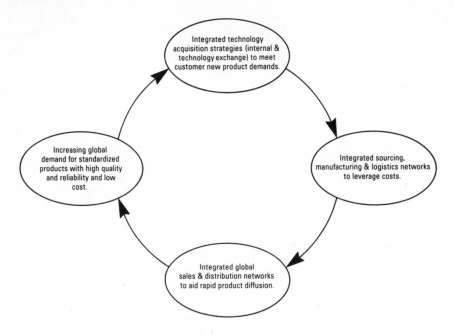

Figure 13.3. The global strategy cycle.

in manufacturing standardized products – were low prices, high quality and reliability. While these attributes ideally suited the demands of the homogeneous Japanese consumer, they placed Japanese companies in a pivotal position to exploit changes in world-wide consumer demand.

The growing standardization of consumer and industrial tastes and preferences in the late 1970s was due to a number of factors. The growth in international communications and travel heightened consumer awareness; changes in attitudes, behaviour and life styles made consumers more cost-conscious and value-driven; and the relative increases in consumer and industrial purchasing power forced the rapid diffusion of new products.

The Japanese realized that this provided them with the opportunity to sell essentially the same products across markets differentiated only by options and accessories to customers with a growing similarity in tastes. However, the Western multinationals frequently misinterpreted these new consumer trends as a need to accommodate more closely local preferences with highly differentiated products, which reinforced their strategy of operating on a country-by-country basis. The early recognition of converging customer demands across national and regional boundaries enabled Japanese companies marketing standardized products to maximize volume and minimize costs by translating these lower costs into lower prices to reach new markets. Coupled with strong consumer franchises for their products, built on quality and reliability, Japanese companies were placed in an unique position to leverage market share on a global scale.

The Japanese were also quick to spot the emerging nature of global competition where competitive position in one country is significantly affected by competitive position in another country[134]. By coupling their increasingly standardized products to meet growing convergences in consumer preference with global sourcing, manufacturing and shipping systems Japanese firms were able to move gradually towards integrating their core activities – production, finance, technology, management, human resources and marketing – into a global network. This enable them effectively to capture the linkages between functions and countries essential to develop competitive advantage and to leverage market position on a global scale.

The effects of a globalized versus a multinational approach are well illustrated by the battle between Makita and Black and Decker. Black and Decker was the world-wide leader of the $1.2 billion professional and do-it-yourself power-tool market with a 50 per cent share. Black and Decker was a consummate customizer offering 400 products in 50 countries manufactured in 50 plants and produced 260 motor sizes engineered in eight product design centres. Makita entered the market with a high-quality drill sourced in Japan, offered at a low price with a very small range of motor sizes for world-wide sale. In three years Makita had equalled Black and Decker's 20 per cent share of the most profitable segment, professional power tools[135].

While business academics in the West pontificated over the virtues and drawbacks of global strategies and advertising agencies advocated their own special interests, Japanese companies quietly advanced on a very broad front in integrating their operations on a global scale to build competitive advantage. Western firms – with a few notable exceptions like Ford, IBM, and Philips – were largely wedded to a multinational, country-by-country strategy, while their Japanese competitors were pioneering integrated global strategies to maximize their strategic strengths and economic advantages to leapfrog their Western counterparts (Figure 13.4).

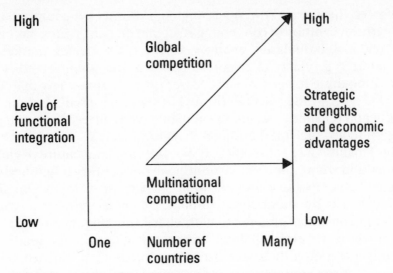

Figure 13.4. By globalizing their businesses ahead of their Western rivals Japanese firms are gaining strategic strengths and economic advantages which will enable them to leapfrog their competitors.

Above all Japanese companies realized that they must become significant world-class players to survive and prosper in a highly competitive future . . . and made the quantum leap to turn this realization into reality. Most Western companies are only now beginning to grasp these new realities and to do something about them. Paradoxically, the Japanese, by virtue of their rapid move to globalized business systems, have set the competitive scene and have taken the new industrial high ground before most of their Western competitors have even identified the battlefields of the future.

14

JAPANESE BEARING GIFTS

In the second wave of competition Japanese firms are addressing a much broader range of strategic issues designed to improve their access to technology, markets and customers in the West.

Western companies have become extremely reluctant to license their proprietary technology to potential competitors. Since the Japanese have now become proficient in developing their own technology this has provided them with more opportunities for cross-licensing technology between Japan and the West on a quid pro quo basis, reducing the West's fears of cloning its future competitors.

- Kawasaki Heavy Industries licensed robot technology for Unimation and exported its own robots, after further development of Unimation's technology, through Unimation's world-wide sales network[136].

- Through their development of advanced process and production techniques and new product development skills, Japanese companies have been able to trade on these abilities with Western partners.

Fujitsu sells its largest series mainframe computer, which runs IBM software, to Siemens for marketing under its own brand in Europe and in return Fujitsu sells the Siemens-developed laser printer[137].

- Honda's joint UK production agreement with Rover provides the former with access to European capacity and the latter with new production technology and models.

- Murata's joint venture in Japan with Bendix gives Murata access to Bendix's machine-tool technology while Bendix benefits from low-cost production using Murata's advanced production processes and techniques to remain competitive in the US machine-tool market[138].

Japanese companies have been able to use their strong financial resources to buy partnerships in major advanced technology projects in the West.

- Ishikawajima–Harima, Kawasaki and Mitsubishi Heavy Industries joined a multinational consortium led by Rolls-Royce in tandem with Pratt & Whitney, Motoren and Turbinen Union and Fiat Aviazione to develop the V2500 jet engine to power a new generation 150-seat jet airliner at an estimated project cost of $3 billion. None of the companies was in a position to develop the engine independently and a consortium was the only viable strategy[139].

- Fuji, Kawasaki and Mitsubishi Heavy Industries were founder members of a Boeing-led consortium to fund the $10 billion development of Boeing's new 7J7 commercial jet airliner. To keep its exposure to between $1 and $3 billion Boeing sought foreign partners and the Japanese firms agreed to fund as much as $1 billion for a 25 per cent share of the project[140].

The USA and Europe still lead Japan in the development of basic technology in many areas of science. Japanese companies are now beginning to bankroll new high-technology ventures in the US and the EEC to gain access to emerging scientific expertise which they can translate into new high value-added products.

- Mitsui invested $20 million in Gain Electronics' gallium arsenide technology, which could have valuable applications in super-computers and satellites, and Nippon Steel has an agreement with Concurrent Computers for the sale and later manufacture of the firm's line of super-minicomputers in Japan[141].

- A number of Japanese companies have bought equity positions and exclusive Japanese marketing rights for products and processes developed by US and European biotechnology companies. Between 1980 and 1983 Japanese companies signed

188 collaborative agreements with US biotechnology companies[142]. For example, Chugai purchased an equity position in Genetics Institute and Green Cross has research contracts with Biogen, Collaborative Research, Genex and Interferon Sciences in a range of genetically-engineered health-care projects.

In the loosely termed 'information technology' (IT) market the key success factor is integrating a range of stand-alone products into completed customer systems. No company possesses the design, engineering and production skills and the technical expertise to compete successfully in a range of converging technologies which have blurred the traditional divisions between industries.

- Toshiba has developed a large number of alliances to support its strategy to develop a diversified IT business on a global scale. It has built alliances with Olivetti (office automation); AT&T (telecommunications); Pitney Bowes, Teleautograph and ITT Europe (facsimile machines); United Technologies (power cells); Westinghouse (cathode ray tubes); Siemens (semiconductors); LSI Logic (semicustom large-scale integrated chips); Hewlett-Packard (new systems applications for memory chips); and with Cie. Générale d'Electricité and Messerschmidt-Bölkow Blohm (robotics).

Trade agreements offer Japanese companies the opportunity to circumvent protectionism and combine lower labour costs and other business synergies to provide competitive advantage.

- Nissan has switched production of four-wheel-drive vehicles from Japan to its 86 per cent holding in Motor Iberica in Spain for sale in the UK. EEC-produced vehicles are not counted as part of Nissan's quota under the terms of the restrictions on UK car imports from Japan[143].

- Lower Canadian dollar value relative to US currency, lower labour and energy costs offering lower production costs and the ability to move finished vehicles tariff-free under the Canada–US Autopact have prompted Honda and Toyota to build their own factories and Suzuki to form a joint venture with GM to produce cars in Canada[144].

- Following a 12 per cent EEC anti-dumping duty levied on Japanese excavators in 1985, Hitachi formed a joint manufacturing venture in 1987 with Fiatallis in Europe. The new plant will manufacture 10 Hitachi designed excavators to be sold under the Fiatallis–Hitachi label and Fiatallis phased out its existing outdated models in 1988. The joint venture will provide Hitachi with access to Fiatallis' strong dealer networks in markets where it is weak, such as France, Italy and Spain, and link its excavators to Fiatallis' much broader range of other construction equipment[145].

- Yazaki has taken a 60 per cent holding with Salvador Caetano in a new company Yazaki–Saltano de Portugal to produce electrical components for vehicles using Portugal's relatively low labour costs to secure a cost advantage and Portugal's new membership as a bridge into the EEC[146].

- Fifteen Japanese companies – including Hitachi, Matsushita, Sanyo and Sony – are using *maquiladoras'* production-sharing facilities in Tijuana, Mexico, to lower manufacturing costs for their US operations. Components produced in the US are shipped duty-free to Tijuana with the requirement that they be re-exported after adding low-cost Mexican labour to the product. Only the value-added portion is dutiable if it returns to the US[147].

While Japanese companies have a growing presence in pharmaceuticals they do not have an international network of medical contacts to perform key local clinical tests, and lack experience in negotiating product registrations and prices with regulatory authorities, and the comprehensive clinical information systems necessary to support an effective marketing effort.

- A number of joint venture arrangements have been made by major Japanese pharmaceutical companies with Western firms to overcome their inherent competitive weaknesses in this highly complex market. Faced with different medical customs, a complex and expensive product approval process and the need to build extensive product and treatment information networks to supply physician and meet regulatory requirements, Japanese companies have almost exclusively used joint ventures, partnerships and collaborative marketing agreements to enter the West. US joint ventures have been formed by Fujisawa with SmithKline Beckmann; Takeda with Abbott; and Yamanouchi with Eli Lilly. In Europe similar alliances have been forged: Chugai with Roussel, Eisai with Sandoz, Fujisawa with Klinge, Takeda with Glaxo, Gruenenthal and Roussel, and Tanabe with Glaxo.

These new strategic alliances offer Japanese companies, with little risk and investment, the opportunity to take advantage of changing technology and shifting customer demands, which can rapidly and dramatically change a firm's competitive advantage. These alliances provide the Japanese with the flexibility to respond to major environmental shifts as well as cooperate with their competitors to maximize their overall efficiency on a global scale.

For many Western companies alliances with the Japanese have become synonymous with significant new opportunities to improve their competitive position by accessing new products, new technology and cash from their competitors. In the UK alone alliances which 'rebadge' Japanese equipment on a reciprocal basis or under licence now cover a wide range of industrial products from construction machinery, forklift trucks and mini-tractors to bearings, diesel engines and machine tools[148].

The enthusiasm which has greeted these alliances in the West has almost totally obscured the fact that the benefits are rarely more than a short-term 'fix' and that nothing is for free. The real cost of the majority of these alliances for Western companies is the long-term deterioration of their competitive position by allowing a Japanese firm low-cost access to their markets – neatly avoiding protectionism in the form of anti-dumping tariffs and VRAs – and access to their customers, distribution systems and technology, which are at the very heart of their competitive strength.

15

SHIFTING THE MONEY

Japanese companies continue to invest heavily in countries with natural cost advantages in raw materials and labour to leverage their costs. However, there has been a dramatic shift in the emphasis of manufacturing investments away from the suppliers of raw material and labour in Asia to the consuming markets of the West in order to support the drive to reduce vulnerability to protectionism and the effects of *endaka*.

Between 1974 and 1986 cumulative Japanese investments in manufacturing in the high value-added consuming markets of the West more than doubled from 21.9 to 53.8 per cent of all manufacturing investments at the expense of increased investments in supplier countries (Figure 15.1).

Offshore Japanese investments increased from $4.1 billion in 1974 to $56.5 billion in 1986 – a thirteen fold increase which accelerated sharply after 1980. While Western manufacturing investment in Japan increased rapidly in the same period, the cumulative investment from the West in 1985 at $5.9 billion was only 50 per cent larger than Japan's total offshore manufacturing investments in 1974. Obviously, while Western companies did face many barriers to entry in Japan, these low levels of investment suggest that they placed little value on securing a strong strategic position in the domestic market of their leading global competitor (Figure 15.2).

While Japanese manufacturing investment in the West is epitomized by car and vehicle component factories and audio and video equipment assembly plants, this is only the tip of the iceberg. Japanese companies invest in sunrise industries such as biotechnology, carbon fibres, ceramics, integrated circuits, computers and silicon wafers as well as in the smokestack industries like flat glass, inorganic chemicals,

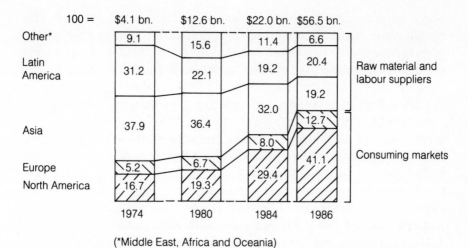

(*Middle East, Africa and Oceania)

Figure 15.1. Japan's shift in investment emphasis from suppliers of raw material and labour to consuming markets.

Source: White Paper on World Investment and Japanese Overseas Investment, Jetro, Tokyo (various issues through 1988).

steel and tyres. As some Japanese firms move into bearings, numerically-controlled machine tools and robotics, others are investing in manufacturing more mundane industrial supplies such as

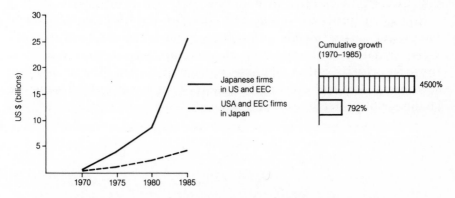

Figure 15.2. The accelerating pace of Japanese direct investments in the US and the EEC, and the low level of US and EEC investments in Japan.

Source: White Paper on World and Direct Investment, Jetro, Tokyo, (various issues through 1988).

105

polyethelyne foam, plastic sheet, screws and industrial fasteners. Even consumer products like fishing rods, golf clubs, instant glue, confectionery, eyeglass frames, stationery, cosmetics and table wear are now targets for Japanese manufacturing investments in the West.

The effects of the rapid appreciation in the value of the yen against the US dollar in 1985–88 and growing protectionist movements in both the US and the EEC were the key driving forces behind the acceleration of local manufacturing investment in the West. However, the transition was made easier by the fact that many Japanese companies had the internal reserves to fund this investment as a result of the huge cash balances they accumulated from the success of their export-driven strategies in the first wave of competition.

At the end of 1985, for example, Matsushita had cash reserves of 1,839 billion yen and Toyota 1,308 billion yen[149]. As the yen appreciated these cash mountains grew in *absolute value* and start-up operations and acquisitions declined in *relative value*, reducing both the risk and the cost of investing in downstream assembly in the US and, to a lesser extent, in the EEC.

Aiding the rapid shift of investment funds was a seminal change in government attitudes to offshore investment. Japanese companies were under strong exchange controls through to 1980. By the early 1980s Japan's trade surpluses had become too large to be absorbed efficiently in Japan's domestic economy and the Japanese government began to help to channel surplus domestic cash into offshore manufacturing as an outlet for reinvesting these underutilized funds. While having the cash available and being supported by their government were key factors in building up manufacturing capacity in the West, the driving force behind Japanese managements was their recognition of vulnerability and their mobilization of resources to overcome the challenge of protectionism and *endaka*.

16

THE MANAGERIAL METAMORPHOSIS

Japanese companies are widely believed to be managed by incrementalism – slow and cautious change based on decisions arrived at through group thinking, and, while meticulously implemented, taken at a snail's pace. This may have been true in the past but the rapid shift of productive capacity from Japan to the West to meet the threat posed by increasing protectionism and the high yen indicate a fundamental change in the way Japanese management operates. Not only has this required a much more entrepreneurial risk-taking style but also rapid and decentralized decision-making demanded by switches to new production technology and the integration of new productive capacity into global networks shifting materials, products and cash.

The undervalued yen, increasing calls for protection in the US and the EEC and pressures to open up the Japanese domestic market were identified by Japanese management as future problems more than a decade ago. However, only limited steps were taken to move into offshore manufacturing until these threats materialized. This was primarily a result of the continuing low level of competitiveness in Western manufacturing and the failure of Western governments to challenge effectively Japanese trade practices. With limited protectionism and an artificially low yen it was cheaper to produce in Japan and to export. Once the rules of the game changed Japanese companies quickly moved into downstream manufacturing to maintain their market franchises. In the first half of the 1980s Japanese companies more than doubled the number of their manufacturing operations in both the US and the EEC (Figure 16.1).

Much of Japan's export success was built on developing large batch manufacturing operations, leaning heavily on economies of scale to provide a competitive advantage. By progressively increasing the scale

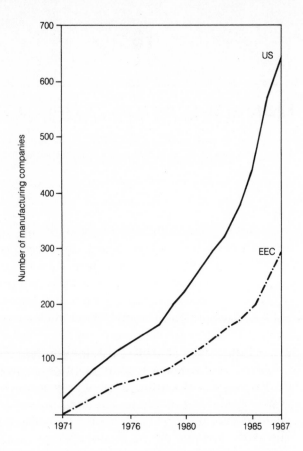

Figure 16.1. The sharp growth in Japanese companies establishing manufacturing operations in the US and EEC (1971–1987).

Sources: Jetro White Paper on World Direct Investment, Tokyo (annual issues through 1988).

of operations greater advantage could be taken of the effects of the learning curve to reduce costs further. By building in a high level of quality and adopting penetration pricing, Japanese companies could continuously open up new market segments which in turn increased volume and again lowered cost, repeating the cycle.

Recent advances in manufacturing technology have had an order of magnitude impact on costs and have eroded the traditional economies of scale based on the concept of large dedicated plants. Computer integrated manufacturing (CIM), incorporating flexible manufacturing systems (FMS), computer-aided design (CAD) and computer-aided engineering (CAE), robotics, numerically controlled machine tools, sensors and telecommunications now offer the opportunity to produce smaller batch sizes in continuous flow without large inventories of components and huge stocks of finished product.

The 'new' manufacturing not only allows companies to monitor the flow of materials but also the flow of information needed to manage production from delivery of raw material through to shipping out finished product. This helps firms to operate in smaller manufacturing plants and increasingly to customize product ranges through small production runs. At the same time they can reduce their break-even point and lower their unit costs. Labour in these highly automated systems has become a far less important component of cost. Japanese companies have been quick to spot the advantages of the 'new' manufacturing and to adopt these new techniques, which allow them to move away from countries with low labour costs to the developed consuming markets without the old penalty of incurring higher labour costs. Japanese companies have also pioneered totally new approaches to manufacturing – for example, 'mechatronics' which combines mechanics and electronics to eliminate mechanical parts by replacing them with electronic components. This has not only eased manufacturing complexity but also provided better precision, more reliability, lower costs and led to better customer features.

Japanese companies using new manufacturing technology are now in a position to move production from Japan to the US and the EEC without losing their competitive advantage in cost over Western producers. At the same time the new manufacturing technology provides another layer of competitive advantage, enabling Japanese companies to accommodate shorter product life-cycles and broaden their product ranges to meet specific customer needs and increase market penetration without suffering the old problem of major cost penalties on small volumes.

Corporate finance has become a network of global systems. Japanese financial institutions during the mid-1980s became a major force in the world money markets. In early 1986 Dai-Ichi Kangyo, with assets of $215 billion, became the largest banking company in the world. Seven of the top 10 banking concerns and 15 of the largest 25 were Japanese. In 1980 none of the Japanese banks were in the top five and only Dai-Ichi Kangyo ranked among the first ten. Similarly, Japanese companies have become a world force in insurance and in securities and financial services. Three out of the largest insurers (ranked by assets) and five out of the 10 major financial service firms (ranked by capital) world-wide are now Japanese[150].

The traditional emphasis on *keiretsu* in Japan with interlinked companies provided many Japanese manufacturers moving production offshore with the opportunity to use their banking partners to extend credit – often at rates below those available to local companies. For example, the Industrial Bank of Japan arranged a complex $600 million financial package in 1983 to underwrite bonds issued by the local county to build a car plant in Tennessee and lease it back to Nissan.

With the availability of highly competitive credit on a local basis from Japanese sources and with limited restraints on the flow of cash to and from Japan, the USA and the EEC, Japanese companies were in a strong position to leverage the global flow of cash to support the second wave of competition based on building up manufacturing capacity in the West.

Japanese management has undertaken major shifts in the allocation of production resources outside Japan in a relatively short time. It has accepted greater levels of downstream risk in the form of investments in local manufacturing as the price for continued growth in the West to combat protectionism and *endaka*. Japanese companies have also displayed the ability to integrate these downstream manufacturing units into global networks to leverage finance, technology, supply and manufacturing. This rapid metamorphosis of Japanese companies from incremental to entrepreneurial management should dispel the myth of a cautious, risk-averse group with a reluctance to shift from predetermined strategies. Paradoxically, Western companies have been so slow to combat Japanese penetration of their own markets that it is difficult to imagine they could move as rapidly and decisively to contain the new threats posed by Japanese manufacturing investments as have the Japanese to reduce their vulnerability to protectionism and *endaka*.

SUMMARY

The West is witnessing a fundamental change in the way in which Japanese industry operates. While Japanese industry is not a unified entity and individual firms do compete vigorously with one another and with external competitors, Japanese companies are making changes in their strategies to accommodate the same basic challenges.

For the first time Japanese firms are moving from low-risk export strategies to high-risk direct-manufacturing investments in their major markets in the West. While this is essentially driven by economic concerns, the yen value and protectionism, the Japanese have managed effectively to integrate this new 'globalism' with existing strengths to create additional platforms to support the transformation. To facilitate this change Japanese companies are beginning to adopt managerial styles to fit the demands of a globalized business system, which requires entrepreneurial rather than incremental management and decentralized structures and meritocracy to foster individual responsibilities and speed up decision-making and implementation.

That R&D is the principal force behind technology and market change – which in turn are the engines powering company survival and growth – is not lost on Japanese management. Technology change has important implications since it largely determines competitive advantage. While Japanese firms invest heavily in developing technology and MITI provides a shove in the right direction and funds research cooperatives, Japanese companies are still behind the West in basic research – the cutting edge of new technologies. Much sooner than their Western competitors Japanese companies realized that cross-border R&D was a fundamental component of global competitive advantage. By forming networks of strategic alliances with key

111

Western companies and with basic research organizations in the US and in the EEC, Japanese firms supplemented their own R&D efforts and gained access to new technology to power their drive for competitive advantage in high value-added industries.

The cement binding together this second wave of Japanese competition is the availability of large amounts of cash from internal sources and from Japanese banks at preferential rates as well as a radically different managerial style from that traditionally attributed to Japanese firms. The level of entrepreneurial risk-taking and the rapid decision-making process necessary to fund and acquire new technology, create joint-ventures, build overseas plants and acquire whole companies illustrate the ability of Japanese management successfully to meet and surmount new challenges.

By coupling overseas manufacturing investments with the selective and highly successful technology leadership strategies pursued for the last 20 years and by creating a web of strategic alliances, Japanese companies have been able to maximize their competitive advantage and market opportunities while limiting their risk exposure. Western companies are still largely in the grip of the old multinational realities of doing business on a country-by-country basis. The Japanese firms are in an advanced phase of integrating functions and countries in global networks which will enable the Japanese to leverage competitive advantage to pioneer the expansion of market position on a world scale.

This globalization of Japanese business will enable firms to capture more effectively the key linkages between functions and countries necessary to develop the strategic strengths and economic advantages to gain competitive advantage on a global scale. While Western firms are still trying to win the last battle of competing on a country level they are being leapfrogged by their Japanese competitors who see the strategic advantage of being able to leverage market position on a global basis as the *new* battlefield.

PART 4

TROJAN HORSE

17

MUDDY WATERS

The surge in Japanese manufacturing investments in the West since the early 1980s, initially in response to protectionism and later coupled to the increasing value of the yen, has been widely accepted as a positive move.

Politicians and many executives view Japanese manufacturing investments as a key force helping to reshape Western economies. These new plants are reckoned to create new jobs, aid the transfer of production and engineering know-how, improve Western competitiveness by stimulating increases in productivity and, through a gradual integration of Japan and the West's economies, reduce trade friction. However, beneath the surface there is growing criticism from organized labour, trade associations and many companies. They view Japanese investments as little more than a deliberate effort to circumvent trade barriers and as an extension of Japan's aggressive mercantilist policies which will put a further nail into the coffin of Western competitiveness.

The truth lies somewhere between these exaggerated positions. However, the 'facts' used to substantiate both the stout-hearted defence and the vitriolic attacks on recent Japanese investments are limited in both scope and depth. The phenomenon of Japanese companies as overseas manufacturers in the West is relatively new and there is little hard data to support either set of claims. The scant information available is obscured by poor or deliberately mixed record-keeping and does not provide a clear view of the amount or trends of Japanese manufacturing investments in either the US or the EEC. Consequently it is difficult to divorce myth from reality and fact from supposition. For example, in the US more than two dozen government agencies are involved in collecting data on money flowing

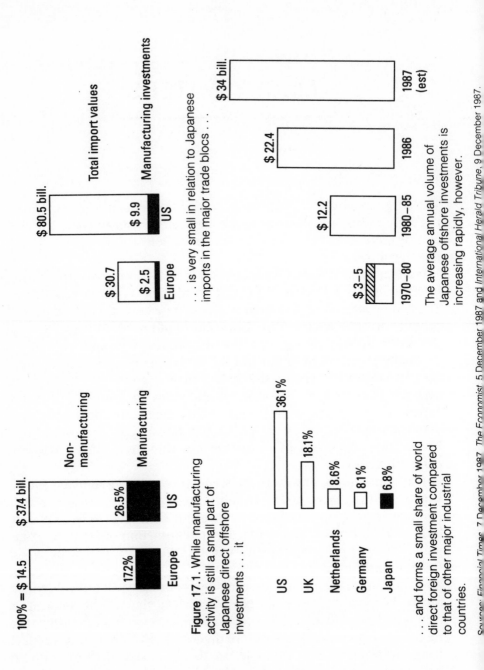

Total import values

Manufacturing investments

$ 80.5 bill.

$ 30.7

$ 9.9

$ 2.5

Europe   US

... is very small in relation to Japanese imports in the major trade blocs ....

$ 34 bill.

$ 22.4

$ 12.2

$ 3–5

1970–80   1980–85   1986   1987 (est)

The average annual volume of Japanese offshore investments is increasing rapidly, however.

100% = $ 14.5 $ 37.4 bill.

Non-manufacturing

Manufacturing

17.2%

26.5%

Europe   US

Figure 17.1. While manufacturing activity is still a small part of Japanese direct offshore investments . . . it

US   36.1%

UK   18.1%

Netherlands   8.6%

Germany   8.1%

Japan   6.8%

... and forms a small share of world direct foreign investment compared to that of other major industrial countries.

Source: Financial Times, 7 December 1987, The Economist, 5 December 1987 and International Herald Tribune, 9 December 1987.

into the US. However, gaps in information, different reporting criteria and legal loopholes allow as much as one half of all foreign investment to go unreported[151].

The data available so far suggests that manufacturing activity is still a limited part of Japanese direct offshore investments and in fact declined from 34.2 to 30.2 per cent of Japanese overseas direct investments between 1981 and 1985 due to massive increases in investments in banking, finance and insurance[152]. It is also very small in relation to Japanese imports into the major trade blocs of the US and the EEC. Japanese investment also forms a small share of world direct foreign investment compared to that of other major industrial countries. (Figure 17.1).

Despite these comforting figures the average annual volume of Japanese offshore investment is increasing rapidly and almost tripled between 1985 and 1987. Significantly, these Japanese direct investments are largely being made in assembly plants sourcing key components in Japan rather than in fully integrated operations. Consequently their economic impact is grossly understated looking at pure financial statistics. Finally, not all Japanese investments are reported and the data does not include start-ups or acquisitions which use local, rather than Japanese, funds.

It is not the size, however, but the combination of the rate of growth and the direction of investments and their type and pervasiveness which will determine the long-term effect of Japanese manufacturing investments on the West.

18

HAVING YOUR CAKE AND EATING IT

The surge in Japanese manufacturing investments in the West is designed to address the two major issues facing Japanese business: the high yen value and the negative trade balances with its major trading partners.

The rise in the value of the yen in late 1985 and throughout 1986 and 1987 cancelled out many of the benefits achieved from the massive streamlining of costs in Japan following the oil shocks and the economic recession of the late 1970s. At 170 yen to the dollar labour costs in Japan equalled those in the US and there were more limited opportunities for further rationalization and increased automation to produce additional cost reductions. Japanese firms quickly found that they were unable to cope with additional increases in the value of the yen which followed in 1987 with largely export-based strategies[153].

Japanese exporters were caught in a catch-22 situation. To maintain market share they had to keep prices to single-digit levels to compete against Western companies. The alternative was to absorb large currency losses which would have an immediate impact on profitability and set the stage for further charges of market subsidization by dumping products at below cost. Conversely they could raise prices and run the risk of surrendering hard-won market share to exports from aggressive competitors from Hong Kong, Korea, Taiwan and Singapore with currencies largely pegged to the dollar and from lower-cost Western competitors. While some of the major Japanese companies with large resources could accommodate a policy of absorbing currency losses in the short term, the small and medium-sized exporters were forced quickly to set up Western manufacturing units. For most Japanese firms manufacturing investments in the West are no longer an option but an imperative for maintaining a viable competitive presence in their major markets.

118

Despite the increase in the yen value against the US dollar the trade balances with Japan's major trading partners in the West remained embarrassingly large and even grew in 1986 and 1987. The US, and to a lesser extent the EEC, are key markets for Japanese exporters. Consequently Japanese firms have a vested interest in maintaining market stability and market access. Local manufacturing investments are visible demonstrations of addressing the trade balance issue and help to diffuse trade friction by overcoming criticisms of dumping. This in turn helps to reduce political exposure to protectionism and circumvents future quotas and duties which could have a significant impact on export-based business.

While the yen's high value and the trade balance issue are the prime movers behind Japan's manufacturing investments in the West, Japanese firms are also securing a number of additional benefits:

- Local manufacturing units place a Japanese firm firmly behind any trade barrier giving protection, and a competitive advantage, over export-based competition from companies from the newly industrialized countries of Asia and from other Japanese firms. Japanese machine-tool companies assembling in the US actively welcome reasonable import restraints to help precipitate a shake-out in an already crowded and highly competitive market, leaving the field to larger 'local' manufacturers[154].

- Industries with rapid technology or customer change a local manufacturing presence helps to keep up to date with scientific, customer and competitive developments and enables Japanese firms to tap local skills and expertise and siphon off this advanced knowledge. The concentration of advanced research, development and production of computers and electronics in the Bay area of San Francisco, for example, has become a magnet for Japanese manufacturing investments. Similarly, Southern California's influence on car design has prompted the leading Japanese car companies to set up advanced design studios in and around Los Angeles.

- By adding a local manufacturing dimension to existing marketing and distribution networks, Japanese companies can achieve better control and a faster reaction to changes in the market with a vertically integrated organization close to the customer.

- In their domestic market Japanese firms have a well organized customer-tracking system based on visits to distribution channels and data on shipments, inventory levels and retail sales which is believed to reflect the behaviour and intentions of consumers better than general attitude studies among an undifferentiated public, as widely used by Western companies[155]. In Japan tight monitoring and control over the distribution channels is possible through networks of exclusive distributors and through independent retailers who have strong links to the manfacturer. This provides a strong vertical integration of market information from the customer through to the producer. Local manufacturing in the West provides the Japanese firm with the final link in the chain, helping to build a competitive advantage over Western firms who are largely wedded to the mass market research approach which has proved to be of limited value in competing with the Japanese.

- By substituting finished imported products for a mix of imported and locally sourced components, Japanese firms can use the reduced costs of duties and freight to increase local profits. Following the typical market investment policies of Japanese firms these additional funds can be employed to leverage product positions to gain market share.

The key local manufacturing issue for Japanese management revolves around the potential economic losses of lower volumes of production, the level of quality and the degree of local manufacturing necessary to offset the low value of the yen and reduce the negative trade balance to acceptable levels.

Any disruption in a manufacturing infrastructure has a potential impact on production economics. Since much of Japan's success has been built on a formula of high-volume, high-quality, low-cost production, Japanese management has strong concerns that local manufacturing will reduce their key competitive advantage: low product cost. While transferring from domestic to offshore manfacturing would *appear* to have a significant impact on production scale economics, this penalty is lower in reality than in theory.

Almost all Japanese manufacturing in the West is in assembly operations which source key value-added components in Japan, enabling Japanese firms to continue to maximize production economics for high value-added components. In reality the Japanese firm is exporting its variable labour costs involved in assembly which, although rarely constituting as much as 10 per cent of finished product cost, have become proportionately more expensive in Japan as a result of the rise in the value of the yen. Consequently the loss in overall economies of scale in production are fairly limited. For example, Komatsu's assembly plant in the UK for excavators and wheel loaders will source most of its principal forged components, engines and much of its electronics in Japan[156].

Japanese firms have generally been able to negotiate hard-nosed agreements securing low start-up and operating costs. These go a long way to offsetting any higher cost which an offshore plant may have over facilities in Japan. Mazda's agreement with the United Auto Workers Union for its new Michigan car plant guaranteed temporarily low wages. Workers were hired at 85 per cent of the going wage at Ford (and would reach parity only at the end of the first three-year contract) and lower benefit costs since it had no retirees to support and its younger labour force required less medical care[157].

In the US and, to a lesser extent, in the EEC the availability and cost of energy, raw materials, land and labour are much more favourable than in Japan. This helps to deflate the differences in production costs by lowering both start-up and period costs.

Finally, the combination of careful employee selection, the installation of new equipment and assembly systems modelled on proven Japanese designs and procedures together with adroit human relations skills has contributed significantly to high levels of productivity and product quality. Sanyo, Sharp and Toshiba's consumer electronics plants in the US have productivity levels similar to those achieved in Japan[158]. Nissan's US light truck plant is running at about 90 per cent of Japanese productivity levels[159] and Honda's Ohio car plant delivers product quality at almost the same level as that in Japan[160]. Given these factors the loss in scale of production economics is limited and costs may in fact be *lower* than manufacturing in Japan. For example, Matsushita's semiconductor plant in Texas and television and VCR plant in West Germany are reckoned to have lower costs than Matsushita's plant in Japan and NEC and Sony's costs in their US plants are such that they even export some components to Japan[161].

A major concern for Japanese management is how far to go down the manufacturing chain in its Western production investments. Transferring the production of major value-added components offshore affects overall corporate production economics *and* consolidated profits and helps to spread critical engineering and production know-how outside the company. Excluding the extractive industries and acquisitions of existing firms, Japanese companies have almost entirely avoided developing fully integrated manufacturing operations in the US or the EEC. For example, one Japanese firm operating an assembly plant for robotics in the UK imports all its engineered parts from Japan[162]. An EEC investigation into Japanese electronic typewriter assembly in the community in 1988 revealed that the weighted average value of Japanese parts used by five manufacturers varied from 75.7 to 96 per cent, with one company's local content being limited to packaging materials only[163].

The reason for this policy is simple: there has been little political pressure on Japanese companies to integrate backward from pure assembly operations. Where local content agreements have been made they are invariably based on ex-factory value, which enables Japanese firms to include all labour and infrastructure costs, locally sourced services and components and even promotion and profits into overall product 'cost' calculations. For example, it is possible to import 60 to 70 per cent of a car's components and still reach a 70 per cent domestic content when direct labour, plant overheads and locally sourced components are added to give an ex-factory 'value'. Japanese car companies have preferred to give up low-value components such as trim, bumpers, aerials, tyres and batteries to concentrate on importing engines and drive-trains where Japanese engineering and technology yield the highest value-added content – up to 30 per cent of a car's cost[164]. By adroitly balancing the mix of components to maximize corporate production economics with local content rules – which are poorly defined and laxly enforced – Japanese firms have been able to limit their offshore facilities to assembly operations.

While production economics and the degree of downstream manufacturing are key decisions for Japanese companies, there is a third, and increasingly important, consideration: the loss of jobs in Japan. Obviously, moving manufacturing offshore transfers employment and MITI estimates that 560,000 jobs will be lost in Japan by the year 2000 as a direct result of overseas manufacturing investment[165] while some 840,000 new jobs will be created in the US alone by Japanese manufacturing investments by the end of this century[166]. With around 20 to 30 per cent of the labour force being made up of temporary employees and only 25 to 30 per cent enjoying lifetime employment and the large volume of employment in *keiretsu*, the Japanese labour force has always been highly mobile. However, the high value of the yen has imposed significant financial penalties on Japanese exporters and for the first time Japanese industry is trying to shed rather than reallocate domestic labour.

The forecast increase in unemployment from 2.9 per cent in 1986 to 5.5 per cent in 1995 is not a vote-getter for Japanese politicians and the transfer of employment to offshore manufacturing and the resulting increase in domestic unemployment is seen as a hollowing-out of Japan's industrial base[167]. For example, the Japanese car industry (including components, equipment and services) accounts for fully 10 per cent of Japan's total employment[168]. Since the car industry is the most visible contributor to negative trade balances in the West any significant transfer of employment will have positive trade implications for the West and negative employment implications in Japan. While it is easier and more acceptable to take 'metal bashing' and other low value-added employment offshore, there are considerable pressures on Japanese companies to retain not only the higher value-added jobs but as many jobs as possible in Japan. The level of unemployment – both current and projected – in Japan, although lower than the West, is higher than the Japanese are accustomed to. While there is a gradual national understanding developing which sees a need to transfer production offshore to meet Western demands and economic imperatives, there are implicit limits to the ability of Japanese companies to transfer production overseas.

To maintain its economic momentum Japan has to secure safe manufacturing bridgeheads inside the increasingly protectionist markets of the West. Changes in manufacturing technology and little pressure from the West over high value-added component imports have enabled Japanese firms to make the transition from finished product imports to assembly plants with little effect on their operating economics or product quality. Using assembly plants to spearhead their manufacturing investments and transferring low value-added low skilled labour-intensive activities to the West, Japanese firms have also been able to minimize the impact of their investments on Japanese employment. Literally Japanese companies have been able to have their cake – local 'production' in the West to maintain market access – and eat it – minimal disruption of production economics and employment in Japan.

19

. . . ONLY THE CRUMBS ARE LEFT

The spate of Japanese companies building production facilities in the West is widely believed to have brought managerial skills, new technology, an increase in employment, a substitution of domestic production for imports and a contribution to improving Western competitiveness. While Japanese manufacturing investments are making a contribution to the West, under scrutiny these advantages are limited and more often than not are potential threats masquerading as immediate benefits.

New Managerial Skills

Probably the main benefit to the West is the direct exposure to Japanese skills of managing human resources. This focuses on the social organization of work, treating people as the key element in production and not as, in the West, of frequently treating people as extensions of machines. Despite obvious cultural differences Japanese companies using greenfield site investments have generally been successful in translating their proven managerial skills to fit differing American and European values of equality and individualism.

The innovative Japanese approach to production with flexible working arrangements, a concentration on quality and just-in-time inventory systems demands a very high level of employee commitment. Japanese managements have built this commitment through a combination of participative work with consensus decision-making, quality circles, group and team work through peer pressure and strong manager-worker interactions on the factory floor. This distinctive hands-on management style has had a significant effect on industrial human relations in acquired and start-up operations on both sides of the Atlantic:

- In the 21 months following Sumitomo's acquisition of Dunlop's European tyre-making plants in 1984, the company achieved productivity gains of up to 22 per cent. Sumitomo invested in new machinery to improve product consistency and reduce waste, cleaned up and rearranged the dirtiest areas to improve the working environment and developed better working practices through briefings, quality circles, suggestion systems and job shedding. The loss-making UK plants broke even in 1986 and the German and French plants had again become profitable. Despite these changes the line and middle management remained almost intact after Sumitomo's acquisition[169].

- Nummi, the Toyota–General Motors joint venture, used a refurbished GM facility in California with obsolete technology and essentially the same workforce to assemble identical Toyota Corollas and Chevrolet Novas. With a flexible assembly line and a just-in-time inventory system Nummi's 2,500 workers produced 240,000 cars a year – what it previously took 5000 people to produce under GM and at a cost comparable to Toyota's Japanese production cost[170]. Needless to say the Nummi plant is the most efficient and has the highest quality in the GM system[171].

However, not all Japanese success can be attributed to better human resource skills. Sanyo's large gain in productivity following the acquisition of Warwick in the US in 1977 can be traced to a $60 million investment in new equipment, product design changes, more labour and a shift from fully-integrated manufacture to assembly operations using components supplied from Japan. Similarly, Sumitomo's improvement of Dunlop's productivity was heavily influenced by an injection of $200 million in new plant and equipment[172] and the fact that the European operations had suffered savage cuts in employment just before the takeover.

In contrast to the strong loyalty patterns typical of manufacturing

125

units in Japan and their largely successful transfer to the West, their Western competitors often have poor relations with their work forces frequently weakened by lay-offs and plant closures. While not all Japanese firms enjoy exemplary relations with their Western work forces – for example, Sanyo in the US[173] and Sumitomo in France[174] – there is little doubt that their operating practices in general are superior and set powerful examples for Western companies[175].

While there is little argument that these new Japanese management and organization models are valid challenges to the status quo in much of Western industry[176] their validity is being increasingly questioned as the West gains more experience in these transplanted practices and systems. While many of them undoubtably contributed to Japan's competitive success they have assumed mythical properties in the West far beyond their real value. It has been suggested that Japan's industrial success has largely been due to exploiting acts of omission in host countries' trade, industrial policy and investment strategies and in domestic competitiveness in the West rather than by superior industrial practices[177] as well as through targetting of specific industries[178].

The most celebrated Japanese industrial practices, particularly those involving human relations, are economically effective. However, they raise human values issues since they have been designed to fit Japanese and not Western cultural values. Vast cultural differences exist between Japan and the West and since the success of many Japanese industrial practices depends on the social organization of the production process it is difficult to replicate Japanese social conditions such as lifetime employment, company unions, seniority-based pay systems and consensus decision-making which underpin the success of these practices[179].

True, Japanese firms starting up from greenfield sites where new work 'rules' were part of the employment contract have generally been successful. However, this success has been driven by Japanese manufacturers in the West using personnel and industrial practices which complement their manufacturing practices[180] as well as by the fact that these greenfield sites are generally in low employment areas with young, non-unionized labour with little or no industrial experience with which to make comparisons. Despite many successes, inter-cultural conflicts are more common in Japanese greenfield sites than is generally appreciated. Honda, Kryocera, Mitsubishi Motors, Nissan and Sumitomo in the US have faced conflicts ranging from overselling promises of job security and layoffs to discriminatory practices with minorities and the lack of promotion and authority sharing with locally hired executives[181].

Japanese firms acquiring Western companies with in-place workforces and Western firms who have tried to emulate Japanese production methods and systems have frequently failed to realize that only a small part of these practices are truly exportable. Where they have not changed their personnel and industrial practices to match these new production methods and systems when whole Japanese systems are transposed to Western manufacturers[182] the need for coercion arises.

The value gains for the West of access to Japanese production methods and systems resulting from transplanting assembly plants is debatable. It assumes that Japanese managerial practices are the key factors for Japan's industrial success to the exclusion of all else. It presupposes that only Japanese firms have mastered the effective management of the interaction between human, physical and capital resources on a global scale. It ignores the massive cultural divide separating Japan from the West and downplays the impact of imposing alien social organizations which are central to effectively replicating Japanese systems. While the West can undoubtably learn from Japanese industrial practices – particularly in the social organization of work – they are not the panaceas claimed and they add only marginally to the value ascribed to encouraging Japanese assembly investments in the West.

Improving Western Competitiveness

Japanese manufacturing investments in the West are expected to offer opportunities to revitalize and sustain declining industries and to improve overall Western productivity through access to new production systems and techniques.

Since most Japanese manufacturing is based on the assembly of key components shipped from Japan on production systems based on proven Japanese designs the transfer of technology has been very limited. The essence of Japanese technology and the skills and techniques developed to transform raw material into high value-added products and the design of production systems and advanced manufacturing plants remain firmly in Japan and are not accessible to the West. Although Japanese consumer electronics firms hold 20 per cent of the colour television market and control 90 per cent of the VCR market in Europe and have had local assembly plants operating within the EEC since the mid-1970s, they employ less than 50 people in development and none in research[183]. While the end results in Japanese manufacturing investments – highly productive facilities and low-cost, high-quality products – are available to the host, the bedrock of Japan's competitive advantage is just as elusive as it was with exports of finished goods from Japan.

An essential component for improving Western competitiveness is the creation of new knowledge and its application through the development of local R&D capability. This spins off new technology and advanced skills, applications and techniques which add value to host countries. A number of Japanese firms have promised to create R&D functions in the West as a second stage following the initial first-stage assembly investment. However, the key questions are when this would take place and what type of capability would be created? Despite the fact that some Japanese firms with a high-technology profile have been operating plants in both the US and the EEC since the early to mid-1970s the creation of local R&D capability has been neglible. Although some development work is undertaken this is minimal and is concerned largely with adapting Japanese products to meet local regulations.

New technology is not created locally by transferring assembly plants for bearings, cars, construction machinery, dot matrix printers, photocopiers, television sets or typewriters to the West since Americans and Europeans pioneered the development and volume production of these products often decades before Japan. The lack of creation of local R&D capabilities in the West is probably due as much to the lack of pressure as to the closely controlled nature of Japanese firms, which concentrate as many key functions in Japan as possible, as well as the standardized 'world' product strategy adopted by most Japanese companies which involves centralized R&D[184].

It is naive to expect that Japanese companies will transfer a substantial amount of production technology, the core of their competitive advantage, to their offshore manufacturing plants or develop substantive local R&D capabilities unless there is significant Western pressure. In turn, without this transfer of production technology and R&D

capability Japanese manufacturing investments will make little or no contribution to Western reindustrialization.

New Employment

The increasing number of Japanese manufacturing units in the West is expected to have a significant impact on the high levels of Western unemployment. By mid-1987 Japanese manufacturing units employed close to 160,000 in the USA and a further 60,000 in Europe[185]. While this is low in comparison to overall levels of employment and has had little impact on unemployment, as the offshore manufacturing presence increases the Japanese contribution to employment is expected to improve. While this is good news for employment, the central issues are the quality of employment being created and the effect on local skills.

Much of the new employment is in low-skilled automated and routine assembly operations and metal-bashing. A study of 20 Japanese assembly plants in the UK, for example, indicated that the portion of direct labour ranged from 50 to 95 per cent of the total labour force, with the majority around 80 per cent[186]. These make little or no use of indigenous skills and do not lead to the development of new or to improving existing skills. Without such development the overall skills base of a country at best remains fixed and at worse atrophies.

There is confusion as to whether the employment created by Japanese manufacturing investments is in fact additional or merely substitute employment. Much of the new employment is literally replacing jobs lost in areas of depressed heavy industry. Japanese assembly investment in Europe is primarily located in Alsace and Lorraine in France, the North East of England, Scotland and Wales and Nord Rhein-Westphalia in Germany, all of which have depressed heavy industries. Since the decline in Western firms' market share in cars and consumer electronics is largely attributable to Japanese export competition, investment in local production in these industries at best produces substitute rather than additional employment. As Japanese firms use assembly rather than fully integrated operations they tend to have lower manning levels and are more productive than their Western competitors; labour substitution is at best only partial and

129

at worst reduces overall employment. For example, the photocopier manufacturers in the EEC suggest that each job in a Japanese company assembling photocopiers in Europe comes at the expense of 4½ jobs in a European firm as the higher value-added – and better paid – jobs remain in Japan[187]. Since much of Japanese assembly plant investment is in slow growth industries with existing overcapacity like cars and electronics the long-term creation of new jobs is highly questionable as each new generation of investment tends to employ fewer people[188].

While this cause and effect relationship can be regarded as somewhat contentious direct examples exist. In August 1986 GM Canada was negotiating a joint venture with Suzuki to produce 200,000 Suzuki designed small cars at a plant scheduled for start-up in 1989. A few weeks later GM was offering incentives to 5 per cent of its 9,000 salaried employees in the Chevrolet–Pontiac–Canada group to leave in 1986 and an equal number to resign in 1987[189].

The case of the European consumer electronics industry is more poignant. Employment fell from 250,000 in 1975 to 120,000 in 1985[190]. Although this was due partially to productivity gains the major impact was the result of increased Japanese competition. Since Japanese assembly operations employed only 10,000 in consumer electronics in 1985 Europe had suffered a net loss of 120,000 jobs, or 48 per cent employment, as a direct result of competition. New Japanese employment provided a substitute for less than 8 per cent of overall employment losses.

Even in acquired companies employment has in fact decreased. In three consumer electronics plants acquired by Japanese firms in the UK employment fell from 4,300 to 1,600, producing a net loss of 2,700 jobs. Similarly, the UK car component suppliers lost 126,000 jobs between 1979 and 1987 largely as a result of Japanese competition[191].

Unless the quality of new jobs created increases and the level of employment generated makes a substantial long-term net contribution to overall employment, Japanese manufacturing investments will have no material impact on Western unemployment.

Trade Benefits

It is generally accepted that significant trade benefits in terms of import substitution, foreign exchange savings and exports to third countries to reduce the negative trade balances with the West will flow from increased Japanese manufacturing in the US and in the EEC. MITI, for example, estimates that Japanese overseas direct investments will increase by an average of 14 per cent annually up to the year 2000 and will reduce exports by $19 billion by 1990, rising to $47 billion savings by 1995[192]. However, since most of these investments are in assembly operations which rely heavily on imported high value-added components, the import substitution is limited to assembly costs such as labour, plant overheads and some freight, plus locally sourced low value-added components. For example:

- Honda, Nissan and the GM/Toyota car plants in the US all rely heavily on assembling high value-added knock-down (KND) kits sourced in Japan[193].

- The Brother typewriter plant scheduled for start-up in the US in mid-1987 was designed to source 30 per cent of the parts locally with most major components being shipped from Japan[194].

- Phase I of Nissan's UK plant assembles 24,000 cars a year from KND kits sourced in Japan[195].

While many of these companies plan to increase local content – Honda's $450 million expansion of its Ohio plant to cast, machine and assemble engine parts, drive trains and brake parts is atypical[196] – the overall levels of integration are very limited.

Exports to third countries also figure prominently in the benefits of Japanese manufacturing investments. For example:

- In France Sony's cassette plant and Clarion's car radio production unit export up to 80 per cent and 70 per cent respectively of their production[197].

- Komatsu plans to export 80 per cent of its UK production to EEC countries[198].

- Nissan expects to source its EEC exports out of its UK plant and Honda and Toyota's planned plants in Canada will use the Canada–US Autopact to move vehicles into the US under tariff-free conditions.

Lower imports due to local investments are also a snare and a delusion.

131

While local production has grown faster than imports of consumer electronics in Europe since 1983, reaching a ratio of 2.5 to 1 for Japan in 1986, the effects on trade balances are illusory[199]. Japanese firms have developed complex logistics systems involving production and transhipment from the NICs which effectively mask the origin of components and deflect the real impact on trade balances.

While export opportunities within trade blocs are based on government-to-government agreements on local content, the methods used to determine content are so vague that the locally sourced value is generally far lower than stipulated. In addition, Western governments have rubber teeth when it comes to enforcing local content agreements and penalizing non-compliance. Overall the amount of import substitution is limited since a high percentage of the value of previously imported finished products is being used to import high value-added components. The net result of Japanese manufacturing investments in the West is a very small dent in Japan's huge trade surpluses.

The final nail in the coffin of the export argument is the flow of trade. Most US and European offshore plants have been designed to ship a large part of their volume production back to their home base to capture lower labour costs. While Japanese offshore plants have also been designed to take advantage of lower labour costs the flow of trade has been focused more on using these cost advantages to penetrate third country, usually Western, and local markets rather than to supply Japan (Table 19.1).

Table 19.1. While US electrical machinery and electronics subsidiaries in Asia have been designed primarily to take advantage of lower labour costs to supply domestic production the Japanese objectives are focused on capturing cost advantages for third country exports and local supply (1982 data).

	US		Japan	
Gross assets (US $bill.)	3.244		2.516	
Number of employees ('000)	162.5		98.0	
Gross sales (US $bill.)	5.099	(100%)	2.263	(100%)
Local sales	0.621	(12.2%)	0.845	(37.3%)
Home exports	3.325	(65.2%)	0.475	(21.0%)
Third country exports	1.153	(22.6%)	0.943	(41.7%)

Source: White Paper on World and Japanese Overseas Direct Investment, Jetro, Tokyo, February 1987

132

Without a strategy geared to multi-directional trade flows it is difficult to visualize just how Japanese assembly plants in the West will be able to deliver significant export benefits to their hosts. Consequently the trade benefit argument is tenuous at best since most Japanese assembly plants are little more than exercises in visible export substitution.

Upgrading the Infrastructure

The high levels of quality and low production cost of Japanese companies are expected to have a major impact on Western competitors, who will be forced to upgrade their businesses to meet the component demands of new Japanese production units. Here the concerns are not only the ability of Western firms to meet stringent demands from Japanese companies but also whether Japanese firms are really prepared to source their major components with Western suppliers.

Many Western firms are unaware of just what Japanese companies expect from their suppliers and that Japanese firms are really buying the supplier and not the components. Close working relationships with suppliers to meet rigid specifications and just-in-time delivery systems, constant investment in new plant and machinery and continuous attention to cost and quality require a high degree of subservience to Japanese manufacturers. To Western suppliers who prize their independence this subservience is alien. While some Western component producers have adapted to Japanese operating procedures many others have not and contend that Japanese demands are onerous or lack reality:

- Komatsu has reportedly told suppliers of forged metal for its UK unit that it is looking to pay $740/tonne while the going price was around $1800/tonne[200].

- YKK is a fully integrated firm where the parent in Japan supplies not only the raw materials for its world-wide production units but also the machinery on which the end product is made. YKK denies, but is often accused of changing specifications to avoid using local suppliers[201].

- Toshiba indicated its surprise that US companies will not bid on contracts where they do not make an immediate profit[202].

Western firms operate on higher local margins than Japanese companies in Japan due to the need to service much higher interest rates. Consequently, low-volume runs with marginal or no contribution have little attraction for most Western suppliers.

Compounding the problem for Western suppliers is the fact that they have to produce components for equipment that has been designed in Japan with Japanese-made components in mind.

While there is agreement that many Western component suppliers are not yet on par with their Japanese counterparts and some of the complaints about the lack of adequate quality, cost, quantity and delivery conditions about Western suppliers are genuine, Japanese offshore manufacturing units have tended to meet the majority of their component needs with Japanese component suppliers or their local units or surrogates.

- Nissan UK has used 27 British manufacturers to supply parts for the first Bluebird cars. However, all of these firms have some Japanese involvement[203].

- In the US at least 72 Japanese vehicle component firms opened plants between 1979 and 1986, and 300 were expected to be operational by 1988 – a number of which will be joint ventures with US component suppliers[204].

Critics contend that Japanese manufacturers prefer to use their own component suppliers in preference to local producers for reasons other than quality and cost. Many Japanese component producers belong to *keiretsu*, where major manufacturers are the key partners. Frequently the manufacturers own stock in component producers and have interlocking directorates. For example, Toyota owns 21 per cent of its major supplier Nippondenso. With familial long-term relationships manufacturers have built strong loyalty and trust ties with their suppliers which are difficult to combat. Toyota, for example, came to the US with an entire support structure of component suppliers to feed its new car plant in Tennessee. In addition to Nippondenso, Aishin Seiki, also linked to Toyota, will supply body parts and Toyoda Gosei steering wheels and plastic components.

While these close manufacturer-supplier links may be strong barriers Japanese companies are in business to produce high-quality, low-cost products and Western firms will have to meet these component demands if they wish to get a share of this new business. Even more important is the fact that Western manufacturers are beginning to impose Japanese-style quality and cost demands on their suppliers in an effort to increase their own competitiveness[205]. If Western component producers cannot meet these demands Western manufacturers will start to source with the new Japanese component suppliers. Nihon Radiator, for example, sells airconditioners and silencers to GM and Ford in the US and has taken business away from GM's own subsidiaries for some GM contracts[206].

The evidence to date suggests that Japanese assembly plants in both the US and the EEC, with some notable exceptions, are largely wedded to using high value-added components shipped from Japan and generally have low local content levels. Where local sourcing does occur the components are frequently supplied by local Japanese component makers or their surrogates and many of these components are shipped from Japan and constructed into sub-assemblies to meet local content requirements[207].

The market reluctance of many Japanese companies to source locally – one company in a UK study even purchased its screwdrivers from Japan[208] – raises strong concerns whether Japanese manufacturing investments *will* help to upgrade significantly the quality of the infrastructure in the West. Even if Western firms do adapt to Japanese quality, cost and delivery requirements there are no guarantees that Japanese plants in the West will source their high value-added components with these suppliers rather than with the flood of Japanese component companies now following their principals offshore. Without the transfer of the technology and skills in manufacturing high value-added components to Western suppliers there is little likelihood that the infrastructure in the West will benefit materially from Japanese assembly plants.

The Hidden Issues

While the West may gain from Japan's shift in production to the West these manufacturing investments raise a number of concerns. In parti-

135

cular the quality of the investment, the subsidies provided, and the competition for investments have a major effect on their value.

Almost all Japanese manufacturing investments in the West are assembly operations. Although plans exist to integrate these plants more fully into Western economies few are self-contained manufacturing operations. This raises the concern that most Japanese investments in the West are little more than 'screwdriver' plants designed to outflank protectionism and the high yen. Japanese firms almost always retain production of high value-added components to capture higher profit margins and key skills and to maximize employment in Japan. Japanese car firms, for example, invariably source engines and drive trains in Japan to leverage costs and centralize high-value income: in addition to 670,000 finished cars Honda exported 326,000 engines and transmissions in 1986, including 70,000 to Rover in the UK[209]. Similarly, Japanese photocopier manufacturers source the crucial high value-added components, the reprographic drum and the lens, in Japan.

To many critics Japanese manufacturing investments in the West are synonymous with exporting low value-added metal bashing and assembly operations which offer marginal if any quality in investment.

Japanese companies have long practised market subsidization using the cash flows generated in Japan, a high-priced market heavily protected from Western competition, to subsidize the penetration of Western markets. Both the US and the EEC regard cross-market subsidization or 'dumping' as unfair competition and have imposed fines, duties, tariffs and restraint agreements to protect local companies.

In the current climate of increasing protectionism and high yen values export price subsidization has lost much of its viability. However, the new globalized approach of Japanese companies offers *indirect* opportunities to maintain cash-flow subsidization. With highly developed networks sourcing, shipping, producing and assembling on a global scale Japanese offshore units became part of a complex logistics system. This provides the opportunity to leverage the flow of raw materials, semi-processed and finished materials, components, sub-assemblies and even finished products between the various manufacturing, assembly and sales operations in different countries. The permutations to continue cross-subsidization of country market share battles with global cash flows to support product positions are almost endless given the complexity of global logistics systems – and almost impossible to identify.

136

Since the Japanese have elevated cross-market subsidization to a minor art form there are strong reasons to believe that they will use the opportunities of complex global logistics systems to pursue sophisticated methods of dumping. Western governments have been struggling unsuccessfully for almost 30 years to come up with a workable solution on the transfer price issue. Given their lamentable record it is highly unlikely that they will be able to tackle the infinitely more intricate task of addressing the issue of cross-market subsidization using global logistics systems with any greater degree of success.

With continuing high levels of unemployment job creation has become a political imperative in the West. Individual states in the US, and regions and even towns in the EEC member states, have been highly active in promoting their attractiveness for Japanese manufacturing investment as a means to create new employment. Considerable concerns are being raised about the level of competition for these investments, the type and magnitude of the inducements and how the money is actually being spent. In essence the lack of guidelines, the superior negotiating skills of the Japanese and the overeagerness to secure new employment have contributed to a disruptive level of competition.

There are no guidelines in the US or in the EEC specifying limits on the type or amount of inducements available to potential investors[210]. Consequently Japanese companies find themselves in a buyers' market where different communities compete by outbidding each other to attract investment. By playing one potential host against another the Japanese company can use 'salami' tactics to obtain significant benefits. Obviously there is a great reluctance to discuss the issue. However, the Department of Trade and Industry is thought to have raised its contribution from £2 million to almost £7 million to enable Telford in the UK to beat competition for a new NEC facility from Hanover in West Germany[211]. Unfortunately, in a largely buyer's market each new package of incentives tends to be the starting point for the next round of plant negotiations. Witness the difference between the $16 million granted to Honda for a plant in Ohio in 1982 and the $125 million incentives offered for Toyota's car plant in Kentucky in 1985[212].

Japanese firms have used highly skilled negotiating tactics to secure subsidies for capital investments *and* ongoing operations. Nissan, for example, in late 1986 announced that it would go ahead with the second phase of its car assembly plant in the UK at a cost of £330 million. This would add a further 2,200 jobs to the first phase, which

137

had cost £50 million and employed 470 people. By moving to the second phase Nissan triggered about £100 million in central and regional government grants – a *subsidy* on capital investment of around 25 per cent on total costs[213].

Honda, Nissan and Toyota's plants in the US have all been located in subzones approved by the US Foreign Trade Zones Board, which allows imports of components for assembly in cars on a customs duty-free basis. It is estimated that the $224 million savings to the US consumer on the 560,000 Japanese cars assembled in the US in 1986 will cost the US Treasury about $1.8 million in customs duties. The average duty on imported parts is approximately 8 per cent of invoice value. However, the Foreign Trade Zone status avoids these charges and the US Treasury collects only 2.6 per cent on the value of the finished car. Toyota, for example, estimates a saving of $30 to $40 on each vehicle assembled in the US due to its subzone status[214]. The net effect of these subzones is a taxpayers' subsidy on each unit assembled in addition to the subsidies paid to secure the plant in the first place.

The eagerness of Western governments to secure new employment and the superior negotiating skills of the Japanese have resulted in a wide range of benefits as well as almost total freedom on how the grants and subsidies are used. In addition to receiving subzone status allowing the duty-free import of components for its knock-down assembly plant Honda received a host of benefits from different federal and local government sources. The Federal Government provided $300,000 for rail improvements, the State of Ohio $2.5 million as a site development grant and the county property tax rebates reduced Honda's tax liability by $90,000. Other perks included subsidizing a cafeteria and tutoring for Japanese employees' children at the State university. Similarly, Toyota's factory in Kentucky, which came on stream in 1988, was the recipient of public largess. Kentucky state provided 1,500 acres of land free, $47 million for new roads and $65 million in training programmes. In addition the local community provided a new sewer system and extra police and fire-fighting resources[215].

The first phase of Nissan's UK car assembly plant cost £50 million, of which £28 million was spent on factory equipment. While Nissan indicates that about 70 per cent was spent in the UK and the rest in Japan much of the UK expenditure was on equipment produced in Japan by associate companies of UK suppliers. Nissan insisted on and, in some cases, arranged for Japanese partners. Haden King, for example, supplied NKC's Japanese manufactured floor conveyor system for Nissan's paint shop[216]. While the first £50 million was at Nissan's expense the second phase will bring total investments up to £330 million. Since the UK will be subsidizing the facility with £100 million there is concern that much of this subsidy will in fact be assisting Japanese rather than UK suppliers.

This largess it not only reserved for large firms. Even small Japanese companies employing no more than 30 people have been able to finance the construction of new assembly plants in the US with the aid of low-interest state-sponsored industrial revenue bonds[217].

While Japanese manufacturing investments have provided exposure to the human relations skills of Japanese management they have contributed little else to the West. Since the investments are largely in assembly plants the amount of technology transfer and the creation of R&D capabilities has been minimal, the employment limited to low value-added activities and the degree of import substitution negligible as a result of imported components. In fact, while Japanese companies have been having and eating their cake the West has largely been left with the crumbs of a few low-skilled low-paid jobs. Adding insult to injury, the West has been furiously competing with taxpayers' money to lure investments which are at best partial substitutes for employment lost to Japanese imports and has no way to counter the effects of this sophisticated form of dumping.

20

THE DOMINO EFFECT

While some view Japanese manufacturing investments as a shot in the arm for Western competitiveness, others are beginning to see a hidden multiplier effect with a significant *negative* impact not only on individual companies but also on the industrial infrastructure of the West.

The Short Term

Short-term concerns are focused on the wisdom of publicly subsidizing aggressive competitors at the expense of domestic industry and of increasing competition in industries already suffering from slow market growth and overcapacity.

Locating in low-cost areas; using greenfield sites; supported by grants, soft loans, subsidies, accelerated depreciation and other perks; using the latest technology; and employing non-unionized young, unskilled and semi-skilled people to assemble components have all given Japanese firms lower start-up and operating costs. In Sanyo's UK plant half the employees are unskilled women and the average age of the work force has been brought down to 20 years[218]. Industry experts suggest that Mazda's agreement with the United Auto Workers for flexible work rules and broad job classifications which eliminate idle work time could cut Mazda's US labour costs by about 15 per cent[219]. By locating in areas with high unemployment and with no history of a specific industry potential employees are more likely to accept lower wage levels and fringe benefits. For example, the plants of Honda (Ohio), Nissan (Tennessee and North East England) and Sony (South

Wales and Dax in France) were all located in areas of high unemployment with no history of assembling cars or electronics. There is also the issue of the social value of the jobs created. Although 16 Japanese firms have created 5,000 new jobs in their assembly plants in Wales the majority are for unskilled women – in a land that desperately needs jobs for men[220].

Western competitors are extremely vulnerable to Japanese assembly operations sited to maximise cost efficiency. Most Western firms have operations which are unionized with inflexible work rules and heavy investment in fixed fully-integrated plants located in high-cost areas. As a result they are saddled with large and aging labour forces (often with a history of poor labour relations) which impose high social security, health care and pension costs. Collectively these expenses impose significant competitive cost penalties. Even acquisitions of existing companies with their in-place work forces by Japanese firms offer no solace for their indigenous competitors. In almost all cases Japanese companies have behaved as if the original work force was fired. This has enabled them to negotiate roll-backs of original pay and benefit programmes, impose one or no union representation with no-strike agreements, single status employment and flexible work groups with lower pay and benefit packages. All of these contribute to lower operating expenses which provide a cost advantage over Western competitors.

Western firms can negotiate similar investment packages. However, they have implicit social and economic obligations with existing investments and labour which largely preclude them from adopting the massive relocation programmes necessary to meet the cost advantage of new Japanese assembly investments. Those few Western companies which have used investment package negotiations have been car manufacturers in the US and Ford and GM in Europe[221]. However, even these companies have not been able to match the operating economics of the Japanese assembly plants since these Western investments are in new fully integrated plants rather than in assembly operations.

Most of the Japanese investments are in slow-growth, mature industries rather than in high technology. As a result they do not create new employment, add to the technology stock of the West or develop high value-added activities. Added to these problems is the fact that many of these mature industries already suffer from over-capacity. New capacity with a cost advantage over existing capacity will obviously secure market share at the expense of existing competitors. The capacity of the new Honda, Toyota and GM/Suzuki plants in Canada will be more than the 1.1 million cars a year the Canadian market can absorb and a large portion of these cars will be sent to the US under the Canada–US Autopact[222]. However, by 1990 the US excess production capacity alone could reach 1 to 2 million cars a year – 10 to 20 per cent of projected sales[223]. These investments are occurring at a time when US car companies are reacting to overcapacity by closing plants[224]. Komatsu's UK plant, designed to assemble 2,400 excavators and wheel loaders in an EEC market of 15,100 units a year, will increase production in a sector already suffering from chronic overcapacity[225]. While Europe in 1986 had 3.5 million units or 24 per cent excess capacity in the car industry Nissan's new plant came on stream in the UK and other Japanese firms were evaluating various sites in Europe for new assembly plants[226].

The Mid Term

In the mid term the key issue is that Japanese assembly operations are creating partial substitute rather than entirely new employment which will help to itensify rather than slow down the 'hollowing out' of Western manufacturing. This erosion of the manufacturing base is undermining the ability of the West materially to increase its value-added output which is essential to maintain headway in a competitive world .

The core concern for the West is the loss of skills and expertise necessary to create, design, engineer and produce new products. Once the set of knowledge in creating and the corresponding set of skills and expertise necessary to convert raw materials to advanced products is lost, it is almost impossible to recreate. Rover's partnership with Honda provides the former with access to badly needed new models and to Honda's expertise in advanced engineering and experience in linking design with manufacturing and engineering. While this has been achieved at a fraction of the cost of developing the internal capability the real cost has been Rover's dependence on Honda. Only the low-cost, low-margin Metro is produced without Honda's expertise[227]. Both Westinghouse and RCA abandoned technologies as a result of competition from Japanese products assembled in the US and have been forced into alliances with Japanese firms to re-enter the market. Westinghouse abandoned development and production of colour video products in 1976. The technology developed so rapidly that the only way back into the business was a joint venture with Toshiba. RCA withdrew from videocassette and videodisc players in the early 1980s. Since both technologies have led to major new products, including video cameras and the compact disc, RCA was forced into marketing Japanese products under its own brand to remain a force in the US home entertainment market.

To plug holes in their product lines and avoid the cost of product development a large number of Western companies have withdrawn from the low-price end of the line and substituted Japanese designed and produced products. ICL and Siemens, for example, market Fujitsu-designed and manufactured small computers in Europe and GM and Chrysler market Isuzu and Mitsubishi-designed and engineered products in the US. Although Ford's Escort was the best-selling US small car between 1980 and 1986, it lost up to $1,000 per car sold. Ford's replacement for the Escort, the CT-20, is to be designed and almost fully engineered by Mazda in Japan and even US-built cars will incorporate substantially more Japanese made components than the Escort. While this will save Ford almost one half of the $1 billion cost of developing a new car, experts maintain that Ford has given up experience applicable to all sizes of car[228].

To a large extent the West stands to loose the capacity to transform complex new ideas into products which will have more value-added capability than assembling and selling products where the differentiating factor is limited to styling. Once a company is locked out of the creative aspects of its business and excluded from new and rapidly changing production processes, its skills begin to atrophy. As the Japanese have demonstrated, production engineering and production development are as essential to overall product economics as is product design, and to transfer these skills to others can wipe out a critical body of knowledge.

While the hollowing-out effect of Western manufacturing appears a purely industrial problem it compounds a set of social, economic and political problems the West is beginning to face. A declining birth rate in almost all industrialized countries in the West and an aging population profile will increase economic pressure on a smaller number of taxpayers to support the increase in social and health care services needed for the growth in numbers of the elderly. At the same time the low growth in Western GNP and the current high levels of unemployment are expected to continue. Since Japanese manufacturing investment is largely in assembly operations it will not create substantial new value-added employment and has the potential to increase unemployment in Western firms, intensifying mid-term economic and social pressures in the West.

The Long Term

For the long term there is a growing concern that increases in the level of Japanese manufacturing investments in the West will lead to an increase in the 'Japanization' of Western industry. While this is generally accepted as encompassing shifts to manufacturing, human resource and industrial relations practices developed in Japan – which have been emulated by many Western companies in an attempt to remain competitive – there is no hard evidence that this will replicate Japanese economic structures in the West[229]. Rather the problem lies in the imposition of techniques, methods and practices developed by Japanese firms in Japan on their Western affiliates which will replicate Japanese industrial and economic structures *within* Western markets. These will help to preclude integrating Japanese firms into Western economies.

This lack of integration of the new Japanese manufacturing plants into the economies of both the US and the EEC is supported by both the attitudes and practices of many Japanese firms towards domestic suppliers and by their attempts to manage their environment totally.

Supply Management: The frequently quoted quality, cost and availability problems of component supplies from Western producers suggest a determined attempt by many Japanese firms to force Japanization onto domestic suppliers rather than a concerted effort to adapt products and components to fit local standards and capabilities. Literally many Japanese firms attempt to clone components, products and even whole plants in the West to duplicate Japanese conditions. Their demands on domestic supplies are focused on having products made exactly as they are in Japan and few Japanese companies are prepared voluntarily to change their designs and specifications to

144

improve local sourcing opportunities. This uncompromising attitude has helped to impose Japanese industrial practices on Western suppliers such as just-in-time production and logistics systems which may not be culturally suited to in-place Western workforces nor to the much higher costs of working capital in the West – two to three times that of Japan – required by suppliers for financing JIT systems.

Both the difficulties in meeting uncompromising Japanese requirements and obvious reluctance on the part of Western suppliers have helped to provoke a follow-my-leader effect as Japanese subcontractors and component suppliers follow their key Japanese clients into the West[230] and become the preferred source of supply for new Japanese assembly plants.

Ecosystem Management: As the size of individual Japanese manufacturing investments reaches significant levels in the West, as in volume car assembly, an 'Ecosystem' management process is becoming evident. Obviously any company will attempt to minimize risk, and the larger the investment the greater the need to reduce risk. However, the deliberate manipulation of the corporate ecosystem – the environment surrounding the company encompassing central and local government, suppliers, labour and the media – covering the entire local polity and economy is a throwback to the coal, iron and steel company towns once prevalent in Europe and North America.

Ecosystem management is a multidimensional process beginning with corporate control over the political system and the media and extending progressively to other aspects such as marginalizing labour and dominating suppliers. An analysis of Nissan's assembly operation in Northeast England indicates that Nissan has used a combination of mechanisms to control its ecosystem[231]. Nissan has been able to reproduce the social *and* material conditions prevalent in Japan and use the same style of management to control the entire production process. This required the subordination of public authorities and their services, land use, organized labour, component suppliers, the media and community opinion. Nissan was allowed to set its own agenda. By obtaining the personal backing of the Prime Minister with her acknowledged hostility towards organized labour Nissan was able, through skilful presentation and packaging, to use the lure of new jobs to impose a consensus and get central, regional and local government, suppliers, trade unions and the media to conform to a pattern determined by Nissan. This was all the more remarkable since the local

145

government and trade unions were politically opposed to the Prime Minister and the trade unions competed among themselves for single-union status and implicit no-strike agreements. As a result Nissan was able to replicate the Japanese model of spatially concentrating the production process in one location down to an extended site owned by Nissan for onward sale to its component suppliers.

This lack of integration has a number of facets. Without integration of the substantial inflow of Japanese manufacturing investment there will be no material improvement of the manufacturing infrastructure. Rather it will lead to a two-tier infrastructure: one driven by Japanese demands for products and services which meet unique Japanese requirements supplied by Japanese component suppliers, their surrogates or 'Japanized' Western suppliers, and one driven by Western firms to meet their specific demands which will be supplied not only by Western component producers but increasingly by Japanese suppliers and their surrogates. If Western industry continues both to decline and to adopt Japanese techniques, processes and systems Western-style infrastructures will continue to atrophy.

This also raises broader issues. At the same time that Japanese firms are castigating Western firms for their lack of success in Japan as their products do not meet Japanese needs and standards and 're-engineering' is necessary to secure supplies of local components, Japanese firms are practising precisely the opposite strategy in the West. It also conveniently glosses over the fact that while most Japanese companies cite poor Western suppliers as the problem in greater integration into Western infrastructures, some companies, like Brother in the UK, have been able to achieve high local content levels with domestic suppliers in relatively short time frames[232].

The long-term issue in the West is whether Japanization is an appropriate vehicle for reindustrialization, given the cultural diversity with Japan and the need to subordinate the state, the community, the media, suppliers and labour to Japanese investment agendas rather than subordinate Japanese needs to those of their Western hosts.

Japanese assembly investments, rather than giving a boost to Western competitiveness, are more than likely to have a domino effect on the infrastructure of the West. Significant cost advantages and over-capacity will help to undermine the ability of Western firms to compete and will increase unemployment. This will help to reduce the skills and expertise necessary to transform ideas into high value-added products, further hollowing out the already fragile industrial base of the West.

146

The West is already moving towards a situation where, unless a quantum increase can be made in high value-added output, a relative erosion will take place in the standard of living of a large percentage of its population. This will not be helped by subordinating the infrastructure and the institutions of the West to Japanese investment agendas, which attempt to replicate Japanese products and systems rather than integrating Japanese manufacturing investments into the economies of the West.

SUMMARY

All the evidence suggests that most Japanese manufacturing investments in the US and the EEC are designed to overcome actual or potential trade barriers and to combat the rising value of the yen.

Japanese plants are invariably assembly operations built with heavy Western public funding using low-cost (largely young, non-unionized and unskilled) labour to bolt together high value-added components sourced in Japan. As such they represent not only a formidable low-cost challenge to Western companies *within* their home market but also the process *maximizes* the offshore component for Japanese firms in the value-added chain.

By constructing a value chain for a typical manufactured product and then applying Japan's share along the chain an appreciation can be gained of the opportunities available to maximize the value-added content offshore through local assembly of components designed and engineered in Japan (Figure 20.1). A number of assumptions have been made in this construction:

- R&D is applied in relation to Japan's world share of high technology.

- Product and process design activities are invariably conducted in Japan.

- Process development, production engineering and key component design are largely retained in Japan with a small amount performed in-market for conversions to local standards and specifications. The US–EEC ratio is based on the relative amount of Japanese inward investment in the two trade blocs.

149

- Assembly normally is approximately 10 per cent with a small
  share performed in Japan largely for subassembly of key
  components with the majority being conducted in-market.
  Again the US–EEC ratio is roughly based on the relative amount
  of Japanese inward investment.

- Advertising and selling activities are always conducted in-market
  with the value being absorbed locally. (This discounts the fact
  that Japanese firms in the West have built up their own selling
  and distribution operations and Japanese advertising agencies
  are also moving offshore.) The US–EEC ratio is as in Figure 20.1.

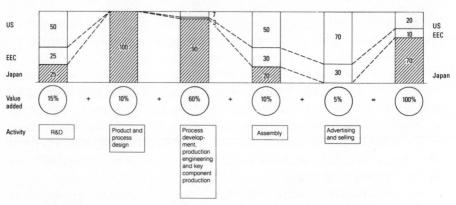

Figure 20.1. The process of maximizing the offshore value-added
component of Japanese assembly plants in the US and the EEC.

While this is a hypothetical case it does illustrate the process by which
Japanese companies *can* maximize the offshore value-added
component in assembly plants located in the West.

In most cases Japanese manufacturing investments will not stimulate efficiency among domestic producers or revitalize and sustain
declining industries. With heavy fixed investments in high-cost loca-
tions, high-cost fully-integrated plants and large aging work forces of
more expensive skilled manpower, many Western competitors stand a
more than even chance of being decimated on their home ground by
new Japanese assembly investments which have a significant cost
advantage.

With the debatable exception of new and innovative managerial
techniques there has been no real generation of new skills or the
transfer to the West of technology of key design, process, production

development or manufacturing skills which are the bedrock of products or the creation of local R&D capabilities which add substantive value to host countries. Experience in the newly industrialized countries of Asia indicates that Japanese firms have been extremely reluctant to transfer any technology or managerial skills to their hosts[233]. This should provide no solace for Western governments.

Japanese firms are also limiting their local purchases to low value-added services which limit Western opportunities to gain substantial linkages to boost local component production in quality and volume. Those components sourced locally are invariably low value-added or are largely supplied by other Japanese firms or their Western surrogates. In fact, Japanese manufacturing investment in its present form of assembly plants may accelerate the transformation of the West into assemblers and sellers, downgrading competences and narrowing the skills base. The loss of a critical body of know-how and allowing skills to flow offshore to Japan will affect the ability of the West to generate enough new ideas and capital to develop the new high value-added products critical to maintain headway in a more competitive world.

In exchange for a few low-paid, unskilled jobs and vague and unenforceable promises of local content the governments of the West have paid taxpayers' money to let their most formidable competitor, Japan, loose inside their home markets with a protected 'domestic' status. This has enabled Japanese companies to add a Trojan Horse in terms of start-up operations, acquisitions and joint ventures *inside* the markets of the West to their formidable array of aggressive trade strategies (Figure 20.2).

While Japanese assembly plants could logically be regarded as first-stage investment followed by second stage (fully integrated production) and third stage (R&D) investment, there is no guarantee that this will occur. The West already has a decade and a half of experience with Japanese assembly plants from high technology firms: the second stage has rarely occurred and the third stage is totally absent.

If Japanese manufacturing investments do not transfer skills to the West and create a large number of new high value-added jobs, they have the potential to threaten more valuable jobs and skills than they will create. The West may not only be sacrificing its short-term competitiveness but also mortgaging its future. Clearly the cost of much of the current wave of Japanese manufacturing investments in assembly plants rather than in fully integrated manufacturing units firmly embedded into the economic infrastructure of the West to meet

Western needs rather than Japanese investments agendas may be too high to bear.

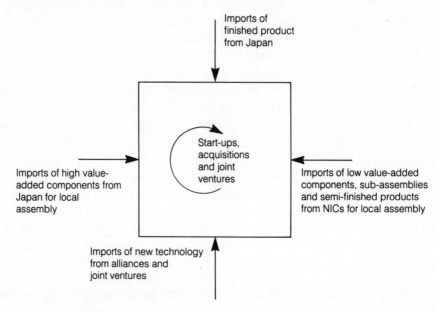

Figure 20.2 The addition of a Trojan Horse (start-ups, acquisitions and joint ventures) to Japanese companies' export-based strategies in the US and the EEC.

PART 5

THE HOUSE OF CARDS

21

'WE HAVE MET THE ENEMY
AND HE IS US'   Pogo

Japanese manufacturing investments in the West, driven by increasing protectionism and the high value of the yen coupled to a rapidly improving technology base and globalized business systems, are only one aspect of the challenge faced by the West. Compounding the problem is that this second crucial wave of Japanese competition comes at a time when the level of competitiveness in the West is approaching its historical low point.

The West has traditionally relied on the free enterprise sector to harness its stock of human, technological, capital and natural resources to provide the competitive advantages necessary to create wealth. Over the last decade the ability of the West to manage effectively its stock of resources to create new wealth has deteriorated. At the same time Japan has been able to improve its economic efficiency, expanding and broadening its position in the world economy largely at the expense of the West. At the core of the West's deterioration in the management of its resources has been a decline in the ability of countries to develop their national competitiveness as well in companies being able to manage their competitiveness in the marketplace.

National competitiveness is a new and imprecise concept coined in the US to reflect a wide range of issues responsible for America's mounting trade and budget deficits. While conventional economic theory suggests that countries, unlike companies and industries, can never lose their ability to compete since the law of comparative advantage dictates that all countries can trade some goods and services, the issue revolves around standards of living[234]. National competitiveness is really being used to indicate the ability of a nation to improve the standard of living of its population by investing adequately in capital, education and technology to improve productivity as the key means to sustain economic growth.

At the heart of the competitiveness issue for the US are two key facts. First, the US has been unable to expand real incomes (to the point where in 1986 they were actually below those of 1982). Increasing poverty and declining aspirations for its population have become major political issues in the US. Second, while Americans are importing increasing amounts of better made and less costly foreign goods which are reducing the country's share of its domestic market, the US has also seen its relative share of world markets for its manufactured exports decline.

Europeans seem bemused by the concern of the US with its lack of competitiveness when it is enjoying its fifth straight year of solid economic growth, low inflation, a high level of new job creation and an unemployment level the envy of much of the EEC[235]. However, Europe has its own set of deep-rooted competitive problems which may even be more difficult to address than those of the US. Much of Europe suffers from intractable unemployment – often double the level of the US; it has largely failed to create sufficient new employment while maintaining protection for a vast range of uncompetitive industries; productivity gains have been low; major pockets of poverty exist – and they are growing; its technology base is eroding relative to that of the US and increasingly Japan, reducing value-added contributions to its economies; and few of its manufacturing companies have the critical mass necessary to compete on equal terms with its US and Japanese rivals.

Changes in the global economic order, the rise of the post-industrial society and economic and industrial mismanagement are at the heart of the West's decline in competitiveness. The West's stranglehold on the keys to comparative advantage in an advanced industrial society – vastly superior stocks of capital, human skills and technology – has been broken. Japan has led the way and has been able to equal and even surpass both the US and the EEC's comparative advantages in a large number of industries. Even more devastating is the fact that the leading NICs – Brazil, Hong Kong, Korea, Singapore and Taiwan – have acquired the cash and technology and have developed human resource skills which come within striking distance of closing the comparative advantage gap with the West in selective areas of high value-added manufactures. In the smokestack and labour-intensive industries, the NICs' own comparative advantages of low wages and high productivity have already exceeded the West's competitiveness.

The West's industrial maturity was a result of its failure to extend its previous lead and develop new comparative advantages. At the same time the rest of the world has been able to come near to matching the West's quality and usage of its stock of national resources which contributed to eroding the competitiveness of the West.

The Western response to the steady decline in its comparative advantage in manufacturing was a steady drift away from manufacturing into services. Of the 11 million jobs created in the US since the 1981–82 recession 80 per cent have been in services – retailing, restaurants, financial and business services, transportation, health and education – and estimates suggest that nine out of 10 new jobs between 1986 and 1995 will be in services[236]. While the US move into services helped to offset the decline in employment in manufacturing, Europe's transition into services has been less successful. Europe cut so many manufacturing jobs in the 1980s and created so few new service jobs that employment growth would have to be increased by a factor of 20 to get down to its pre-recession level of 5.4 per cent by 1990[237].

The move out of manufacturing has had depressing effects on Western competitiveness. First, service jobs generally pay 10 to 20 per cent less than the manufacturing jobs which they replace and generate very low levels of productivity. One survey, for example, indicated that since 1985 some $160 billion had been invested in computers and communications to improve US service sector productivity but that this had produced no broad-based savings[238]. The move to a larger service sector with lower wages and negligible productivity gains has a negative impact on national competitiveness and an immediate depressing effect on standards of living.

Second, the health of service industries is linked to their ability to support the productive sector. As manufacturing employment declines the demands for services as diverse as consulting, construction, finance, health, transport and utilities atrophy. General Motors' major supplier is not a steel, tyre or electronics firm, but a health insurance company[239].

Finally, few service industries offer significant export opportunities. Since services are not regulated by GATT almost all countries operate trade barriers which control service industries and restrict or discriminate against foreign competition. In essence, the Western move from manufacturing into service industries helped to compound rather than solve its problems with its competitiveness.

Government and industry in the West have been unable to develop or implement effective strategies to maintain their competitive position. Western governments have been incapable of countering Japan's long-term goal of maximizing the value-added component of its exports at the expense of short-term gains in standards of living. Western industry has been equally inept in combatting the objectives of Japanese companies of maximizing their market share rather than taking short-term profits. Both failures are central to the West's decline in its relative competitiveness. While the US and Europe were busy managing their national and corporate response to Japanese challenges by the traditional rules of the game they were unable to compete effectively as Japan had changed the nature of the game and was playing by a different set of rules.

The competitiveness of the West is not just an issue of trade balances and exchange rates but increasingly of making less of the things that others want to buy. Japan has developed more new products and made them more efficiently at a higher quality and at a lower cost than either the US or Europe. The painful reality is that more and more Western consumers vote for Japanese products with their wallets – which is reinforced day after day. Unless the West can improve its competitiveness against Japan it will continue to suffer declines in real wages, which will not only lower the standards of living by giving less cash to spend on goods and services but will also erode the quality of life by providing less money to spend on the infrastructure and essential services.

The truth is that Western governments and companies are their own worst enemies. To blame Japan for maximizing its opportunities is like berating a horse for running away after you left the stable door open. Nevertheless, allowing Japan to slip a slew of low value-added assembly plants unchallenged into the West at time when the West's competitiveness is in decline will superimpose a new set of competitive problems which have the potential to accelerate the competitive crisis in the West.

22

THE COMPLACENCY OF
THE ELECTED

In most respects Western governments have mismanaged their responsibility to develop their industrial bases and this has led to poor industrial performance and declining competitiveness. Almost all countries have a national industrial policy. Industrial policies are the economic practices covering taxation, the funding of R&D, reinvestment, industrial credit, trade, employment and competition. Collectively these practices can exert powerful influences on the direction and rate of industrial development, on national competitiveness and ultimately on the standard of living.

Western governments have been unable to develop *and* implement sound and workable approaches to creating strong and sustainable national competitiveness based on national industrial policies. The inability to match Japan's purposeful approach to creating long-term industrial wealth is the result of a set of short-sighted, poorly focused and uncoordinated approaches pursued with less than total commitment by governments in the West.

The West is rich in private and public institutes devoted to forecasting the future. However, the policies and practices of Western governments rarely reflect anticipatory long-term vision for industrial development coupled to a coherent plan to leverage the present to exploit the future. In contrast, MITI in Japan has developed a series of detailed strategic 'visions' for each decade. These identified the key factors driving industrial development and provided the framework for concentrating national resources to improve the value-added component of Japanese industry to enhance its long-term industrial wealth. The fact that MITI's visions have successfully made the transition from plan to reality as industrial development policies has been due to the way in which they were developed. By reaching a broad consensus of agreement between the key players – government, industry and labour – on the national interest, on the speed and direction of change and its impact on the economy and society, on the development of specific technology, and on the role and potential rewards to the individual players MITI's visions have become living industrial policies.

In the West a lack of mutual respect and even mistrust between key players has all but precluded agreement on scenarios of the future and on the problems and the opportunities that change will bring. As a result the implementation of cooperative approaches to develop the industrial base to the mutual benefit of all the players has rarely occurred. Since 1945 Western governments have consistently fallen into the trap of subordinating industrial policies to social goals. That is, they have attempted to meet short-term social demands rather than leveraging their human, technological and capital resources to improve productivity and competitiveness over the long term[240]. National competitiveness ultimately determines the standard of living and the quality of life that a population can enjoy. The West's priority for short-term social gains has been made at the expense of its ability to earn long-term industrial wealth and security.

Japan has taken the opposite approach and has concentrated on developing the productive efficiency of its industrial base to ensure the economic growth necessary to provide future security for its population. Probably Japan, rather than the West, has more ably managed the distribution of income and wealth and the linkage between productivity and economic incentives. Japan's recent economic performance suggests that the West has greatly over-estimated the importance of the trade-off between social justice and economic efficiency since Japan is now more egalitarian and more efficient than the West[241]. While it is true that Japanese work longer and harder, live in smaller dwellings, save more, and pay higher consumer prices than their counterparts in the West, they also enjoy a standard of health care second to none and suffer a crime rate well below that of any country in the West.

Japan's overall economic strategy of moving progressively from recovery and reconstruction through internationalization to readjustment to changes in energy costs, environmental pressures and to technological change has been supported by a flexible industrial policy. This has enabled Japan continuously to select higher value-added industries for development and exploitation within an overall framework designed to improve its long-term industrial profile. Despite the fact that MITI's visions are available in English there has been little appreciation in the West of the intention or of the implications of Japan's industrial policies. The Western response has been poorly coordinated by governments and left largely to the private sector to develop and implement. Since Japan's challenge has been based on a cooperative approach by government, industry and labour the haphazard Western responses by industry alone have been weak and ineffective in meeting Japan's challenge.

Compounding the problem is a widespread lack of understanding by government of industry and of the need for effective policies to steer industry to adapt to continuously changing market forces. As a result Western governments have not been able to rationalize their positions in low value-added industries, or to develop a sustained approach to moving capital, labour and technology away from sunset industries with declining comparative advantages into sunrise industries offering high value-added opportunities. Rather governments in the West have bowed to partisan demands to protect and subsidize the less competitive industries at the expense of accelerating the funding of new industries which offer potentially greater future rewards. Consequently support for new industries has largely been left to a private sector dominated by a fixation on short-term rewards. Without the push and pull of government-driven policies forcing industry to adapt quickly to changing market needs much of the West's industrial base has been locked into producing more and more product which less and less people are willing to buy.

In the West most national industrial policies are not coupled to fiscal and monetary policies. These complementary linkages are essential to regulate the money supply, the national debt, interest and exchange rates, consumer credit and savings and taxes – all of which are powerful mechanisms helping to direct the movement of capital, labour and technology to meet industrial development goals. In Japan strong linkages have been forged between industrial, fiscal and monetary policies, which has helped to support economic goals designed to improve national competitiveness and ultimately standards of living. Fiscal policy has been used as the main instrument to improve the infrastructure and to develop the industrial base, capital accumulation and exports. Similarly, monetary policy has guided industrial development by channelling funds to strategic industries[242].

The strong linkages in Japan between industrial, fiscal and monetary policies have helped to create and sustain a producing economy while weak linkages in the West have caused a steady drift into a consuming economy, retarding the manufacturing base.

Centralized economic management is an anathema in the West since it is regarded as the antithesis of a free market system which allows market forces to allocate resources. There is widespread political and industrial hostility to policies which increase the role of the government in directing private sector investment in the West and which are seen as limiting the freedom of the private sector to allocate resources. Obviously the West can point to the monolithic plans of the Communist bloc and their monumental failures as the folly of centralized economic management. However, the consensus approach, with shared visions and responsibilities between government, industry and labour in Japan and Japan's sustained industrial success suggest that the hit and miss approach of the West has been less than effective in sustaining competitiveness. The West's economies are a reflection of partisan politics and pressures by interest groups rather than a planned manipulation of natural comparative advantages to develop a more productive and effective industrial sector to improve national competitiveness[243].

Japan's industrial policy has succeeded not because it is highly planned but because it is a disciplined approach to achieving consensus between government, industry and labour. Government's role in Japan is a facilitator, using administrative guidance to allocate resources to meet market forces. In Japan industrial policies link the virtues of planning with the virtues of the market and do not use one to thwart the other as in the West[244].

A lack of long-term vision; concentrating on the effect (social needs) rather than the cause (increased productivity and competitiveness); protecting and subsidizing the past determinants of comparative advantage rather than focusing on future opportunities; poor linkages with fiscal and monetary policies which have helped to promote consumerism and reduce production; and the inability to get industry and labour to buy-in to shared futures, values and responsibilities have ensured a haphazard approach to industrial policies in the West. Japan's ruthless practice of a disciplined, integrated approach to planning and implementing a long-term flexible response to changing domestic needs and international market forces enabled Japan to reach and even surpass the competitiveness of most Western countries by the early 1980s.

Governments in the West have failed to appreciate the crucial linkages between capital, education and technology and their multiplier effect on industrial competitiveness. The West has largely assigned the task of determining priorities for funding industrial capital investment to the private sector, education to the public sector and technology to a mix between the public and the private sector. Since agreements between government, industry and labour on national industrial goals are almost non-existent and those cornerstones of industrial performance are designed and managed almost compartmentally they tend to serve different goals. In contrast, Japan recognized the essential nature of these linkages, the glue cementing its industrial policies, and with a planned and consensus approach has been able to harness these assets to drive its industrial development much more successfully than the West.

Capital promotion is essential to fund investments in new businesses and to increase the volume and quality of plant and equipment available to labour to increase productivity. The West has suffered continuous problems with capital formation and its use due to limited government industrial policies, a failure to manage the issue of relative costs and the orthodoxy of industrial management – each of which has contributed to the West's persistent productivity problems.

Policies in the West for direct tax incentives and subsidies to encourage investment have been haphazard and rarely sustained over the long term. Rather than promoting to industry the necessity of continuously reinvesting to upgrade productivity, capital investments have been widely used by industry as a means to reduce corporate tax. Japan has consistently pursued a policy of direct tax incentives with investment tax credits, accelerated depreciation and special depreciation allowances. As a result it has been able to channel a large percentage of its GNP into industrial investment[245]. Japan has also managed to focus this investment to drive productivity gains and to develop new competences in targetted industries to upgrade the value-added profile.

Capital investment growth rates respond to changes in relative costs. Relative costs are a function of the availability of capital and labour, which are regulated by the linkages between national industrial, fiscal and monetary policies. Since these linkages are weak governments in the West have been unable effectively to manage relative costs to promote industrial investment. High unemployment has created a large labour pool which has depressed relative wages, giving industry the excuse to use less efficient but less costly labour rather than more expensive capital[246]. Capital expenditures in the West are largely driven by retooling for new products rather than for added capacity and little is spent to increase productivity[247]. The ineffective management of relative costs as a direct result of the poor linkages between industrial, fiscal and monetary policies has enabled Western industry to pursue policies of squeezing old equipment to the last drop rather than investing in new machinery to improve the tools for labour to increase productivity.

Western industry has followed an orthodox approach and the line of least resistance rather than innovative policies and practices to confront its problems directly. By following traditional approaches to maximize short-term profit which dictate that as long as the marginal cost of production on old depreciated machinery is less than the full cost of producing on new equipment, Western firms have retained existing plant and equipment. Japanese companies follow market share policies for long-term profit. These are based on leveraging the experience curve to drive down costs with increasing volume so that price can decline parallel to cost, continuously opening up new market segments and adding to volume. Consequently Japanese firms have abandoned existing machinery just as soon as new technology became more efficient, giving up short-term profits in the interest of far greater long-term returns. Rather than confronting high domestic wages and rigid work rules, Western industry has frequently outsourced production to the Asian NICs, which have a comparative advantage in labour costs. Essentially this has resulted in the export of jobs in exchange for lower labour costs at the expense of investing for domestic productivity gains to enhance the standard of living.

The capital issue runs across industries and countries in the West and even the high-technology area, widely believed to hold the key to improving the West's competitiveness, is not immune from capital investment problems. Europe appears to suffer more than the US in its growth of capital formation in high technology. Gross fixed capital formation in high technology in the EEC increased at an annual 4.9 per cent *lower* than in Japan between 1972 and 1982; productivity grew annually at 8.1 per cent in Japan compared to only 2.6 per cent in the EEC between 1973 and 1983. As a result, high technology output increased in the EEC by only 3.8 per cent while it grew in Japan by 12.2 per cent annually. The EEC has been unable to win export orders, or meet domestic demand, due to poor capital formation in high-technology industries where world demand has been strongest and profit margins high[248].

Industrial competitiveness in the West has been severely hampered by its approach to the formation and use of capital. Limited encouragement and direction of capital investment, poorly supported by fiscal and monetary policies allocated by a private sector managing for the present, have contributed to falling productivity and standards of living.

The talent or level of human capital of a population, the quality of abilities and skills, is a key factor in national competitiveness. The higher the quality the better the nation is able to exploit its stock of capital, technological and natural resources to maximize its wealth. Both the standard and the focus of the educational system are central to the level of human capital. Education in the West has been unable to meet the challenge posed by Japan with an educational system designed to equal and surpass that of the West and has failed to prepare itself for changing educational needs created by the decline of its basic industries and the rise of new technology and service industries.

Japan's competitive success is firmly rooted in high-quality schooling and advanced vocational training. Numerous studies in the US and in Europe attest to the fact that Japanese schoolchildren attain substantially higher skills in mathematics and science than their Western counterparts and more emphasis is placed on the development of technical skills[249]. Japanese recognition of the importance of human capital as a major factor in catching up with the West resulted in a very high priority and investment in education. By establishing clear national standards open to continuous improvement, providing adequate and evenly distributed resources, according a high status to the teaching profession and fostering a highly competitive system Japan has been able to make significant progress in developing the quality of its educational system.

As a result of Japan's concentration on building human capital, by the late 1970s Japan was setting the competitive standard in world education. By grafting a high level of education onto a disciplined, cooperative but individually competitive population accustomed to hard work Japan forged a competitive advantage[250].

The West has not accorded the same degree of priorities to the education system and in particular to basic education. The result is that while the elite centres of education produce a small number of outstanding graduates the majority are educated to minimum levels of literacy. Functional illiteracy, for example, is estimated to run as high as 20 per cent in the US.

The fiercely competitive standards of Japan's vocational training have been pursued with the same vigour as that of basic education. With an industrial policy based on continuously increasing productivity and improving the value-added profile there has been a heavy concentration on developing a large cadre of engineers and scientists to serve industrial needs. Japan has outproduced the West in the supply of these professionals and as early as the late 1970s was employing proportionately more engineers and scientists in its labour force than leading Western nations[251] (Table 22.1).

Table 22.1. By the late 1970s Japan was employing proportionately more scientists and engineers than its major Western rivals.

Percentage of labour force		
	Scientists and engineers	R&D workers
Japan	11.5	1.4
Germany	5.3	1.0
US	3.0	0.8

Source: *Economic Prospects: East and West*, J. Winiecki, CRCE, London 1987

In the West engineers and scientists rate low in industrial esteem and reward while the best brains are attracted into more visible and higher-paid professions like law and occupations like merchant banking and investment services. It is little wonder that the US and Europe cannot compete as equals in manufacturing with Japan given its emphasis on technical vocation backed by social and industrial systems which reward scientists and engineers.

Much of the West's education has been designed to produce workers for economies based on labour-intensive manufacturing industries. As basic manufacturing industry declined and knowledge-intensive industries and services grew the qualitative demands for labour, educational levels and skills changed. For example, increasing computerization and automation has created demands for more workers with specific skills. However, the West has not responded fast enough in refocusing its education systems to meet the rapid rise in demand for new and more skills created by these new industrial needs and there is a gap between demand and supply. Paradoxically, as basic manufacturing industries in the West continue to shed workers who end up swelling the ranks of the undereducated, undertrained and underskilled there is not enough skilled and trained labour available to meet demand. As the industrial base of the West changes low-wage jobs will disappear and the minimum level of skills which will be required will start to overtake the knowledge of employees who entered the labour market within the space of a decade. In fact, the half-life of people's knowledge is reckoned to be contracting so fast now that it almost equals the time taken to acquire it[252].

Western economies in the process of transforming into a post-industrial society based on knowledge-intensive industries are faced with two educational problems. The first is to switch the welfare resources being used to keep the unemployed off the streets into massive retraining for upgrading skills and education to improve the economic contribution of the idle. Without this retraining more and more resources earned by fewer and fewer people will be devoted to welfare, which will further erode productivity and standards of living and ultimately add to social discontent. The second is the need to refocus educational needs to anticipate continuously a labour market being driven by the switch of emphasis to new technologies that are creating demands for new skills and higher levels of basic education. Without a change in education the West will not be able to sustain its competitiveness, which will increasingly be determined by improving productivity and creating and harnessing new technology. The lack of attention to educational quality and a delay in switching educational emphasis to match the demands of post-industrial society in the West have been major factors in declining productivity and standards of living.

Technology, the methods and materials used to apply science to industrial objectives, has long been recognized as a key component of national competitiveness. The amount and quality of technology has a direct effect on the level of national comparative advantage and the value-added level of industrial output. While the West has led the world in the development and introduction of new technology it has begun to see its lead decline. The erosion of the West's once unquestioned leadership in technology has been due to underestimating the ability of Japan rapidly to build up a world-class technology base and a failure to develop efficient systems to manage the transfer of scientific knowledge into usable products to compete effectively in world markets.

Japan regards technology as a major force in its industrial policy. This is reflected in the allocation and use of its resources and in the degree of cooperation between government, industry and academia. Japan's funding of R&D as a percentage of GNP has grown continuously at the same time that its GNP registered substantial gains. Japan now outspends its trade rivals as a percentage of GNP spent on R&D to drive its technological development (Figure 22.1). Japan recognized that although changes in the use of labour and capital investment had a significant impact on overall productivity growth, the key element driving productivity was rapid adaptation to new technology (Table 22.2).

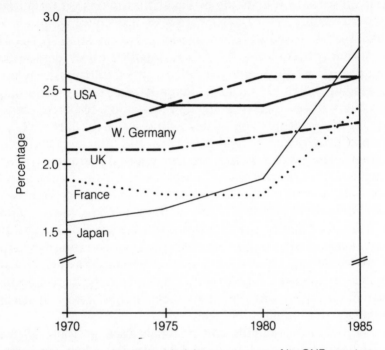

Figure 22.1. Japan almost doubled the percentage of its GNP spent on R&D in a rapidly growing economy while its trade rivals registered at best small gains on low growth economies.

Source: *International Management*, October 1987.

Table 22.2. Overall productivity growth determinants in conventional manufacturing are weighted more heavily towards adapt-ation to new technology than other elements.

Determinants	Percentage
Changes in use of labour	15
Capital investment	25
Technology change	60

Source: *The Economist*, 20 December 1986

Government in Japan takes a pivotal role in guiding and directing technology in the national interest by helping to fund advanced R&D and promoting close collaboration between government, industry and academia. For example, MITI set aside yen 26 billion in 1981 to finance R&D in private industry over a 10-year period in biotechnology, widely regarded as a key technology with a high value-added content.

Driving the whole process is a high level of technology management. Firms in Japan have concentrated on developing a flexible attitude to technology to promote horizontal communication. This is centred on building cooperation between science and production to move concepts smoothly from the laboratory to the production line. This helps to minimize the psychological barriers in managing technology and creativity[253].

The commitment in the West to technology lags behind Japan. While Japan's major trade rivals were all spending more of their GNP on R&D than Japan in 1970, slow growth or even declines in expenditure reversed the picture by 1985. The training and employment of scientists and engineers in industry in the West falls behind Japan's commitment. Traditional antipathy between the players – government, industry and academia – and more limited communications between the research and the manufacturing functions as a result of the tendency in Western industry to compartmentalize activities have helped to hinder the efficient exploitation of new technology.

Japan has consistently linked its R&D efforts to visionary long-term goals focused on developing specific products and their essential production processes and systems. By emphasizing the transformation process, moving products from concept through automated mass-production systems capable of producing complex advanced technology products at high quality and low cost on a scale large enough to meet world demand, Japanese firms have been able to secure significant competitive advantage. Probably more than anything the Japanese realized that integrated product and production research are essential to move concepts to the market place quickly to meet demand at prices that people can afford[254].

The West, while continuously creating and developing advanced technology, has seen its share of markets for complex products ranging from machine tools and medical electronics to semiconductors and robotics erode. A failure to develop the systems to promote the rapid transfer of products from concept to the market and to develop processes to manufacture at high volume and quality and at low cost lost the West its early

169

market lead in many new technologies. Japan has concentrated on organizing its resources and integrating activities effectively to use advanced technology to maximize the value-added content of its industrial output. The West has maintained a much more diffuse approach to managing technology. This has suboptimized its resources and lowered its competitiveness. More quickly than the West, the Japanese realized that research complexity now dictates that the application of technology to make marketable products is less a product of individual genius and serendipity and more an outcome of an organized and integrated approach to managing technology.

Much of the fault for the West's declining competitiveness stems from a lack of integrated industrial policies and differences between the objectives of the public and private sector. The fact that the West has fallen behind Japan in its management of capital, education and technology is a reflection of the failure of Western governments to develop effective industrial policies. Literally, when you don't know where you want to go it is impossible to plan effectively to get there.

Japan's strong industrial growth was inevitable given the state of its economy in the late 1940s. However, Japan has been able to sustain an economic growth rate consistently higher than that of the West for over 40 years. It has reached an economic position second only to that of the US and dominates the world market for many advanced manufactured goods. Japan's performance was not merely the result of a combination of catching up with the West and of leveraging favourable circumstances. A large measure of government complacency together with hostility to disciplined industrial planning and management of the West's capital, human and technological resources is at the heart of the problem. This complacency enabled Japan, with a flexible set of industrial goals and an integrated and organized approach to using its national resources, to undermine Western competitiveness.

23

MANAGEMENT MEDIOCRITY

The way firms are managed and how companies have responded to the challenge of Japanese competition and to economic and technological change have played a central role in the decline of Western competitiveness.

In the quarter century from 1950 Western industry enjoyed almost continuous non-inflationary growth where the key management skills centred on outproducing competition and introducing new products for which pent-up demand and growing consumer affluence produced almost limitless opportunities. Under these conditions it was not difficult to prosper and as a result management gained a reputation of mythical proportions for business success and for skilled professionalism. However, this success was a result of competing largely on an empty field and masked growing arrogance, complacency and mismanagement in much of the corporate West.

The failure of many companies in the West to address the recession of the early 1980s and to compete successfully against Japanese firms has called into question the very ethos of Western management – the way in which management has responded to its owners, customers, competitors, employees and to the discipline of the financial market.

The Rise of 'Corpocracy' and the Ownership Issue

The conventional wisdom is that companies are governed by those skilled in the practices of management – 'corpocrats' – who direct the development of firms in the interests of their owners.

171

This accountability is theoretical as in practice control and ownership are almost always divorced in companies of any size. Most public companies had little concentration of stock ownership and most shareholders were effectively absentee owners. The result was that management exercised an exclusive right to control companies with little input from the real owners. With diffuse shareholder power a 'protected' management with little personal stake in the business became self-perpetuating, determining who would run the company and how it would be run. In numerous cases managements lost sight of their basic responsibility to the owners and became obsessed with exercise of personal power, bigger budgets and expanding empires. Since management elects itself it enjoys life-time tenure. This has led to entrenchment and the creation of redundant bureaucracies – more layers of management – where the process, massive control systems and complex procedures and sophisticated analytical techniques considered necessary to run large companies assumed more importance than the results. Apart from increasing the depth of the hierarchy and creating inefficiency this produced two significant trends.

First, this encouraged a move away from hands-on experience and from people with in-depth multifunctional backgrounds towards narrow specialization which increasingly proved to be the route to the top[255]. Historical trends in the US over the last 50 years show a progressive change in emphasis from production to marketing to finance and legal backgrounds of company presidents[256]. As a result companies in the West became increasingly managed by pseudo-professionals rather than by individuals with broad-based operating skills and experience. Managerial responses became more superficial and more concerned with conflicts over turf than the fundamentals of winning in the market place; companies became less able to maximize the use of their productive resources – human skills, plant, equipment, technology and cash – to compete effectively. In contrast, Japanese companies have long adopted rotational functional training starting at the lowest levels to provide a cadre of well-rounded individuals schooled in perfection through the mastery of detail. This gave Japanese firms a depth of management with the broad-based experience and skills necessary to run complex companies efficiently and effectively.

Second, management – like all bureaucracies – has a fear of any change which will upset the status quo. This bred an aversion to taking risk and increasingly led to taking the line of least resistance and of adopting orthodox responses to new and innovative challenges. When push came to shove – strong challenges from superior Japanese products – Western firms largely avoided taking the actions necessary to compete more effectively by improving quality and cutting costs. Generally they took soft options by abandoning products and markets to the Japanese and moving up-market into more secure but smaller-volume, higher-value niches. Those companies which finally did respond by improving quality and cost competitiveness failed to interpret correctly both the depth of Japanese competitive strength and long-term intentions. Japanese quality and cost competitiveness resulted from the use of innovative manufacturing techniques, sophisticated production equipment, effective labour practices and customer-driven product development – not just lower wage costs. Many Western firms failed to recognize that it does not follow that you will become more competitive if you just lower your costs and increase your quality. Competitive advantage is a more complex issue and is built on managing converging competences in production, finance, quality, design, technology and service. Japanese strategies are designed to produce strong future competitive positions for global brands with the potential for cross-market subsidization[257]. A small number of Western companies have realized that competitive advantage has now shifted in dimension from the country to the global level. However, most have not been able to implement meaningful global strategies of their own.

Management's autocratic behaviour to its owners and customers was not important so long as business was growing and earnings took care of themselves in expanding markets; managerial failures generally went undetected. The impact of the recession in the early 1980s and the continued loss of market position to the Japanese in their home markets had a major impact on corporate financial performance. At the same time institutional shareholdings began to increase. In the US alone by mid-1987 one third of all stocks were reckoned to be held by institutions[258] and in Europe the deregulation of financial markets and the growth of pension funds, insurance companies and banks substantially increased institutional shareholding.

This concentration of ownership, combined with poor company performance, raised serious questions in the financial community about the ability of entrenched management elites to run their businesses in the interests of their owners. Managements began to come under increasing pressure from institutions due to the size of institutional shareholdings. Institutional investments in many companies had begun to reach a level where institutions could no longer just sell stock and walk away from companies where the management was incompetent or feathering its own nest at the expense of creating sustained value for shareholders. Institutional frustration led to confrontation and conflict and managements began to suffer from the first effective challenge to their hegemony as institutions attempted to reduce managements' power.

Competing by Running Away

Western reaction to Japanese competition has largely been to avoid confrontation and to retreat – disengaging from the market by abandoning products, market positions and manufacturing skills.

Some firms moved their labour-intensive assembly operations and component supplies offshore to capture lower costs to improve their cost competitiveness. By the 1980s the US semiconductor industry had 80 per cent of its assembly operations carried out in South East Asia and Latin America[259] and major companies like Apple Computer, Chrysler, GE, IBM and Philips were sourcing significant amounts of their component requirements in the Asian NICs.

Other firms moved to their Japanese competitors to supply lower-cost, higher-quality OEM products to keep their product lines alive. US car firms, for example, started to buy their small cars from Japanese producers (Chrysler and Mitsubishi) or by building small cars using designs and major components from Japan (Ford and Mazda[260]). In the photocopier market Pitney-Bowes and 3M in the US and Gestetner in Europe abandoned production and became distributors for Toshiba, Ricoh and Mita, respectively[261]. To stay in the consumer electronics business in Europe AEG-Telefunken, Thorn/EMI and Thomson all built local plants to assemble VCRs to JVC's designs using many JVC-sourced components. To penetrate a market that it had failed to spot Kodak marketed camcorders, a combination of 8mm videotape and recorders, using tapes purchased from TDK and hardware from Matsushita[262].

Many firms driven by the need to access new products, new markets, new technologies and low-cost manufacturing know-how increasingly turned to joint ventures with Japanese companies. These agreements spanned a wide range of high-technology industries ranging from aerospace (Boeing with Fuji, Kawasaki and Mitsubishi Heavy Industries) and carbon fibres (Elf Acquitaine and Pechiney with Toray) to computers (Honeywell and Groupe Bull with NEC), robotics (IBM with Sanyo Seiko) and advanced semiconductors (RCA–GE with Sharp).

Rather than address the real problem – the lack of competitiveness – Western managements preferred to take the easy solutions of leaving the market or of cooperating with their Japanese competitors. This added to the decline in competitiveness by reducing the capability to design and manufacture complex, innovative products and helped to hollow out the manufacturing base and turn many Western manufacturers into assemblers, distributors and marketers of Japanese products.

Many of these strategies reduced costs dramatically. It was estimated in the US that the cloning of a car design could save as much as $1000 per car in development costs, and by using foreign-sourced components a further $700 could be saved[263]. However, these strategies did nothing to halt and even contributed to the erosion of the West's manufacturing base and, in turn, its industrial competitiveness. By retreating and cooperating Western managements added additional dimensions to the problem of competitiveness. Component and OEM supply and joint ventures with Japan have helped to transfer employment skills, experience and profits off-shore to Japanese labour and Japanese companies. This has left Western workers with the peripheral parts of the product process – assembly, marketing and logistics – which do not produce the high value-added income needed to support rising standards of living. More problematically, this has provided Japanese competitors with the opportunity to control the next generation of production and product technology[264].

At the same time the Western obsession to form alliances with their most dangerous competitors has given Japanese firms more opportunities to acquire Western technology and greater access to Western markets. As protectionism increases in the West to limit Japanese market penetration by exports the shift to alliances with Western firms provides Japanese firms with market access which cannot easily be regulated with traditional duties, tariffs and quotas.

The Customer as Peasant

In theory the customer is king. In practice Western managements have long been guilty of treating customers more as peasants than as the sole reason for their existence.

The driving philosophy of Western companies in the growth era through to the mid-1970s, fuelled by pent-up demand and growing consumer affluence, was that of a producer bureaucracy. Cosy, inefficient oligopolies were able to impose long-term policies of selling what they could make and charging premium prices for the privilege. There was little fear of a real competitive challenge since competition was based on trying to outproduce other companies and speeding product through the distribution system. This 'competitive' policy of a producer focus began to unravel as market forces and Japanese pressure changed the dynamics of competition. Consumers in the West came into contact with an increasing volume of well-made and inexpensive Japanese products. Used to poorly designed, badly engineered, carelessly manufactured and indifferently serviced domestic products at high prices these better made, more innovative and cheaper Japanese imported products came as a revelation. Western consumers began to vote increasingly with their wallets for what they saw as better value.

At the same time a new individualism and a new affluence began to shape the demands of Western consumers. Changes in interests, tastes, life styles and aspirations began to move consumers away from fixed, inherited values to individualism and to discovered values. Increasing affluence made consumers more sophisticated and purchase decisions moved towards products with greater style, better quality and higher value[265].

Western industry for years dismissed Japanese products as shoddy and imitative and their low prices as a function of low labour costs. Management compounded these errors by continuing to adopt production-driven policies rather than market-focused strategies. Premium pricing policies and waiting for competitors to make their products obsolete only created an umbrella over Japanese market penetration. However, the real problem stemmed from their appalling ignorance of what customers want and the way in which they approached the marketing task. Conventional wisdom suggests that customers buy products and services because they offer benefits perceived to be greater than those offered by competitors. Many Western companies with successful track records of producer-driven policies had never got close to their customers and lacked the commitment and the sensitivity necessary to organize themselves to concentrate their efforts on customers to deliver better product value[266].

Japanese companies succeeded because they anticipated customer needs and built better products by adding value – quality, design, style, delivery, suitability, reliability and after-sale service. This better met customer needs and delivered greater levels of perceived product value than Western competitors. Essentially Japanese firms have concentrated on using strategies which couple their accumulated *invisible* assets – their knowledge and experience of customers, the distribution system, competition and the market environment – with their efficient usage of their fixed plant, human, capital and technological resources to match product closely to customer needs to secure competitive advantage[267].

Modern marketing theory evolved in the US and became well accepted in Europe in the early 1960s. While the approaches taken by most Western companies can be termed 'marketing-oriented' they are rarely customer-focused. For example, some companies are more concerned with the short-term elements of the marketing mix – advertising, selling, promotion and distribution; others concentrate on organizing the internal flow of products from raw material input through to physical distribution to improve their efficiency; some managements adopt formula approaches to marketing designed to control the organization's response to changes in the market created by competitors' actions; while other companies base their marketing decisions largely on short-term financial criteria related to the bottom line and to returns on marketing investments. All of these approaches can be considered marketing-oriented but they are preoccupied with internal issues. Nowhere is this better illustrated than in the radical difference in pricing philosophy adopted by Japanese firms compared with most of their Western competitors. Japanese firms tend to use market-driven accounting practices which enable them to do away with estimating product cost based on prevailing engineering standards and with designing products to make better use of technology and workflows. Rather they design and build products that will meet a competitive market price which is usually well below currently achievable costs based on standard techniques and processes and requires innovative solutions to deliver a profit[268]. In contrast their

Western competitors are often wedded to simplistic 'cost-plus' formulae which foster neither low-cost production nor creativity by management or labour.

These and other ostrich-like approaches have helped to isolate many Western firms from the market place rather than helping them to focus their attention on reacting to customer needs to generate sustainable long-term success. The inevitable result has been a growing gap between what customers want and the products supplied by Western companies, and this has been reflected in their declining market shares.

The appalling ignorance of customer wants is due to corporacy and to the legacy of past successes which have played havoc with the competitiveness of Western firms. Large bureaucracies became inward-looking, form took precedence over substance and as the real rate of return on investments declined risk aversion set in and companies in the West suffered declines in their ability to respond effectively to changing market dynamics. For example, the economic dislocation of the early 1980s caused by the recession increased unemployment and made Western consumers much more cost-conscious and value-driven. However, Western firms continued to adopt their producer philosophy and their internally driven marketing policies.

By establishing strong customer franchises based on superior value perceptions for their products Japanese companies were ideally placed to capitalize on these shifts to more discerning demand in the West. This not only helped Japanese firms to increase their penetration of Western markets but also set the scene for them to begin to move up-market to the higher margin, more profitable, segments. Ironically, this served to increase pressure on Western firms who had moved up-market to escape from early Japanese competition in the lower-priced segments. Many Western companies have myopically continued to attempt to sell what they could make and have failed to switch to a policy of making what they could sell. Literally, they have failed to find out just what the customer wanted and have not been able to shift the organization to fulfilling these needs. This lack of customer focus has given away niches, segments, markets and whole industries to Japanese competitors who better understood the new imperatives for success.

The legacy of past successes is a powerful hindrance to change. Companies in the West continue to adopt producer-driven strategies long after the market has shifted to customer-driven demand. GM's new Quad 4 motor, heralded as a major breakthrough in car engine design, is a typical producer-driven product[269]. Available as an option at extra cost on a limited number of GM models in 1988, the Quad 4 fails to take into account that twin-cam, four-valve engines have been available for years as standard equipment on Japanese cars.

Japanese goods have transformed the lives of Western consumers with cheap, well made and reliable products and Japanese goods have frequently come to set the standards against which other products are measured. The wheel has come full circle. Thirty years ago Japanese firms westernized their brand names to build customer confidence. Now Western companies are using Japanese brand names in the West to signify quality and superiority. Curry's and Dixon's, consumer electronics retail chains in the UK, have achieved an unqualified success in marketing their Matsui and Saisho 'house' brands complete with rising sun logos – although the products are made anywhere but Japan[270]. Unless Western companies can regain leadership by dumping their historical producer-driven orthodoxy and move to offer consistently superior products they will continue to suffer market erosion at the hands of Japanese companies who better understand their customers and their markets.

The Disposable Employee

The greatest asset of any company is its stock of human resources. How well labour is organized, trained and motivated and the amount and quality of the tools at its disposal have a major impact on a firm's competitiveness.

Managements in the West frequently view labour as inefficient, expensive and obstructive while labour has clung to unions with rigid work rules and job classifications to protect itself from managements which are widely perceived as exploitive. The inability to forge an effective dialogue between management and labour has had a signifi-cant impact on Western competitiveness. Effective management of human resources depends on creating and sustaining a set of common goals based on the principle that wealth has to be created before it can be distributed, a willingness on both sides to invest in the long term and to share sacrifices. Many Western companies have slid into increasing wages and benefits to keep labour peace without obtaining a compensatory increase in productivity.

The autocratic style and the hierarchies and bureaucracies of many managements in the West have prevented companies from making and executing productivity and management decisions based on participation and consensus agreement between managers and workers. Without a management initiative to democratize the work place companies have been unable to change work practices and to get labour to adopt the flexibility necessary to increase productivity[271].

Although Japan is heavily unionized, the unions are largely company rather than functionally based and cover white and blue collar workers and are more cooperative with management. However, Japanese management has worked at becoming a master of human relations and has built structures which create teamwork and encourage the will to work. As a result it has been able to harness individual selfishness and group loyalty so that workers gain morally, financially and socially when their efforts help the group as a whole[272]. While autocracy in the West has helped to create barriers between management and labour, Japanese managements have fostered equality to build a mutuality of trust and values which has helped to motivate employees to compete and to cooperate with each other rather than to pursue individual financial gain. To further equality personal success in Japan is tied to the success of the company and promotion and pay are linked to age and expertise – the status and skills of the employee. The Western system emphasizes elitism with the above-average performer rapidly getting to the top with pay and promotion linked to performance – which has a negative effect on the morale of the majority.

Western managements have compounded their labour problems with their reaction to adversity. Faced with downturns they have adopted slash-and-burn tactics to unload their most expensive asset – labour. While this has led to short-term cost reductions it has reinforced fear and mistrust and led to the widespread perception among labour that it unfairly bears the brunt of managerial failures. Since morale has long been recognized as pivotal to productivity gains fear and mistrust are hardly likely to increase management-labour cooperation. Japanese employees are loyal to the extent that their employers take care of them. Management in Japan attaches great weight to its social responsibility to preserve job security and goes to extraordinary lengths to absorb the shocks of downturns. Redeployment within the *kaisha* or *keiretsu*, the creation of anti-recessionary cartels to provide a common cushion for all firms and, when layoffs are inevitable, providing adequate compensation are typical corporate responses in Japan to adversity.

In short, while Japanese managements accept their social obligations and are prepared to pay the penalty for their mistakes and misfortunes by erecting self-imposed barriers which limit their ability to dump labour, Western management is more prone to lay off labour with minimum compensation to cut its short-term costs. Since labour legislation in the US is more flexible than that in Europe American workers have tended to suffer more from slash-and-burn approaches than their European counterparts.

Managerial reactions to downturns in the West also include paring investments in training and in new plant and equipment to reduce costs and the asset base. As a result companies burdened themselves with obsolescent skills and aging capital, neither of which helps to increase productivity and both of which compound their competitiveness problems. In contrast, in times of adversity Japanese companies continue and even increase their commitments to improving productivity through the development of new and better skills and the acquisition of more efficient capital equipment. The Japanese approach of using labour as a key asset with a managerial focus on equality and participation has led to a flexible and efficient allocation of labour and built the morale necessary continually to improve productivity and product quality.

The managerial obsession with autocracy and a widespread approach to regarding labour as a troublesome, expensive and disposable asset has had a predictable effect on loyalty and productivity in the West. While the West has demonstrated its ability to redeploy its capital it has been unsuccessful in redeploying its labour to build the firm base needed for superior growth. Many Western managements have failed to appreciate that much of Japanese firms' success can be directly traced back to the effective use of the knowledge, skills and experience of committed people.

Penny-Wise and Pound-Foolish

Companies in the West are moving closer to managing the business for the short term at the expense of long-term rewards. While this was once a US phenomenon many European companies are adopting the same short-term approach to managing their businesses. The narrowing of horizons to the short term has been driven by a combination of factors.

The shift in corporate control progressively away from those who made and sold products to those who handle the purse strings changed the focus of many companies from the goal of creating and keeping satisfied customers, a long-term process, towards managing the business to maximize the return on investment, effectively a short-term fixation. A recent comparison of the objectives of US and Japanese companies indicated that US companies are essentially managed to maximize their short-term performance while their Japanese rivals are managed to build their businesses to harvest long-term rewards (Table 23.1).

Table 23.1. By managing for the short term US firms are sacrificing their ability to compete successfully in the long term.

Managerial objectives	
The short term (US firms)	The long term (Japanese firms)
1. Return on investment	1. Market share
2. Share price	2. Profitability
3. Market share	3. New products

Source: *Forbes*, 6 October 1986.

A UK study confirmed that short-term profit was twice as important for American and British companies as for Japanese firms; Western firms were willing to reduce costs and allow their market shares to erode if necessary to boost short-term profits[273]. Even when presented with a golden opportunity when Japanese companies were forced to increase their prices to combat *endaka*, Western competitors invariably raised their prices aggressively to increase profits rather than maintain or lower them to capitalize on the situation and increase market share. US exporters, for example, raised prices in 1987 by an annualized rate of 12 per cent – the largest quarterly increase since late 1983 – and US domestic producers followed suit.

With little price incentive consumers continued to select Japanese products with their higher quality image[274].

These practices go a long way to explaining the poor record of Western industry in defending its domestic markets and its failure to exploit its past leadership positions, first in overseas and later in domestic markets.

Since pay and incentives for top management in the West are often linked to profit performance it provides an additional incentive to give priority to short-term earnings and share prices rather than long-term growth. This increases the obsession with quarterly earnings. When earnings come under pressure there is an obvious reluctance to invest in R&D, capital equipment and employee skills enhancement – the key building blocks for developing a competitive edge and increasing productivity. As a result, many Western companies easily slipped into the trap of underfunding their future. With pay and incentives in Japan largely uncoupled from short-term earnings managements have more freedom to set objectives and to invest to develop their businesses to produce long-term value appreciation.

The lacklustre performance of many Western firms produced strong pressures from the financial community on management to improve the quality and quantity of earnings. The reaction to these pressures was to concentrate even further on maximizing short-term earnings. Major programmes were adopted to boost cash flows, shareholder value and productivity by cutting wages, laying off employees, exporting jobs offshore, reducing investments in R&D, capital equipment and training and by merging, selling off and dumping inefficient plants and by restructuring their businesses. In most cases these were once-for-all shakeouts. While cost-cutting, streamlining, downsizing, merging, restructuring and selling off assets have a valuable role in business and produce short-term productivity gains, this corporate *Perestroika* has not added quality, products, services or jobs to the economy. Nor has it led to the more intelligent use of capital, human skills or technology to create superior products to sustain those long-term productivity improvements vital to regain a competitive edge.

In cold financial terms it also became increasingly apparent that it was far cheaper and offered lower risks and higher profits to buy established products and their customers than it was to invest in conceiving, developing and producing new products and in creating new customer franchises. Literally, companies in the West began to move away from the old-fashioned way of making money –

developing and producing superior products – to buying up cheap market shares developed by others and making profits by moving money around. Inexplicably this flew in the face of Japanese success, which is firmly focused on the conventional wisdom of organic, internally driven growth.

The deregulation of the European financial markets, easier exchange controls, conservative governments with relaxed attitudes to antitrust and relatively inexpensive share prices made cross-border acquisitions a reality and fuelled the overall growth in takeovers. As a result of the increase in acquisitions the growth in fixed capital investments central to improving long-term productivity to increase competitiveness was shifted to the buying-up of other firms and their market shares[275]. Whether the spate of acquisitions will increase the overall long-term competitiveness of Western industry is open to question. A study between 1950 and 1986 of the 3,788 acquisitions, joint ventures and start-ups made by 33 US companies, many with reputations for good management, indicated that on average they divested more than half of their acquisitions in new industries and more than 60 per cent of their acquisitions in entirely new fields[276]. While these acquisitions probably added to shareholder wealth, a similar study of 1,800 acquisitions made over the same time frame in the UK indicated there was no data to suggest that any of these acquisitions had a positive impact on the acquiror's competitiveness[277].

In many respects Western management has responded to pressure from the financial community by boosting the quantity of performance – that is, current earnings – rather than improving the quality, long-term competitiveness of their businesses. Managerial thinking in the West is dominated by the belief that the financial markets are focused solely on the short term and money moves to short-term yields. This played havoc with long-term industrial development. Empirical evidence suggests that the financial market *does* reward well managed firms and meaningful long-term investment. One US study, for example, showed that company stock prices increase by an average of 1 per cent per annum on announcements of increased R&D expenditures while those that did not invest in their future were vulnerable to being dropped by institutions and became easy meat for predators. The study also surveyed 217 companies taken over between 1980 and 1984 and found that 160 did not list any material R&D and the remainder spent an average 0.77 per cent of revenues on R&D – less than one half of that spent in those industries by companies that had successfully eluded predators[278]. The amount of venture capital invested in new businesses with long-term payouts like advanced electronics, biotechnology and new materials, was over $10 billion in the US alone between 1982 and 1986[279], and the fact that predators have rarely acquired high-technology businesses would also suggest that the market values future-oriented investments much higher than incumbent management.

However, this is not to say that the market mechanism is flawless in the West since there is an obvious bias towards short-term gain over long-term value appreciation. In reality long-term prospects are determined by market managers and traders who are forced to churn their portfolios to meet market performance. Consequently the real imperative for management in the West is to balance both short- and long-term prospects to maintain the financial community's interest. While managements in the West have become increasingly focused on generating short-term earnings to satisfy the perceived demands of the financial community, the market has really been focusing on the ability of managements to satisfy short-term needs – generating cash for shareholders and reinvestment – *and* long-term requirements – creating new products and developing and maintaining customer relationships – while taking on little debt. This misperception by management as to the real agenda of the financial community is at the heart of the short-term managerial fixation and its devastating effect on the development of long-term competitiveness in the West.

Japanese firms are rewarded with higher stock prices when they improve their long-term strengths, not on how their managements maximize short-term earnings. A comparison of US and Japanese stock performance in local currency over the 16 years between 1969 and 1985 indicated that Japanese companies grew sixfold while those in the US only doubled. This suggests that while US companies provided short-term benefits the Japanese firms with little emphasis on paying shareholders in the short term were rewarded with increased market confidence[280]. While there are obvious structural and institutional differences between the two markets and differences in the degree of patience between Western and Japanese financial markets, and the cost of capital is lower in Japan than in the West, both seek to ensure that companies are well managed.

The new activism of the financial community in the West is due largely to the belief that managements have been mismanaging their responsibility to build long-term shareholder wealth through their inability to manage their businesses efficiently for the short term and effectively for the long haul. In many companies the sum of the parts is greater than the whole: they have break-up or liquidation values greater than their share valuations. Corporate raiders on both sides of the Atlantic have been quick to spot this anomaly and started acquiring undervalued companies to strip out their undervalued assets and sell them off at a profit. This prompted management to focus on manipulating the gap between the share price and the estimated break-up value of the assets and building defences against raiders at the expense of improving their competitiveness.

The result has been a massive misuse of corporate assets and of executive time. Assets have been used to pay huge investment banking and legal fees, golden parachutes to management and greenmail to pay off corporate raiders rather than to negotiate the best price for the shareholders[281]. To render companies indigestible assets have been squandered and debt has been taken on to make dubious acquisitions – the poison pill – to prevent the target company's assets being sold to finance the debt. In 1986 alone US companies sold $263 billion of debt, double the 1985 figure and five times the 1982 amount, much of it to foil raiders[282]. By taking on massive levels of debt these managements have robbed their companies of the future by using earnings to repay current borrowings rather than to fund new technology, plant equipment and skills vital to long-term competitiveness.

As a final misuse of shareholders' assets managements have resorted to buying back their outstanding shares to reduce the opportunity for raiders to buy the stock and make a run on their companies. This also boosted stock prices and spread earnings over a smaller stock base to satisfy shareholders. Again this diverted funds away from improving the business to protecting management. It was estimated that US industry in 1987 was spending $80 billion a year to buy in its equity and only $50 billion on new capital investments[283].

Elaborate measures, including staggered boards and dual classes of stock to stack voting power in friendly hands, have been used to foil potential raiders. By mid-1987 three quarters of the largest 500 corporations in the US had introduced clauses in their constitutions to prevent share raids[284] and a number of states adopted statutes to curtail predators.

The net effect of these corporate manoeuvres has been to deflect management attention away from its primary purpose – creating long term shareholder wealth by increasing competitiveness through improved customer satisfaction. Management responses are widely seen as measures to evade the discipline of the market, to limit the rights of shareholders, to keep companies independent and to preserve managerial jobs. Manoeuvring assets to produce short-term gains has little or no linkage with improving competitiveness to provide long-term value appreciation of the business. Predators have had an energizing effect on management and have provided a badly needed shake-up of entrenched corpocracies – and shareholders have made net gains in the short term. Nevertheless, there is no consensus on whether this will provide the vitality that companies will need in the West to compete successfully in the long term or whether this is more a process where 'companies run by fools fall into the hands of knaves'[285]. Transferring assets between owners creates worthless casino money since it is a zero sum game where no one gains except at the expense of someone else – and it has little to do with improving corporate competitiveness. It also adds little economic value to society and enriches only a small number of arbitragers, bankers and lawyers. However, while the financial market does bring a measure of discipline to management the financial market itself is hardly a paragon of logic. No one, for example, can explain the logic (other than greed) behind the bidding for RJR Nabisco in late 1988. One day the stock was worth $55, the next day the stock was valued at $75 by its management who attempted a leveraged buyout. RJR Nabisco was finally put out of its misery being sold at auction for $109 a share at the end of November to Kohlberg, Kravis and Roberts – a major acquiror of companies[286]. Either the shareholders were incapable of understanding the value of the firm, or the management tried to steal the company, or the acquirers ran amok and overbid to maintain their ego.

Management in the West has been performing poorly for decades and must bear a direct responsibility for the decline in industrial competitiveness. Companies got fat and inefficient in cosy oligopolistic markets and became risk averse when confronted with innovative competition. They neglected their customers and labour relations and focused increasingly on producing short-term rewards to fend off growing frustration on the part of their dissatisfied owners. Japanese industrial success has not been due only to lower wage costs, luck or taking unfair advantage but is a result of hard thought and the ability to recognize and exploit new opportunities driven by a consuming policy of continually striving to meet customer needs. The most troubling fact is that Western management is aware of its own failings. Almost 90 per cent of the responses to a questionnaire in the *Harvard Business Review* in 1988 from nearly 4,000 executives in 35 countries placed the primary responsibility for the lack of competitiveness in US industry squarely on the shoulders of management[287].

While there are many well run companies in the West that have been able to face and beat Japanese competition, the sad reality is that the majority have failed. The intractable competitiveness problem in the West is largely to do with ingrained attitudes of mind, outdated management concepts and inefficient working habits which have allowed equipment to age; design, engineering and manufacturing to be relegated to poor relations; investments in new technology to be reduced; and relationships with customers and workers to deteriorate[288].

SUMMARY

Western competitiveness is badly holed below the waterline and, if not sinking, is fast taking in water. Its long-term comparative advantages in the scale of operation, access to low-cost capital, cheap resources, superior infrastructure and advanced technology – the bedrock of its competitiveness – have largely vanished. Government and industry have compounded the problem through their inability to work together to develop new policies and practices which meet the new determinants of industrial success.

Governments in the West have not yet come to terms with changes in the global economic order which have helped to precipitate the decline in their relative competitive advantage. Since most Western nations have had no clear long-term commitment to an industrial vision they have not been able to decide in a rapidly developing post-industrial era whether they want to retain a manufacturing sector, and in which industries, and what policies are needed to develop these industries. Western governments have been handicapped by political and industrial attitudes to government intervention based on antiquated assumptions that a centralized planning role for government is bad. The lack of consensus national industrial policies has led to the piecemeal management of national stocks of capital, technological and human resources and haphazard fiscal, monetary and trade policies.

By adopting a coherent national industrial policy built on internal consensus, emphasizing work, saving and investments flexibly administered to accommodate shifts to those activities bringing higher value-added opportunities, Japan's industrial growth has consistently outperformed that of the West. Bolting this strong, focused set of national industrial priorities to a socially cohesive population with a strong

189

competitive ethic has provided Japan with a long-term advantage over the disparate, uncoordinated government practices which loosely pass for industrial policies in the West.

Industry's competitive problems are deeply embedded in the psyche of Western management. As a protected species largely immune from censure, management has been able to run companies as personal fiefdoms and has come to believe that it has a divine right to use shareholders' assets as it wishes. It has failed to get people to work effectively together making products people want to buy at prices they can afford and when the going gets tough it expects government assistance, protection and the taxpayers' money, to manufacture products at a loss that no one much wants to buy. Management's response to improving competitiveness has largely meant a 'scorched earth policy' of cutting labour and closing plants and manoeuvring assets to further its myopic infatuation with short-term profits. Rather than coming to grips with important issues that influence competitiveness – R&D, capital investment and effective human skills and working practices – it has pursued programmes suited to its immediate survival. As a result management in the West is facing a growing credibility gap with its customers, owners, employees and with government. Managements' ability, commitment, control and even legitimacy are increasingly being questioned, so helping to compound the West's problems with its competitiveness.

It is hard to overstate the impact that this litany of errors of omission and commission by government and management has had on the level of competitiveness in the West. Evidence suggests that much has been achieved in attempting to improve Western competitiveness. However, this has been accomplished by tackling the easiest problems first and the West is now facing an increasingly difficult uphill battle[289]. The heart of the West's competitiveness problems is structural rather than cyclical and requires major changes in the attitudes, value systems and working practices in government, industry and labour.

Japanese manufacturing investments in the West have the potential to place a further nail in the coffin of the West's competitiveness. The West has no effective controls in place to gauge the *quality* of Japanese investment, which is invariably in the form of assembly facilities for high value-added components sourced in Japan. Nor does it have procedures to measure the *utility* of the investments, which are increasing industrial overcapacity. The fact that Japanese firms have

190

relative freedom to invest in the West to maximize taxpayer support, minimize labour costs with young, semi-skilled, non-unionized labour and to leverage productivity with proven assembly practices and new equipment increases the compression effect on Western firms. While Western companies are busy trying to increase their competitiveness by cutting costs within their traditional fully integrated structures, Japanese assembly investments in the West, using very limited integration, lower period and subsidized capital costs, are able to compete on an even lower cost plane than their Western rivals.

The West urgently needs to develop effective government and managerial responses to these new challenges to its competitiveness created by Japanese assembly investments in the West. Without effective policies and practices Western management will continue to take the line of least resistance and will scale back manufacturing, export more labour and skills offshore, dump plants and employees, seek more trade protection and form additional alliances with their Japanese rivals. These will lead to further decreases in competitiveness and more long-term structural unemployment depressing the standard of living in the West. Competitiveness in the West is a house of cards. Unrestricted market access with low-cost and low value-added Japanese assembly plants could well be the single new card toppling the West's fragile competitive system.

PART 6

FIGHTING BACK

24

THE SEVEN DEADLY MYTHS

Japan's second wave of competition and in particular Japanese manufacturing investments in the West, coupled with aggressive globalization, have the collective power further to reduce the West's already
faltering share of high value-added world trade. The net effect will be
to depress the standard of living and add to unemployment in the
West.

The implications of Japanese manufacturing investments are being
obscured by the growing emphasis on Western 'competitiveness' in a
very broad and unfocused sense, diffused by conflicting opinions on
the extent of the West's decline in its ability to compete, and responses
are being delayed and watered down by convenient excuses and
self-serving arguments. Japanese competition is not going to go away
and there is every indication that Japanese manufacturing investments in the West will intensify the competitive pressures on Western
industry.

What to do about Japan's second wave of competition and Japanese
manufacturing investments in the West is an infinitely more complex
issue than establishing how the West got itself into its predicament.
The polemics of right and wrong in the trade and industrial squabbles
with Japan have clouded the issues. Half-truths have become substantive facts and it has become extremely difficult to divorce myth from
reality.

False hopes are pinned on the value of a more open Japanese market
and on the impact of *endaka* on Japanese industry. Archaic views are
ascribed to the power of protectionism and to new technology. Anti-
thetical but fashionable opinions are growing on the decline of global
economic interdependence and the rise of the national economy.
Inflated beliefs are prevalent that Western industry is in the midst of a

self-generated renaissance. Exaggerated self-serving values are attached to the problems that Japanese management will face in moving production offshore. Each of these myths needs to be shattered before the West can mount a credible and effective response to the second wave of Japanese competition.

Opening Up the Japanese Market Will Plug the Trade Gap

Governments and companies in the West have conveniently pursued opening up the Japanese market in the belief that this will go a long way to closing the US and EEC trade balances in Japan's favour. This was valid in the 1960s and 1970s while Japan had a growing domestic economy and small-scale companies but has now become a matter of honour in the West rather than a major opportunity for expansion for a number of reasons.

With a population of 122 million – half that of the US and around one third of that of the EEC – how much import volume can Japan reasonably be expected to absorb? Although domestic prices are high volume is limited by the relatively small number of consumers. Japanese consumers, private and industrial, are already well served by Japanese companies. As a result of a successful import substitution policy in the 1960s and 1970s Japan's industrial needs are heavily concentrated on commodities, selected advanced technology products and licences. In 1986, for example, Japan was absorbing only 7 per cent of the world's manufactured exports compared to 63 per cent by the US and 23 per cent by the EEC[290]. Japan's consumer demands for Western products are centred on packaged goods, the service sector and luxury products. Neither industrial or consumer product imports for Japan's home market offer the volume and value necessary to make a significant dent in Japan's trade imbalances with the West.

Japan's overwhelming consumer and industrial preferences for domestically produced goods are a rate-limiting step in increasing the import of finished goods in volume. Japanese government agencies are promoting greater consumption of imports, which helped to increase exports by 20 per cent in yen values and 30 per cent in volume between September 1986 and August 1987. However, how much more can Japan absorb given cultural pressures which were deliberately built up over 40 years to limit imports?[291]

Compounding the problem is Japan's divide-and-conquer response to trade pressures. While Japan is a firm believer in multilateral trade it has pursued bilateral trade agreements with the US on items like beef and citrus imports, semiconductors and even US participation in Japanese construction projects that have left the EEC out in the cold. The result has been an increase in tension between the US and the EEC, which has deflected attention away from Japan.

Japan obviously has both the capability and the capacity to increase imports as a share of GNP and manufactured goods as a share of imports. However, it is unlikely that the inbuilt resistance to imports can be overcome in a period short enough and in the volume necessary to make a significant impact on the West's trade imbalances (Figure 24.1). Even though Western imports have increased in 1987 and 1988 as a result of strong domestic demand, low prices when denominated in yen and political pressures from the West, much is illusory since it is narrowly based and often low value-added. For example, one quarter of the EEC's export increase in 1987 was accounted for by high-priced cars and much of the US imports is made up of low value-added agricultural products[292].

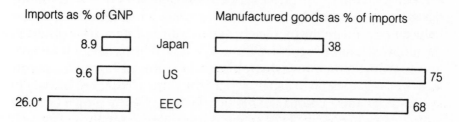

Imports as % of GNP   Manufactured goods as % of imports

8.9 ☐   Japan   ☐ 38

9.6 ☐   US   ☐ 75

26.0* ☐   EEC   ☐ 68

Figure 24.1. Japan's economy has a high level of resistance to imports in general and manufactures in particular as a result of long-term import substitution policies and cultural preferences for domestic production (all data 1987, *1986).

Source: GATT, Geneva, September 1988.

Japanese preferences for locally produced goods reinforce the need for local manufacturing facilities and this increases the cost and the risk for Western companies to compete successfully in Japan. A comparison of US and European investments in Japan with Japanese investments in the US and in Europe through 1984 suggests that the combination of limited market opportunity, high levels of internal competition, the costs of fully-integrated plants – all of which increase risk – has inhibited major expansion of Western manufacturing in Japan.

Conversely, the relative freedom of investment with low costs – generally assembly operations heavily subsidized by governments – and the ability to build on brand franchises established by finished product exports have encouraged the expansion of Japanese manufacturing operations in the West. Between 1980 and 1984, while Japanese firms invested $6.9 billion in the US and $2.9 billion in Europe, US firms invested only $1.1 billion and European companies a mere $310 million in Japan (Figure 24.2).

Despite the desultory level of Western investments in Japan a number of companies have made significant commitments to developing the Japanese market with local fully integrated operations. Some Western companies like Dow Corning, Du Pont, W.R. Grace, IBM, Kodak and DEC from the US and ICI and Ciba-Geigy from Europe have even invested in large-scale R&D facilities in Japan in the belief they can better meet the needs of demanding customers with on-the-spot research facilities[293]. Significantly, Japanese companies investing in offshore R&D to serve their customers in their far larger Western markets are almost non-existent.

Finally, Japanese companies are a formidable force in their domestic market as a result of three decades of intense competition which has helped to eliminate the inefficient and to concentrate market power in the hands of large, progressive firms. If Western firms have a hard time in competing in their own domestic markets against Japanese imports how well will they do in Japan, where the cards are stacked heavily in favour of Japanese companies? People fail to grasp the simple fact that how cheap and how well you make your product is totally irrelevant if barriers of any kind keep them out of a market.

Despite these problems there are opportunities for Western firms to compete successfully in Japan, particularly since Japan has now dismantled most of its tariff barriers – in 1986 alone Japan eliminated or reduced by 20 per cent tariffs on 2,000 items – and its tariffs on industrial and mining goods at 2.1 per cent were less than half those of the US at 4.4 per cent and the EEC at 4.6 per cent[294]. However, the opportunities are far narrower than is generally believed and have been constrained by the passage of time. One study found that eliminating all barriers to US imports would increase exports to Japan by

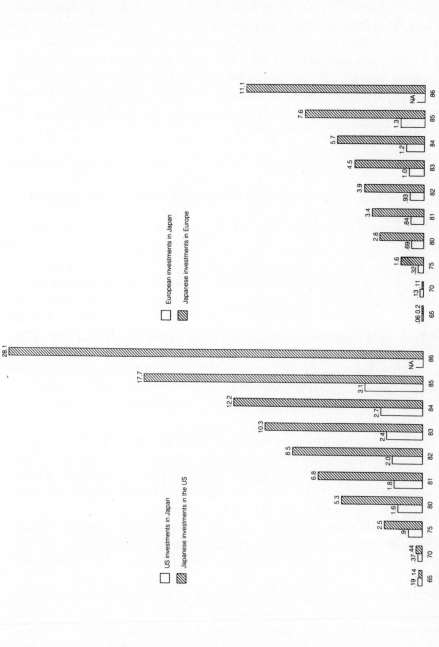

Figure 24.2. Japanese companies are investing considerably more resources in the US and in Europe than their major trade competitors are investing in Japan. (Equity investments only, no debt, US $ billions.)

Source: Ministry of Finance, Tokyo and Jetro White Paper on World Direct Investment, Tokyo (various issues through 1988).

between $5 and $8 billion – about one tenth of the US trade imbalance with Japan[295]. Japan would have to achieve a totally unrealistic growth rate of over 30 per cent a year in its import values just to wipe out the present level of trade imbalances with the US – let alone the EEC. It is naive to believe that complete freedom of access to the Japanese market at this late stage in the trade game would have a signficant deflating effect on Japan's positive trade balance with the West since Japan's domestic market alone cannot solve such a massive problem even in the long term.

Endaka has Seriously Affected the Competitiveness of Japanese Firms

The visible effects of *endaka* – widespread cuts in corporate profits for exporters in 1985 and 1986 and increased unemployment in smokestack industries – have been striking. However, the impact of *endaka* has been exaggerated, possibly deliberately, by the Japanese and through wishful thinking in the West. While the marginal and the mediocre have suffered the net effect suggests that major Japanese manufacturers have the situation well in hand and will emerge *stronger* rather than weaker as a result of *endaka*.

Rationalization – including the shedding of labour, massive cost reductions, product mix changes and selective price increases – and the widespread move to developing global technology, finance, manufacturing and sourcing networks have already begun to bear fruit. Many Japanese exporters are now in a position to compete comfortably in the range of 120–140 yen to the dollar and Honda has even factored an exchange rate of 120 yen to the dollar for its next five-year plan[296]. With relatively fixed European currency rates against the yen Japanese firms have even increased their margins in Europe as a result of their cost improvements to meet the challenge of a lower value dollar.

Since most Japanese exporters are dependent on adding value to imported raw materials, the sharply lower costs of commodities denominated in dollars have significantly benefited Japanese firms. Japan's iron ore costs fell by about 40 per cent in 1987 over 1986 and procurement cost savings on imported raw materials reduced

Yokahama Rubber's costs by 9.5 billion yen – about 9 per cent of total sales[297]. Japanese industry in fact turned the corner in 1987. In the fiscal year to March 1988 corporate profits increased by an average 28 per cent against a 2 per cent rise in 1986. Companies which suffered sharp earnings declines or even losses were virtually all posting strong recoveries. Growth in domestic demand more than offset declines in exports and higher volume led to big cost reductions due to increased use of existing capacity[298].

The hope that *endaka* would expose the fragility which Japan's export success has masked – the grafting of sophisticated technology and large-scale productive capacity onto archaic labour and distribution systems – did not materialize. Rather *endaka* has given Japanese companies the strength and the opportunity to overcome domestic social and political pressures essential to carry through major rationalization programmes to address the short-term issue of high costs. Since much of Japanese industry has been able to adapt successfully to lower costs this will produce a level of cost which will enable Japanese firms significantly to underprice their Western competitors.

Protectionism Will Cut Japanese Imports and Increase Western Competitiveness

Protectionism is building a strong political following in the West since it is easier to buy votes by blaming the Japanese for unemployment than it is to castigate governments and companies for their mismanagement. Few in government or business in the West appreciate the high levels of protection that already exist, the direct and indirect costs of protectionism or its unpredictable results.

Public procurement in the EEC discriminates against the US and Japan, US defence purchases discriminate against all non-US firms and all three trade blocs have blatantly protectionist agricultural policies[299]. Protection has been increasing. In 1975 some 8 per cent of US imports were restrained by some form of protection – $7.9 billion of a total of $99.3 billion in imports. By 1984 protection had risen to 21 per cent, $67.9 billion, of a total import bill of $329 billion and by 1986, despite the fall in the value of the dollar, protection covered fully 25 per cent of all US imports[300].

Tariffs are a tax surcharge on consumption unless the revenue raised is recycled to consumers in the form of tax cuts. The UK voluntary agreement with Japan to limit car imports to 10 to 12 per cent of the market ensures that UK consumers pay about 15 per cent more than they need to for Japanese cars[301]. Between 1981 and 1985 the International Trade Commission calculated that US consumers paid $15.7 billion in higher car prices as a result of the Japan–US Voluntary Export Restraint Agreement. Although the quotas saved 44,000 jobs in the US car industry it would have been more economical at $357,000 a job to pension off the workers[302]. Significantly, during the 1981–1985 period US car manufacturers covered by the Export Restriction Agreement registered record profits.

Protection literally increases consumer costs and reduces standards of living and at the same time redistributes income from consumers to shareholders and workers. In almost all protected industries shareholders have a higher average income than the consumers being forced to pay higher prices for their protected products. In many protected industries in the US, like cars and steel, the workers earn well above average industrial wages[303]. Protectionism effectively helps to transfer income from the relatively poor to the relatively rich.

Numerous studies show that the cost of saving jobs through protection is high and the overall cost of supporting uncompetitive industries is phenomenal. Each job saved in the clothing industry in the US and in Europe as far back as 1980 cost $193,000 and $124,700, respectively, per annum[304]. In the US in 1985 alone the cost of protecting the bulk steel industry amounted to $7 billion, cars $6 billion, dairy products $5.5 billion and textiles and clothing $27 billion[305]. The cost of keeping the non-leather shoe industry on its uppers in the UK in 1985 was estimated at $3.5 billion[306].

Although it is widely believed that industries receiving protection are able to compete more effectively reality hardly bears this out. A long-term study in the US of 12 industries receiving tariff and quota protection between 1954 and 1979 indicated that only one firm, Harley-Davidson, was successful in defending its position once protection was removed[307].

Few protectionists understand the cause and effect relationships of protection. By protecting the steel industry in the US and the EEC end users were forced to pay higher prices as tariffs and duties were applied to bring Japanese steel prices up to the level of subsidized Western costs. This undermined the competitiveness of large Western end users such as the car, consumer durable, construction, machinery and shipbuilding industries selling in international markets. As Japanese steel companies continuously applied cost leadership and quality improvement this compounded the competitive problem for Western users, who generally saw the gulf between the world market price and their protected supply prices for steel widen and their access to Japanese steel become more restricted through the use of protective quotas.

International trade is increasingly centred on multiple-sourcing arrangements due to growing intercompany trade, joint ventures, licensing and out-sourcing. Consequently protectionism is creating bizarre situations. In 1987 the US imposed a set of 100 per cent tariffs on certain electronic products and components to punish Japanese firms for dumping semiconductors. US computer companies found themselves paying heavy tariffs on imported computer components which they had sourced offshore to reduce costs. IBM was estimated, for example, to source $30 to $40 million in motherboards for its PS/2 personal computer with Matsushita which were subject to the 100 per cent tariff[308].

Protection in the West is being driven by a combination of home-made problems – balance of payments deficits, overvalued currencies, uncompetitive industries and unemployment. However, to focus on these problems is not appealing politically or industrially since it is much more difficult to address these complex issues in the short term than it is to add a 'quick fix' of an extra layer of tariffs and quotas. Protection has a multiplier effect far greater than traditional trade theory suggests and threatens to dominate trade policy as the West attempts to achieve positive trade balances. Improvements in trade positions tend to push currencies higher, making exports less competitive. Offsetting some of the improvements in the trade balance counteracts the very purpose of protection. To keep monetary growth constant higher interest rates would be needed, which would reduce the reinvestment necessary to restructure and to increase and improve production, technology and productivity[309].

Protection in the West safeguarded inefficient industries by shielding them from competition and has delayed the inevitable by helping to postpone badly needed restructuring. All evidence points to the fact that industries come to depend on the addictive effects of tariffs and quotas and are rarely able to compete without continuing and increasing levels of protection. Protection is a zero-sum game and an increased dose of protection when the West desperately needs to compete more aggressively will compound rather than ease the problem.

More protectionism will hurt Western consumers and give Japan a moral advantage of being a victim.

Technology Will Continue to Provide the West With Sustainable Competitive Advantage

Technology is seen as a major opportunity to increase Western competitiveness. While the development and application of new technology is a vital factor in changing value-added contributions, the West is no longer the dominant force that it once was in all forms of technology. Both the US and the EEC have major problems with their approach to technology at a time when Japan is broadening its technology focus. In essence the West is suffering a crisis in its commitment to R&D and in the linkage of R&D to economic and political goals.

In the US industrial commitment to R&D is on the decline. While double digit increases in funding new products and processes have been common since the late 1970s it peaked at 14 per cent in 1984. In 1985 and 1986 the increase barely reached 10 per cent and although US firms spent a record $54.3 billion or 3.4 per cent of sales on R&D in 1987, when corrected for inflation the real increase was less than 4 per cent over 1986[310] and half the rate of gain in the preceding decade. Real spending has also suffered due to a refocusing on short-term profits by management in the face of pressure from the financial community. The increase in mergers and acquisitions with sharply increased debt servicing costs and the high-risk long-term syndrome of R&D has resulted in a slowdown in private sector commitment to R&D, which has often become a postponable expense. As a result this has frequently led to an R&D budget of acquired or merged companies of less than the sum of the R&D expenditure of the two companies prior to the merger or takeover.

Japanese firms, although hard hit by *endaka*, excluded R&D from their massive cost reduction programmes and have maintained and even increased their R&D commitment from smokestack through to sunrise industries in the belief that funding technology is the most effective measure of guaranteeing future survival and growth[311].

The fact that Japan's financial community is patient and does not press for short-term returns supports Japanese industry's long-term commitment to R&D. This provides a major competitive advantage over Western managements, who are increasingly pressed (or believe they are pressed) to deliver short-term profits.

In the West government supports much of the R&D while in Japan industry is the major driving force behind the development of new technology. In Japan clear national industrial policies exist and seed money is available to channel industrial R&D into areas which build on national needs. However, in the West national industrial priorities are obscure and while considerable sums of public money are available the use of resources is not directed towards achieving identified industrial and economic objectives.

The EEC suffers from even greater problems than the US. While EEC expenditure in total is almost double that of Japan much of its R&D efforts are duplicated. Scarce resources are poorly utilized, much of the effort is conducted in public laboratories and universities with few links to industry and R&D is not concentrated on areas producing the highest value-added opportunities[312].

In two decades of all-out technological effort Japan has caught up with, and even passed, the West in selective areas of technology. Japan is now moving towards developing significant competences in basic research in pure science and has labelled the 1980s as 'A decade of innovation'[313]. To support this growing technological sophistication Japanese companies have used the high value of the yen in the US to secure strategic stakes in small, high-technology companies and to fund long-term basic research at US universities at bargain basement prices to gain deeper insights into new technologies[314] (Table 24.1).

The West is no longer the sole developer of new technologies and is limiting its commitment to developing technology. At the same time Japan is single-mindedly improving its technology and increasing its access to the West's stock of new technology. Given Japan's formidable capabilities to transform new technology quickly at low cost and high quality into preferred consumer products it is unlikely that the West can base its survival on the fallacy that the *possession* of new technology alone will guarantee its survival and success. Historically the West has created new markets with new technology but loses them because it is not able to meet consumer demand. Above all Japan has realized much more quickly than the West that technology is highly mobile – witness the rapid transfer of technology and market share

Table 24.1. Japanese firms have begun to acquire cutting-edge technology through aggressive acquisitions of small, high-technology companies, particularly in the US.

Investor	Invested in	Business	Holding (%)	Investments ($ m)
Computer Software	Foothill Research (US)	Computer software	50	N/A
Dainichiseika Colour & Chemicals	Pope Chemical (US)	Pigments and colouring agents	100	22
Eiko Kogyo	Educational AV division of Bell & Howell (US)	Optical instruments	100	20
Kobe Steel	Laser test equipment division of GCA (US)	Laser test equipment for chip manufacture	N/A	N/A
Kubota	Dana Computer (US)	Computer venture	25	20
Kyocera	Conterpoint Computers (US)	Manufacture of computers	N/A	N/A
Mineaba	Keytronic (US)	Computer-input systems	30	64
Mitsubishi Metal	Siltech (US)	Silicon wafers	100	33
NGK Insulators	Beryllium copper division of Cabot Corp. (US)	Beryllium copper	N/A	45
Nippon Seiko	Motornetics (US)	Hi-tech machine tools	40	3
Nippon Steel	Stabilizer business of Hughes Tool (US)	Oil exploration equipment	N/A	N/A
Osaka Titanium	US Semiconductor (US)	Chip materials	100	N/A
Otsuka	Phospho-Energetics (US)	Spectral analysis equipment	40	3
Rohm	Exel Microelectronics (US)	IC memories	100	57
	Xetel (US)	Design and manufacture of chip parts	63	4
Shizuki Electric	Condenser division of TRW (US)	Condensers	N/A	N/A
Sokisha	Pyramid Optical (US)	Industrial prisms	100	3
Tateho Chemicals	Fused magnesia division of Combustion Eng. (US)	Fused magnesia	100	6

Source: *The Financial Times*, 12 July 1986

away from the Western inventors of semiconductors and video recorders, to the Japanese – and that sustainable long-term success is primarily built on *people* working effectively together.

Unfortunately the West still clings to outdated notions that Japanese technology remains behind that of the West. A decision in 1987 by the Massachusetts Institute of Technology (MIT), one of the premier computer research centres, to buy a supercomputer from NEC – since it concluded that the 20-year lead in supercomputing had been wiped out by Japan's first generation – was dropped only after strong representations by the US government[315].

Maintaining the fiction of technological superiority, while playing to national sensitivities, detracts from the overriding goal of attaining *competitive* advantage and is both a snare and a delusion for the unwary. Technology is only one facet of a competitive strategy and needs to be seen in the full context of design, delivery, price, production economics, reliability, service and, above all, customer utility. By concentrating on only one aspect – technology – which is vulnerable to the increasing mobility of knowledge to the exclusion of other competitive imperatives, the West is increasing its vulnerability.

The Rise of the National Economy and the Decline of Global Economics

Western politicians are beginning to believe that the world is increasingly dominated by national economic policies rather than the competitive, open environment put forward by international trade economists who advocate that market forces dominate trade flows. As the trade deficits with Japan increase political pressures to close Western markets to Japan escalate. In fact, the reverse is true. The world is becoming economically *more* rather than less interdependent.

While the growth in international trade has been slowing down since 1980 there has been a growth in international investments focused on increasing domestic production which has substituted for trade growth (Figure 24.3). The changes in the dollar's value, the recycling of Japan's massive trade balances, protectionism, the globalization of business and shifts in comparative advantage are the triggers for the surge in international investments.

207

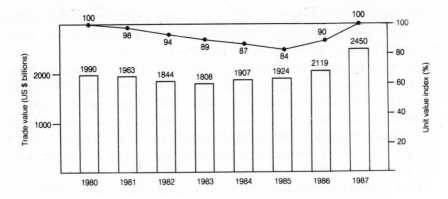

Figure 24.3. International trade in both value and unit terms has remained in a trough through the 1980s. (Although difficult to prove it is believed that the growth in international investments has partially substituted for trade growth.)

Source: GATT Geneva, August 1987.

In the late 1970s and early 1980s the overvalued dollar was the driving force behind US offshore manufacturing and service investments. Between 1976 and 1981 US direct investments overseas increased from $136.4 billion to $226.4 billion. By the mid-1980s around 25 per cent of US manufacturing assets and productive capacity were located outside the US, with three quarters of the output for offshore sale and the remainder intercompany trade for export back to the US to be sold in, or incorporated in, products for the US domestic market. Similar levels of assets of US banks, insurance companies, financial service firms and advertising agencies were also located outside the US by the mid-1980s[316]. The overvalued dollar was instrumental in precipitating the hollowing out of the US manufacturing base. US firms moved production offshore to capture lower costs and avoided taking the more difficult but infinitely more important decision necessary to sort out their domestic productivity and cost problems.

The decline in the dollar against the yen and major Western European currencies in the mid-1980s reduced the costs of investing in the world's largest market, the US, and created a surge of foreign direct investments. Between 1980 and 1985 foreign direct investments in the US increased from $68.4 billion to $183 billion – ranging from manufacturing companies to real estate and from vineyards to mineral deposits.

208

Since US manufacturing industry had already shifted a significant part of its labour-intensive operations offshore in the late 1970s and early 1980s the undervalued dollar began to increase offshore manufacturing costs for products and components for supply to the US. At the same time new highly efficient and lower-cost assembly investments in the US by Japanese competition began to pressure US domestic manufacturing operations. With limited reinvestment opportunities in its own domestic market Japan embarked on a major foreign investment programme in the early 1980s to recycle its trade surpluses. By the end of 1987 it was estimated that Japan's external assets exceeded $500 billion with much of the investment in the US. In 1986 alone Japan invested $40 to $50 billion in US government, federal agency and corporate bonds; this helped to underwrite the economic growth of the US, which would have slowed without this support[317]. Although Japan's direct foreign investments in the West have traditionally been passive – in bonds and property – a major shift occurred in the mid-1980s as Japanese firms began to invest directly in stocks, in acquiring companies and in building local assembly plants.

The growth of protection in the West has had a seminal effect on manufacturers. While US companies were already well established in the EEC, Japanese firms began to invest directly in assembly plants in Europe and both Japanese and European-based firms increased their productive capacity in the US as a hedge against increased protection. These investment decisions were made in the belief that it is better to be *in* a market rather than *outside* trying to get in when protectionist measures are threatened. With much Japanese manufacture being transferred away from finished good imports to local production in assembly plants, the effects of new and major protectionist initiatives in the West against Japanese imports are becoming window-dressing rather than key competitive legislation.

Competitive advantage is increasingly determined by attaining a global leadership position rather than by securing leadership on a country-by-country basis. Global leadership is based on capturing the linkages between functions and countries and requires sophisticated networks to move technology, cash, products and managerial and human resources on a global scale. The growing globalization of Japanese companies at a faster rate than Western firms has led to an increase in the international investment of funds necessary to acquire new technology, build plant and finance the logistics systems to move raw materials, components, sub-assemblies and products world-wide to leverage global market positions. In many respects the more rapid globalization of Japanese industry has lifted competition to a new plane where battles for market share are being won and lost on a world scale rather than on a national level.

The traditional concept of comparative advantage based on wage differentials is fast disappearing as a result of rapid changes in production economics created by advances in manufacturing technology. Production is effectively being uncoupled from labour as knowledge and capital are increasingly being substituted for employment[318]. Even though Western manufacturers are increasingly using the Asian NICs and Mexican *maquiladoras* to supply labour-intensive services due to their significant labour cost differentials compared to the US and the EEC, this is only a short-term fix. In the mid-term increased productivity through improved manufacturing technology will make suppliers of labour-intensive services much less important in the production process since labour costs in only a few manufacturing industries account for more than 10 per cent of overall product cost.

Traditionally investment followed international trade patterns. However, investment is becoming the driving force in the world economy and trade is beginning to follow international investment[319]. As a result the national economy is giving way to an interdependent global economy. While Japan has based its economic policy on exploiting global economic change the West has largely ignored subtle shifts in the world economy, preferring to focus on exploiting national economic change. The West's indifference to the growing interdependence of national economies and narrow concentration on individual economics has made Western firms less able to compete effectively on the global economic stage.

Western Industry is on a Roll

There is a high degree of optimism that Western industry has finally got its act together and is becoming much more competitive and able to take on and beat Japanese companies. This optimism is based on the fact that many Western firms are progressively restructuring, shedding surplus labour, rationalizing production and increasing productivity and product quality – all of which will make them more competitive.

Unfortunately, the reasons behind the restructuring frequently have little to do with competition and the strategies adopted are often unworkable.

Much of the change in Western industry is *not* driven by an appreciation of a recognized need to become more competitive to survive and grow in the mid to long term. Rather restructuring is driven by an obsession to preserve the jobs of management by keeping companies out of the hands of corporate raiders who pounce on those with poor performance or under-valued assets – or from other companies who see opportunities to maintain earnings growth or boost market share with cheap acquisitions. While many Western companies are attempting to restructure to increase their competitiveness, even more companies are adopting the 'quick fix', short-term measures to protect themselves from the capital market, rather than long-term policies designed to place them in a strong competitive position moving with rather than against market forces. Much of the movement to increase Western competitiveness is illusory and is helping to focus managerial actions on the short-term while their Japanese rivals are wedded firmly to achieving and maintaining long-term competitive advantage[320].

The performance of many Western firms is constrained by their approach to business strategy which makes them extremely vulner-able to their Japanese competitors. Companies in the West invariably lack a clear commitment to a consistent long-term strategic intent for their businesses – and those few that do allow their strategic goals to change direction radically every few years. In contrast most Japanese firms have very clear commitments of strategic intent which provide a long-term framework for opportunistic behaviour[321].

Much strategic thinking in the West is based on slavish conformity to simplistic strategic concepts and tools which are intuitive rather than innovative[322]. Western managements have fallen into the trap of accepting that the process of formulating and implementing strategy responds to fixed imperatives, follows preordained patterns and has a set logic. Consequently, form dominates substance and strategy becomes a ritual. While Western firms focus on jockeying for position under these rules Japanese competitors are inventing new ways of competing and building several layers of competitive advantage which provide multi-dimensional opportunities both to attack their Western rivals and to defend in depth against Western competitive response[323]. Japanese firms have pioneered new strategic concepts which focus heavily on using accumulated experience, information and reputation with customers, the distribution system, competitors and the market environment to provide competitive advantage. These 'invisible assets' take time to accumulate, cannot be easily duplicated and provide firms with a real source of sustainable competitive advantage[324]. Bolting these invisible assets to the efficient usage of fixed assets – high-quality, low-cost products made by highly skilled, educated and committed employees – has given Japanese firms significant strategic advantages over their Western competitors.

Western firms need to restructure with the emphasis on securing a *sustainable* competitive advantage and adapt their strategic thinking to the new rules of the game, which are increasingly dictated by the Japanese. Unless restructuring enables Western industry to work within the new game plan it will never be able to compete successfully against Japan over the long term.

The Problems of Globalizing Japanese Industry

Experts believe that the rapid shift away from exporting finished products to exporting productive capacity to the West will produce significant problems for Japanese management. There are concerns that while Japanese manufacturing with offshore plants has achieved impressive quality and productivity gains by imposing Japanese systems and disciplines, coping with complex decisions involving several layers of management in a number of countries is of vastly different magnitude[325]. While there are obvious cultural differences between Japan and the West it is very easy to overestimate the problems that Japanese industry is facing in globalizing its business and the relief that this may provide to Western competitors.

Many Japanese companies already have multinational managerial experience through production ventures in the Asian NICs from the mid-1970s. Most of these are more manufacturing-intensive than those they currently operate in the West. Since Japanese manufacturing investments in the West are largely assembly plants bolting together components sourced in Japan most of the key decision-making resides in Japan and there is limited need for independent complex decision-making on a local level. Assembly operations are less manpower- and skills-intensive than fully integrated manufacturing operations, and small numbers of people with lower levels of

212

skills performing simplistic and routine tasks are easier to manage with fewer layers of management than large groups of highly skilled people performing complex tasks with high levels of independence. As most local content agreements with Japanese companies are designed to increase slowly management has a leisurely opportunity to phase in necessary adjustments to its style to adapt to local conditions. Also, the number of plants required in the West is vastly overrated. Depending on the industry and product proliferation, one plant can often meet total US demand and by 1992, with full market integration, one plant could meet demand from all the EEC countries.

Obviously Japan does face new challenges to its traditional managerial style, not only from its move downstream to its end markets but also from the potential clash of cultures and numbers in more complex and larger organizational structures. In the same spirit in which Japanese industry responded successfully to the impact of the oil crisis of the 1970s management reacted in a broad and purposeful way to both *endaka* and the growth of protectionism forcing the move to offshore production. Companies have begun to decentralize their organizational structures, to focus on basic research, to change their compensation and promotional policies to merit systems and to adopt much more enterpreneurial styles of management[326].

It is extremely naive to believe that the 10 to 15-year lead that American and European companies are claimed to have in understanding how to operate on a multinational basis over Japanese firms will translate into a competitive advantage[327]. Many Western multinationals have been outmanaged by their Japanese rivals in world markets for a decade which seriously questions whether they *really* do understand how to operate competitively on a world scale.

The constant interchange of fact with fallacy has led to the development of a number of myths which have helped to foster a level of optimism minimizing the threats of Japanese manufacturing investments. This has contributed to overestimating the capability of the West to overcome the problems which these investments will create. Even more damaging is the fact that the ambiguous nature of the threat posed by assembly plants coupled to the credibility which many of these myths have gained has helped to delay an effective Western response. Unless these myths can be shattered they will become a series of dogmas which will crush any attempt to react quickly to the Trojan Horse of Japanese assembly plants.

25

INDUSTRIAL JUDO

'YOU CAN'T BEAT SOMETHING WITH NOTHING'

Leo Durocher

Through a mixture of apathy, arrogance, complacency, default, incompetence and plain negligence the West has allowed Japan to dictate industrial battlegrounds. By giving Japan the freedom to take the high ground, without much of a contest, Western companies have made life easy for their Japanese competitors and consigned their role to making futile gestures when the war was essentially lost.

To counter the growing threat of Japanese assembly plants the West has to adopt a much more aggressive attitude towards Japan. This means changing the rules of the game to provide the West with a competitive edge. To develop this competitive edge the West has not only to create new mechanisms to channel Japanese manufacturing investments into *supporting* the industrial development of the West but it must also make radical changes in its attitudes towards Japan.

Attitudes in the West are entirely conditioned by Japan's successes. Japan's increasing vulnerability and the cost, rather than the price, of Japan's access to the lucrative markets of the West needs to be factored into Western responses to help to change the rules of the game. Conventional wisdom in the West is to regard Japan's success as a natural course of events. However, behind the flood of Japanese manufacturing investments into the US and the EEC are several inescapable facts which have tipped the scales of competitive advantage in favour of the West.

Today *no* company, Japanese, American or European, builds an overseas manufacturing plant unless there are *unavoidable* political and/or economic imperatives for doing so. If you can export finished products and capture economies of scale in manufacturing and purchasing, retain technology and skills in-house and maintain close managerial control over research, quality and productivity from a central base then you do so – for as long as it is feasible. To do otherwise would be naive. Unlike US multinationals in the 1960s and their European counterparts in the 1970s, geographical expansion is no longer an option for most Japanese companies since volume opportunities are constrained by economic conditions, increasing competition and protectionism. Japanese firms are setting up assembly operations *only* because protectionism in the EEC and a combination of protectionism and currency valuation problems with the dollar in the US make it expedient to do so. Japanese strategy is now defensive not expansionist and is dictated largely by the need to maintain market access.

Japan's manufacturing base has rapidly shifted away from making commodity products – where it has lost its comparative cost advantage to the Asian NICs – to technology-intensive high value-added specialty products. Japan's industrial policy of continuously moving up-market with high-technology products to gain higher value-added returns is *dependent* on maintaining access to markets which can absorb the quantity and quality of Japan's output. The US and the EEC are the only markets with the volume of sophisticated customers with the disposable income to absorb Japan's growing up-market product portfolio and allow Japan to maintain economic headway.

The cash generated by Japan's trade surpluses and its high level of domestic savings have outstripped investment opportunities in Japan. With trade surpluses of $94 billion and £96 billion in the fiscal years 1987 and 1988 created at a rate of between $7 and $9 billion a month, Japan was forced to recycle these funds offshore since its own economy was unable to absorb the cash. The only opportunities for investments on this scale – whether in real estate, commodities, bonds, stocks and plant and equipment – are the large developed markets of the West, which have the added advantage of political and economic stability.

Japanese manufacturing investments in the West are largely a façade since they are almost always designed to assemble components sourced in Japan with local content largely limited to services and labour. There are very few Japanese manufacturing investments in the West which can be classified as fully integrated manufacturing operations using domestic sources to supply most of their needs. Even components sourced locally are provided by Japanese suppliers who have opened-up local assembly units or by their surrogates – licensees or joint venture partners. In almost all cases it is blatantly obvious that Japanese assembly operations in the West are not genuine investments but purpose-built to circumvent protection.

Japan has a long history of trade friction with the West. It has been long on promises – to open up its own market, boost domestic consumption by changing the quality of life to match Japan's wealth and to reduce exports – but it has been short on delivery. Japan is perceived in the West as not playing its full role in the world economy and of being a trade predator by taking as much as it can out of the international trade system and putting back as little as possible. As the trade deficits with Japan increase and Western companies are still largely unable to make headway in the Japanese market and continue to lose ground in their home markets, Japan's credibility falls further and confrontation increases. Today there is a strong and growing body of opinion in the West that Japan will only react positively by confrontation and that negotiation is basically a dialogue with the deaf[328].

The majority of Japanese industry is in a very vulnerable position. It can no longer rely on shipping finished products to its major markets and is being forced to open up production in the West to outflank the effects of protection and the low dollar value. With an increasingly up-market product portfolio and growing protectionism in its major markets Japan is in danger of becoming a victim of its own policies of targeting high value-added industries. The vulnerability of Japan's industry is directly proportional to the degree of access that it has to Western markets to meet the needs of its high value-added product portfolio (Figure 25.1).

The balance of power has shifted decisively in favour of the West. Japan's economy is now inextricably enmeshed with those of its two major trade partners who consumed 91 per cent of Japan's 1987 trade surplus of 11.59 billion yen[329]. Practically all major Japanese exporters are heavily dependent on the US and European markets; two thirds of Japan's exports consist of high-value cars, consumer electronics and semiconductors, most of which go to the US and Western Europe; and 15 to 20 per cent of all Japanese jobs are reliant on exports[330]. Adding to Japan's problems is the fact that the West offers the only long-term safe havens large enough to absorb the cash recycled from Japan's trade balances.

Japan cannot survive without access to the markets of the West. The

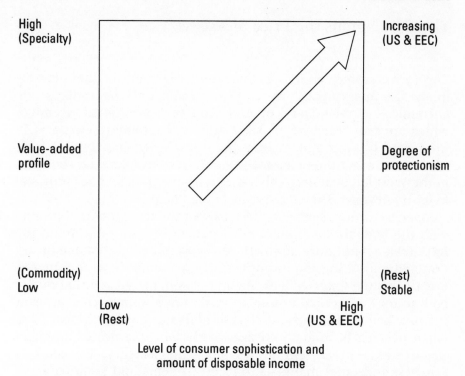

Figure 25.1. Japan's move up the value-added chain to secure higher margins requires continuous access to sophisticated consumers with high disposable incomes . . . which brings it into conflict with increasing levels of protectionism in its key markets – the US and the EEC.

loss of the Japanese market to the US or Western Europe, while serious, would not be a fatal blow. Ironically Japan now needs the West *more* than the West needs Japan for both trade and investment. Consequently, the spectre of increased protection against Japanese imports of products and cash into the US and the EEC is met with considerable apprehension by Japanese politicians and industrialists. Industrially and economically Japan is probably more vulnerable than at any time since the late 1940s. Any appreciable contraction in its access to the two Western trade blocs, which collectively account for 38 per cent of the World trade, would have significant structural effects on Japan's industrial base and its economy. To change the rules of the game Western governments must factor Japan's vulnerability into their approach to Japanese industrial investments.

217

The Cost Versus the Price of Access

The conventional wisdom is that you must pay and compete for industrial investments. As a result industrial investments are encouraged through layers of local, regional and national incentives which are distributed with a large degree of autonomy, vary widely from case to case and increase in response to competition from offers from other potential hosts. States, regions and even countries in the West fall over each other on a beggar-my-neighbour principle to entice new investment to create employment.

Japanese companies were quick to spot the imperatives of dealing with the 'Balkan' investment environment in both the US and the EEC, divided authority and with the egos and political ambitions of those administering the incentives. Consequently, Japanese investment has often followed a divide-and-conquer strategy using rivalry both to up the economic 'ante' as well as to minimize controls over the investment. Similarly, unions in both the US and the UK have fallen over each other to do deals with Japanese firms for single-union status in an era of declining membership. By courting Japanese industrial manufacturing investments and securing them at almost any cost the West has surrendered its trump card: that Japan needs North America and Western Europe more than the West needs Japan. The Western mindset of overbidding for the privilege of securing even the most dubious Japanese manufacturing investments has masked the growing vulnerability of Japan and the necessity of Japanese companies to secure production beachheads in the West.

Western governments need to move away from begging for internationally mobile investments to treating access to their markets as a valuable asset worth more than an investment funded largely by taxpayers' money to create a few low-paid, low-skilled assembly jobs. The West is in a position to reverse conventional wisdom and to place the onus on inward investors to convince the host of the value of their investment. Ironically, the West needs to learn economic lessons from the Asian NICs like Korea, Singapore and Taiwan, who all adopted strong policies towards inward investors to improve the quality of their industrial investments.

Using industrial judo to place the West's strength − large volume and value markets with wealthy, sophisticated consumers − against

Japan's vulnerability – the need to access these markets – inward manufacturing investments could become much more substantive and add *genuine* industrial and economic value at much lower costs to the West.

26

PUTTING STEEL INTO RUBBER TEETH

The West is noted for the rubber teeth it uses to administer its few controls over inward investment. To channel Japanese manufacturing investments to benefit the West a major change is needed in the scope and content of inward investments and the incentives used to attract them. By changing the rules of the game the West can alter the whole game plan to a much more favourable state.

Market Access

Inward foreign investment approval in the West is designed more to smooth the way to keep investors happy and politicians to garner votes from the newly employed than it is to ensure that the investment and the terms negotiated are favourable to the nation or trade bloc as a whole.

Since the procedure is focused on speed of approval there is virtually no framework for evaluating the impact of manufacturing investment. Using market access as a mechanism selectively to control inward investment to improve the quality of benefits the West needs a framework to evaluate the effects of the investment on competition and trade and its utility or essential worth. This framework needs to address a number of key issues.

How will the manufacturing investment affect competition? This is complex since it concerns the breadth, depth and width of the investor's competitive profile.

Breadth issues arise because apart from finished product imports most major Japanese firms have developed a complex web of networks to access Western markets. Figure 26.1 illustrates the partial web of strategic networks used by one Japanese company, Matsushita, to access Western markets.

Intercompany networks include finished product imports, local assembly of Japanese-made components and other forms of global supply. Intracompany networks cover joint ventures, technology exchanges and dual production, marketing and supply agreements. With the exception of finished product imports none of these market access tactics are measured, far less controlled, under conventional agreements regulating bilateral trade. The variety and flexibility of competitive opportunities provided by these networks enable penetration of Western markets far more extensively than import statistics record. To gauge the impact of a manufacturing investment it is essential to understand the significance of the investment within the context of the investing company's broad range of competitive activities within a host country.

Depth issues concern the impact of the investment on local competition. Capacity levels are crucial since there is little economic justification in using scarce resources to add to existing production levels which already exceed current and foreseeable market demand. North America and Western Europe are already awash in capacity for cars, compact discs, microwave ovens, motorcycles, photocopiers, televisions and VCRs into the foreseeable future. With world demand for cars forecast to increase at 1 to 2 per cent per annum overcapacity will reach 6 to 7 million units by 1990, equally split between the US, the EEC and Japan. Much of this is the result of offshore Japanese investments. In North America alone 10 Japanese plants capable of producing 2.5 million cars a year will come on-stream by 1990[331]. Does it make sense to add more capacity in mature industries? It could be argued that there is a greater need to rationalize capacity to improve existing industry economics than there is to add new capacity. If GM's share of the US domestic market continues to decline it will be forced to close down more plants than the 11 currently planned which employ 29,000 people in four states[332]. Given the overcapacity in the US market, by closing its plants GM would be giving up its capacity to new Japanese assembly plants.

Long term the problem becomes more acute since the Japanese do not view local assembly as a substitute for imports but rather as *additional* business. In 1988 finished Japanese car imports as well as cars assembled in the US from Japanese components held a 25 per cent share of the market. Extensions to existing and new Japanese assembly plants

221

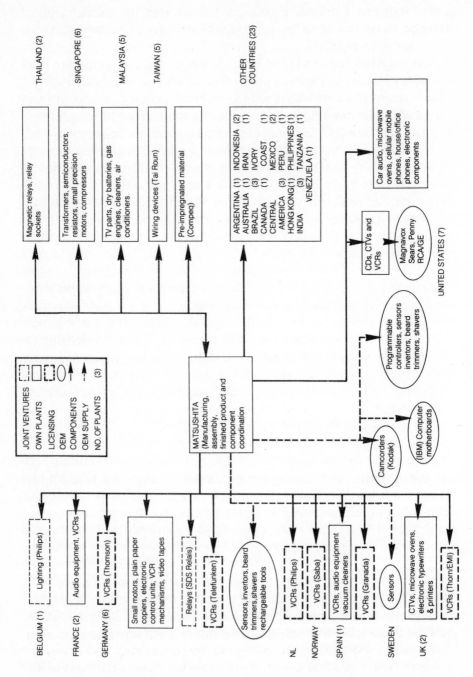

Figure 26.1. Matsushita's strategic network (1987 data).

coming on stream will produce 2.5 million cars a year by the early 1990s. If imports remain at the 1986 and 1987 levels Japan's total share of the US car market could reach 40 to 45 per cent by 1990. Japan's planned 12 plants in the EEC and five local assembly bases in Portugal will increase local assembly capacity to over 800,000 cars a year by the mid-1990s. If Japan retains its current high levels of imports of finished cars into Europe this, together with local capacity, would result in Japanese penetration of the European car market at over 2 million units a year, increasing market share from 11 per cent in 1988 to almost 17 per cent by 1993[333]. Such massive overcapacity would squeeze out small-scale producers in both the US and Europe.

Japanese estimates suggest that by 1992 a radical shift will have occurred in the location of Japanese manufacturing capacity, with up to one third being located offshore (Table 26.1). With continued protectionist pressures from the US and the EEC a large part of this new capacity is destined to be located in the West. With existing overcapacity in many of these industries in the US and Europe and low growth in demand this new Japanese capacity has the potential to drive out domestic capacity.

Table 26.1. Japanese firms plan to locate up to one third of their production capacity offshore by 1992

Industry	Offshore productive capacity (%)	
	1988	1992
Office machinery	12.1	39.0
Consumer electronics	25.0	37.0
Cameras	14.0	31.0
Cars	11.5	30.0
Machine tools	5.2	27.0
Computers	5.7	25.0
Semiconductors	2.5	12.0

Source: Japan Machinery Exporters Association, Tokyo, Japan 1988 (*Forbes*, 22 August 1988)

Under the free market system the efficient drive out the inefficient – but is this absolute or relative efficiency? A new plant using state-of-the-art equipment, developed production processes, a low-cost, young and non-unionized labour force assembling components sourced from Japan in a facility subsidized by public funds is obviously going to be *more* efficient than that of a fully integrated local competitor. Absolute efficiency comparisons do not provide a level playing field for local competitors. If a highly efficient new investment puts an existing plant out of business because its costs are structurally lower is this providing the greatest good for the greatest number? Will displacement enable the West to reap the benefits of greater efficiency . . . or are these investments merely providing additional unskilled employment using public funds which will create mid-term social costs in unemployment and industrial costs in the loss of highly developed skills?

The 1988 strike at Ford UK was a direct result of comparing 'apples and pears'. Ford management, with a productivity level of 17 cars per man year in a fully integrated manufacturing operation, compared this to Nissan UK's expected productivity of 40 cars per man year on an annual production run of 200,000 cars in 1992. In attempting to improve productivity to Nissan levels Ford lost sight of the fact that Nissan's operation was based entirely on component assembly. Since no fully integrated plant can compete with a pure assembly plant in terms of productivity Ford was essentially chasing an unattainable goal. While American and European firms have labour forces which are less disciplined than those in Japan, social welfare costs are high – particularly in Europe. Heavy unionization exists and controls over suppliers are much looser; there is also a complete lack of appreciation by politicians that the costs of integrated domestic producers must be structurally higher than Japanese assembly plants which operate under totally different economic conditions.

There is also the spectre of loss-leadership competition. The Japanese assemble colour televisions in 17 plants and VCRs in 25 plants in the EEC. However, only one plant reached the generally accepted minimum economic scale of production of 500,000 units a year. These Japanese assembly plants, as a result of poor operating economics, show a return on sales below 3 per cent throughout Europe. Hitachi, Mitsubishi, Sanyo and Sony have all declared large losses on their UK operations[334]. By selling at or below cost from subscale plants (facilities which have a total output below that generally accepted as a minimum economic scale of production) which circumvent conventional trade controls Japanese companies can weaken the competitiveness of domestic firms. Can the West afford subscale manufacturing which is designed primarily to weaken Western competition?

These concerns need to be balanced against the costs of protecting Western companies from highly efficient Japanese competition. Without a competitive stimulus Western firms with their cosy oligopolies can easily revert back to their producer-driven strategies and tyrannize their customers with a limited choice of shoddy, high priced goods.

Width issues involve the cross-impact of these investments on competition. The growing presence of Japanese assembly plants in the West raises two issues.

First, Japanese products assembled in the US will qualify as US products and can be shipped to Europe while Japanese products assembled in Europe can be exported to the US. Honda, for example, is committed to exporting 70,000 cars a year from the US by 1991, of which 50,000 will go to Japan and the rest, almost certainly, to Europe[335]. Since European car companies are heavily dependent on value and volume exports to the US, Honda has a strong chance of succeeding without being challenged. This type of cross-market supply raises the spectre of the US government and the EEC fighting to protect the rights of 'their' Japanese assemblers who are sourcing a large portion of the value of their product content outside *both* trade blocs. There is strong potential for future trade conflicts between the US and the EEC over exports from Japanese assembly plants. The EEC, for example, was faced with a major problem in 1988 with photocopiers imported into Europe by Ricoh from its US assembly plant. Ricoh was quoted as saying that the US-assembled photocopiers contained 90 per cent Japanese content and Ricoh was felt to have been trying to circumvent EEC anti-dumping duties by supplying the European market from its US plant. In the wake of strained US–EEC trade relations in 1988 the EEC deferred judgement and requested its member governments to agree in 1989 on a regulation of rules of origin for photocopiers. Since the draft regulation proposed a 45 per cent local content to qualify for local origin this would allow the EEC to treat Ricoh's re-exports from the US as if they were Japanese and impose duties. Supporting Washington's questioning of the EEC's right to impose duties on re-exports were not only Japanese firms like Sharp, who were waiting in the wings, but also Japanese surrogates like Nashua that exported Ricoh photocopiers to Europe under its own brand name[336].

Trade conflicts have also occurred within the EEC. Triumph Acclaims assembled under licence from Honda by British Leyland with a 60 per cent local content and rebadged as British Leyland cars were accepted into Italy only after strong UK government pressure in 1982 to fulfil a pledge to Honda[337]. The most serious clash occurred in September 1988 when the French government, supported by Renault, refused to allow Nissan Bluebirds assembled in the UK with 60 per cent local content as

'European' cars and insisted that they be treated as part of France's unilateral quota restricting Japanese cars to 3 per cent of the market. This was rapidly followed by protests from Fiat and the Italian government, who claimed that 20 per cent of the Bluebird was clearly European, 32 per cent of the origin was ambiguous and could not be clearly established and the rest was clearly of non-European origin[338]. The issue was particularly sensitive. On the one hand the UK government had made considerable efforts to secure Nissan's plant location in the UK and was honour-bound to support the exports of Bluebirds within the EEC. On the other hand the French believed that the Bluebird was nothing more than a Trojan Horse which needed to be stopped to avoid creating a precedent. Sandwiched in between was the EEC, faced with adjudicating in a case of dubious legality viewed from both international trade law and Community competitive law.

Second, Japanese firms have already demonstrated their ability to shift production from country to country in the Asian NICs following changing wage levels, exchange rates and tariff and quota agreements[339]. Western hosts may be forced into situations where they become the recipients of the rewards of Japanese firms playing the game of international wage and exchange rate competition – changing levels of employment and ultimately local tax contributions – which will have more negative than positive effects on the host country. Sanyo, for example, purchased Warwick, an OEM supplier to Sears Roebuck, in the US in 1977. Sanyo rapidly built up production, added new product lines and increased its labour force to a high of 2,400. However, by early 1988 Sanyo had transferred all but large TV set manufacture to lower cost *maquiladoras* in Mexico and retained only a token labour force of 190 at its Arkansas plants[340].

Does the investment *substitute* for imports? One of the key advantages touted for local manufacturing plants is their trade benefits – that is, their ability to substitute for imported finished products which will help to reduce trade deficits. The substitution effect requires careful analysis since there are a number of factors which can reduce and even reverse the effects of promised trade benefits.

Almost all Japanese manufacturing investments in the US and in the EEC are in plants assembling a high content of Japanese-made components and little or no substitution has taken place. In the US, for example, it is estimated that imported components for Japanese vehicle assembly plants can add as much as $20 billion a year to the trade deficit[341]. There are few quotas or tariffs on imported components, few checks appear to be made on the level of import substitution and reported checks on policing local content agreements are almost non-existent. As a consequence the operators of component assembly plants have the freedom to manage trade flows in their own self-interest. With no effective control mechanism in place component assembly plants have increased rather than cannibalized imports.

When finished product quotas coexist with component assembly plants, as in the US car market, Japanese firms have been able to use this flexibility to improve overall operating economics at the expense of trade benefits[342]. Finished product imports have been switched to higher-value, higher-margin products to cushion the impact of the fall of the dollar against the yen. The assembly plants have been focused on low-value, high-volume products using imported components which capture the benefits of off-shore production economics for high-value components, lower in-market labour costs and a 'domestic' status.

Finally, some assembly operations are used merely to change product status. The Japanese are meant to restrict imports of mini-vans to the US to around 115,000 units a year. By leaving out the back seat they can be imported into the US as light trucks, so escaping the restriction. A back seat is added at a local assembly plant and the product can then be sold as a mini-van. Through the year to the end of March 1987 Japanese firms had imported 234,000 'light trucks' into this fast-selling market segment[343].

What is the *utility*, or *essential worth*, of the investment? The value-added component of an investment is central to the issue of utility. What will the investment bring in terms of new or better use of existing skills and new technology, manufacturing, process and managerial skills and does this enhance the stock of national wealth? Utility analysis is essential given the multiple impact of assembly operations using large volumes of imported components.

Assembly plants require less labour than fully integrated operations and the number of new jobs created tends to be relatively small since they are more labour than skills intensive and the type of job created is low or semi-skilled due to the fact that these plants are generally highly automated or are involved in routine assembly operations. Assembly plants using imported components and pre-developed systems do not require investment in advanced skills training as they do not transfer new manufacturing techniques and production processes. Consequently, the expertise to develop complex components and processes –

the guts of high value-added products – remain firmly anchored offshore. Local purchases for assembly plants sourced with offshore components are largely services and low value-added components which do not help to build up the manufacturing infrastructure. Imported components containing built-in profit margins help to lower local tax payments, again reducing the positive effect on the local economic infrastructure. Finally, the lower structure costs of assembly operations compared to fully integrated manufacturing, together with subsidized start-up and often on-going subsidization, can displace higher-cost fully integrated domestic competitors.

Utility analysis is essential to identify the impact of assembly operations on the number and type of skills generated and in the transfer of vital new skills and techniques to the host. However, they must go much further and pinpoint the erosion effect on vital skills and the potential for replacing existing high skills with lower value skills.

A composite view of potential effect on competition and trade and the overall utility of the investment provide an opportunity to link market access directly to the relative quality and quantity of benefits which the investment produces. Where selective industrial policies exist this linkage can be extended to compare the investment's fit with national industrial goals.

Access can be controlled on the basis of the investment's potential effects on capacity and on value-added contribution. For example:

- Limiting the number and productive capacity of new investments to avoid adding to existing capacity which already exceeds demand. However, access restrictions should only cover a fixed period – say, three years. This would serve notice on Western competitors that they have only a limited time in which to restructure and rationalize to become more competitive. Fixed periods of protection will help to overcome building permanent walls around inefficient industries which inevitably force consumers to pay the price of uncompetitive businesses – high prices and restricted choice. It also ensures that Western industry does not conveniently maintain its traditional uncompetitive cost structures and poor productivity levels.

- Approving investments based on economic scale manufacturing to ensure that subscale production is not used as a competitive weapon to weaken local firms, as well as promoting fully integrated local manufacturing. In turn this would require a higher degree of knowledge transfer to local suppliers through increased local content levels.

- Basing approval and the incentives offered on the quality of the investment – that is, on the level of local content, the number of new jobs created and the level of skills involved, the amount of import substitution, the level of technology transfer incorporated in the production process and the creation of substantive local R&D capability.

Attitude changes in the West are crucial to using market access as a key control mechanism. Access to markets must be regarded as a valuable asset in its own right. Those investments which provide high-quality benefits with a stimulating rather than a conflicting effect on domestic competition should be encouraged. Conversely, those investments that are designed primarily to circumvent conventional trade barriers should be discouraged as they have a negative impact on national economic and social infrastructures.

Local Content

A key mechanism to control the input of manufacturing investments on local industry is the amount of local content contained in the finished product.

Unfortunately the definition of local content is extremely vague. GATT, for example, has no provisions which define when or whether local content requirements can be used as an instrument of trade policy, let alone the definition of local content – or the specific percentage. There is no international convention on how to define where a product originated. The EEC defines a product as of Community origin if the last substantial process or operation that is economically justified was performed in the Community – and was carried out in an undertaking equipped for the purpose – and represented an important stage of manufacture.

While GATT can take action to prevent circumvention of anti-dumping duties it is doubtful whether this extends to local content requirements. Adding insult to injury, the levels of local content agreed between hosts and investors (since they are designed to secure investments) may be illegal, set too low and with the time frames given to improve the content levels being liberally interpreted.

Nevertheless local content agreements will play a growing role in international trade as cross-border investment becomes the rule rather than the exception and the increase in globalization forces companies to draw from multiple sources.

To improve host country benefits major changes are necessary in the approach to inward investors' commitments to local content. Unfortunately, its measurement is open to wide interpretation, and this provides ample opportunity for abuse.

Two main methods are used. The first is based on the ex-factory *cost* of production less the cost of imported parts, while the second is calculated on the ex-factory *price*, which includes margins for profit, promotion and distribution minus the cost of imported components. However, there are wide variations as companies have different ways of calculating their costs. This helps to mask the real effect of imported components in the cost mix. Ford in the US, for example, estimates that new Japanese assembly plants producing cars with a 50 per cent North American content are really using only 20 per cent local value, with the high value-added components (worth up to 80 per cent of the total value) being shipped from Japan[344]. Nissan, which has a local content agreement in the UK based on ex-factory price, will be able to reach an 80 per cent local content level *without* the engine or transmission (about a third of the ex-factory cost) being sourced in Europe[345].

Complicating measurement of local content is the creativity used by Japanese firms to justify their content level. This has ranged from the simplistic claiming of costs at an FOB or CIF value rather than on an into-factory duty paid basis in the host market, to highly imaginative propositions. One EEC investigation of typewriter assembly in the community identified a range of ploys used by Japanese assembly plant operators to demonstrate high local content levels[346]:

- Importing all the parts from Japan, delivering them to a third party for exclusive assembly for a fee, then selling the returned finished product within the community as EEC 'origin'.
- Having high value-added sub-assemblies constructed entirely from parts imported from Japan by an EEC subsidiary of a Japanese firm (which normally manufactured these products in Japan and supplies them to the Japanese assembly plant's mother company in Japan).

- Selling high value-added components directly from a mother company in Japan to a domestic EEC company which then carried out sub-assembly and sold the resulting 'product' to the EEC assembly plant of the Japanese mother company, which claimed the entire cost of the component as community value.

- Creating sub-assemblies by putting several imported components together to generate a unique added value and claiming this as community value when in reality the sub-assembly did not exist in normal production.

- Using inflated transfer prices, often at replacement or spare parts levels normally charged to independent purchasers incorporating heavy profit margins, from the mother company in Japan to its EEC assembly plant.

There is an obvious need to fix local content definitions at a standard which eases comparisons between products and trade blocs and makes the role of imported components much more transparent in the cost mix. A measure based on ex-factory cost would be appropriate providing that it captures *only* those elements like direct materials, components and labour traceable to the finished product plus indirect costs associated with production such as variable costs (power, supplies and indirect labour) and fixed factory overheads (rent, insurance, taxes and depreciation) involved in the manufacturing process. Margins covering promotion, distribution and profit should not be allowed since they are not costs involved in production. R&D activities performed in host countries are rarely directly attributable to production and have a global rather than a country specific effect. However, they are vital added-value components to hosts since they help to transfer skills and contribute to improving the quality of the infrastructure. R&D costs could be incorporated into ex-factory cost definitions as incentives to encourage skill and knowledge transfers. However, these must be substantive. Claims for R&D which involve gathering market research information, technical visits to Japan by Westerners for training and claims for transferring assembly technology when the knowledge of assembly of products has been known often for decades in the West do not constitute R&D activity or technology transfer[347].

A switch to a standard local content definition in the West based only on costs involved in the manufacturing process would have a dramatic effect. This would identify the real benefits to the host country by washing out non-production expenses which effectively obscure the role played by imported components in the cost mix.

In practice the West depends almost entirely on the largess of inward investors for the level of local content used in the final product. The US and the EEC have no legally defined local content levels. While the EEC has used a rule-of-thumb 40 per cent[348], and there was a loose agreement in May 1988 that a 60 per cent EEC-sourced content qualifies for free circulation within the EEC, there is wide disagreement between the member states on what constitutes an appropriate level of local content[349]. Since states in the US and countries in the EEC negotiate individually with Japanese companies the low levels of content agreed are reflective of the host's political anxiousness to secure inward investment to create new jobs at almost any cost rather than a desire to obtain the best deal in the national or trade bloc interest. When the European Commission attempted to get agreement in mid-1987 on higher levels of local content Greece, Ireland and Spain refused to ratify levels over 40 per cent local content. However, these are not the only cases favouring low local content in the EEC. Both the UK and France are notorious for agreeing to investments which have local content levels falling well below EEC Guidelines[350]. In fact the UK's success in attracting 65 different assembly operations, accounting for about 30 per cent of all Japanese manufacturing investment in Europe through 1987[351], is believed to have been strongly influenced as much by its liberal aid packages as by its accommodative inward investment practices.

The spate of Japanese assembly plants for plain-paper copiers built in Europe in anticipation of EEC anti-dumping duties – provisionally set at up to 15.8 per cent in August 1986 and finalized at up to 20 per cent in February 1987[352] – is symptomatic of the problems of non-policing of content levels. A subsequent evaluation of the assembly plants of Canon, Konica, Minolta, Panasonic, Ricoh, Toshiba and Sharp found that local content averaged only 12 to 13 per cent[353]. A similar EEC study found that the effective local content at five Japanese plants assembling electronic typewriters varied between 4 and 25 per cent. In one case the only local material used was the packing cases used to ship the typewriters[354].

Agreements are common where investors promise to increase the level of local content over time. For example, Mazda has announced that its US assembly plant on stream in 1988 will increase the content level for locally sourced products and services to between 70 and 75 per cent by the 'early' 1990s[355]. None of these 'time delay' local content

232

agreements has been challenged on the grounds that an existing domestic infrastructure is available already supplying domestic manufacturers and can meet component needs of the assembly plant virtually from start-up. The original agreement in the UK gave Nissan a five-year breathing space to bring car production up to a 60 per cent local content level defined at ex-factory price. This was subsequently modified in 1986 following a scale-up of output to an 80 per cent level by 1990, giving a seven-year time frame[356]. No concerns appear to have been raised over the long period allowed Nissan to convert to higher levels of local sourcing. The local content level was relatively low since the content was defined at ex-factory price and the UK and the rest of the EEC have a developed infrastructure supplying quality automative components in volume.

Forcing the achievement of high local content levels within short periods of time is essential to dissuade investors from building assembly plants whose primary purpose is circumvent trade barriers on finished products. Enforcement will contribute to decreasing trade surpluses and to improving the quality of the host country's infrastructure.

Local content levels can be positively influenced by a number of measures:

Punitive duties can be imposed on component imports to reduce the economic attraction of using large amounts of imported components for local assembly. However, punitive duties would only be a significant factor if:

- They become an integral part of all new agreements and were retrospectively applied to all inward manufacturing investments which had five or more years of local production and had not met an 80 per cent local content level at a defined ex-factory cost of production. (This 80 per cent level would oblige almost all manufacturers to transfer high value-added components to local production.)

- They are retroactive to avoid drawing out the impact through stockpiled supplies.

- They were imposed at 2 to 3 times the percentage levied on finished product imports to produce a strong economic penalty for non-compliance.

- Extra duties would be triggered if the assembler attempted to absorb the cost of duties rather than pass them on in the form of higher prices to end users to avoid nullifying the price impact.

- They would be imposed worldwide with the exception of those sourced from within a trade bloc with a rider that trade bloc supplies must also reach an 80 per cent local content at a defined ex-factory cost of production. This would prevent the use of indirect imports to circumvent local content requirements and avoid the use of components supplied from Japanese affiliates or suppliers in third countries, particularly those with undervalued currencies which lower artificially the cost of imported components.

Almost all Japanese assembly plants have been built to secure market access in the face of actual or threatened protectionism and the revaluation of the yen. Inward investment agreements need to be linked to import constraints to ensure that local content levels are improved, export substitution does take place and the degree of manoeuvrability of investors is limited in practice rather than in theory. Voluntary Export Restraints (VERs) based on *value* measures could form an integral part of any inward investment agreement. This would enable the host to:

- Count the value of all imported components from any non-trade-bloc source as part of the overall VER value. This would overcome the present situation where component imports are excluded and consequently have an additive effect on imports.

- By using value measures the host would be protected against the investor dumping labour-intensive low value-added assembly operations for high-volume products in the West while maintaining imports based on volume but switching the mix of the imports to high value-added products capturing the higher value and complex skills offshore.

Inward investment agreements could also employ *unitary ratios* to improve the value-added, employment and skills content. For example, the ratio of value-added, the number of people and the level of skills employed compared to sales in the host country could be fixed at levels equivalent to those same ratios achieved by the investor on a global scale[357].

Local content levels can also be linked to increasing *export commitments* to spur a more rapid integration of inward investment into the host country's infrastructure and to achieve a positive effect on trade balances.

The case of Japanese manufacturing investments in Taiwan is particularly relevant. Prior to the 1982 ban on more than 1,500 Japanese consumer product imports the local VCR industry was limited to local assembly with less than 20 per cent local content. To promote domestic producers Taiwan progressively imposed higher local content levels coupled to exports and stopped finished product imports until 1987. By 1984 most Japanese firms had upgraded their operations to joint ventures and technical cooperation agreements with local firms. In 1985 Taiwan increased local content requirements to 55 per cent and by mid-1986, as a result of the success of the programme, lifted the ban on imports one full year ahead of schedule.

By progressively forcing higher levels of local content coupled to aggressive export policies focused *outside* the host country's economic bloc the West could improve the quality of investment and gain a net trade contribution.

The *time frames* allowed to move from start-up to high levels of local content need to be restricted. Given the capabilities of component manufacturers in North America and in West Europe a maximum of three years would be sufficient time for assembly plants to reach agreed maximum levels of local content. However, component content should be clearly defined at, say, 80 per cent of the ex-factory cost level to avoid surrogate supply. Speeding up the time frame would help the investment to make more significant contributions more rapidly to the host country's infrastructure.

Local content levels are extremely important to host countries. They provide a wide range of net contributions ranging from using existing and developing new skills and substituting for imports to building up manufacturing infrastructures which have been eroding in the West during the 1980s. Without a firm commitment for high levels of locally manufactured components as part of the approval process for new investments, particularly high value-added supplies, most assembly plants will continue to be shell-like operations with the benefits flowing largely to the Japanese investor.

Incentives

The inward investment decision is heavily influenced by both the size and the scope of the financial package and the non-cash benefits offered by host countries. States in the US and countries in Western Europe are firmly in the grip of the belief that they must 'buy' inward investments in competition with others and the level of subsidy offered has reached absurd proportions. This has enabled the bride to select among suitors on the basis of the largest dowry.

New attitudes and approaches are necessary to reverse the situation:

Incentives. The practice of competing for inward investment ensures that financial packages are used to subsidize both start-up and ongoing operations, which are rarely to the host's advantage and frequently lead to 'sweeteners' like free education for Japanese children and driving lessons for the wives of Japanese executives to close investment negotiations which have no place in industrial investment aid packages. These are not real incentives since they do not direct investments into patterns of local content levels and skills and technology transfers which provide measurable benefits to hosts.

By linking incentives directly to specific goals and objectives the hosts can gain significant improvements in the quality of inward investment agreements. For example, incentives can be applied in proportion to the level of local content and the speed at which it is reached and can be paid retrospectively to ensure a punitive effect for non-performance. Similarly, training grants can be made available only for schemes which create skills such as accredited apprenticeship programmes and for upgrading skills through advanced training at approved technical institutions.

As an alternative the West can apply strict reciprocity and grant incentives strictly in line with those offered to Western companies in the same industries or at the same magnitude of value in Japan.

Harmonization. To counter the begger-my-neighbour syndrome used to compete for internationally mobile investments, incentive packages should be harmonized in terms of content and scope throughout trade blocs. A standardized approach to incentives, with special provisions to meet social goals of development in depressed areas, would go a long way to controlling the types of incentives offered as well as reducing the overall level of subsidization. By subjecting inward investments to federal (in the US) and to European Commission (in the EEC) advance approval instead of the prevailing blanket clearance process, this would exert a much higher degree of control over host state or country incentives in the national or trade bloc interest.

Capital equipment. Almost all inward investments receive grants and tax breaks to cover initial capital equipment purchases. However, these are used mainly to favour the investor's own domestic suppliers or those suppliers' surrogates in the host country. Since the US and Western Europe have sophisticated and advanced capital equipment suppliers there is little justification in using taxpayers' money to fund the purchase of Japanese-made equipment for use in their Western assembly plants.

To ensure that these public funds are recirculated within the host's economy and used to support the local manufacturing infrastructure they should be applicable only to local purchases incorporating at least 80 per cent local content defined at the ex-factory cost level.

Subsidies. To minimize the impact on domestic competitors no operating subsidies should be given – such as long-term tax holidays and duty-free import zones status – which effectively lower period costs and undermine the cost structure of local competitors who have no or limited access to the same benefits. While trade zones status created 4,400 new jobs in car assembly plants in the US their duty-free component imports caused the loss of 14,600 jobs in the US autoparts industry[358].

There also seems little point in subsidizing inward investment when the profits generated are largely exported offshore through the transfer price mechanism on component supplies and represent a cash transfer from consumer and taxpayers in the host country.

By coupling incentives to benefits, harmonizing incentive programmes, ensuring that these incentives are used to support the infrastructure and avoiding subsidization at the expense of domestic industry inward investments can be channelled into patterns offering much greater benefits to host countries and minimize the cost effect on Western industry. To put this into place governments in the West will have to put a considerable amount of steel into the rubber teeth which they currently use to control inward investment.

27

BOLTING THE BACK DOOR

Much can be done to improve the quality of Japanese manufacturing investments in the West. However, full benefits will only be achieved if the West plugs the loopholes which Japan can use to circumvent new controls.

Discriminatory practices. Although Japan is the main exponent of 'screwdriver' assembly plants designed to circumvent protection any penalties must be equally applicable to firms from all countries. This will not only prevent Japan from appealing to GATT over discriminatory treatment[359] but will also apply to Korean and Taiwanese firms who are beginning to build assembly plants in the West to overcome the same problem – growing protectionism. The Koreans already have assembly plants in the US, Canada and Europe and by 1991 Taiwanese companies will have spent $2.4 billion on direct equity investments in the US[360].

Conflicting regulations. Governments in the West need to ensure that their legislation supports rather than conflicts with overall quality improvement goals for inward investment. For example, the UK's Export Credit Guarantee Department's decision to ease foreign content restrictions from about 15 per cent of total value to higher levels[361] offers the opportunity for assembly plant operators sourcing high levels of content offshore to use the host's taxpayers' money to finance re-exports.

To avoid compromise inward investment regulations designed to improve host country benefits must pre-empt conflicting legislation or practices.

New routes. Faced with a strong probability of increased controls over the quality of inward investments Japanese companies are likely to change tactics.

Investment emphasis can be shifted to *lower-cost* hosts within trade blocs such as Greece, Ireland, Portugal and Spain in the EEC or to those countries with a close *proximity* and *preferential trade agreements* with a host

such as Canada and Mexico with the US or a number of developing countries with the EEC. To prevent Japanese firms using the soft underbelly of
low-cost sites and surrogate countries inward investment controls must be
enforced across trade blocs to prevent divide-and-conquer tactics and to
ensure that high local content levels become an integral feature of all
preferential trade agreements.

Collaborative agreements involving joint ventures and OEM and
component supply can be increased with Western firms to improve penetration through surrogates. The large number of semiconductor joint ventures, joint development and equity investment deals made by Japanese
firms in the US in 1986 were a direct response to circumvent the US–Japan
semiconductor pact[362]. Similarly, the joint ventures incorporating large
amounts of imported components with German vehicle manufacturers in
1987 (Toyota–VW, Isuzu–Opel and Mitsubishi–Daimler Benz) were
designed to counter concerns over the growing penetration of the German
market by Japanese vehicle manufacturers. While some advocate that global alliances are the new strategic imperative[363], others suggest that the
naivety of most Western firms in collaborative deals with the Japanese,
often negotiated from a position of weakness, results in the annexation of
Western competences and technology at low cost and low risk and provides uncontrollable forms of market access[364].

To prevent Japanese firms from using Western surrogates to circumvent
pressures to improve the quality of Japanese manufacturing investments
collaborative agreements could be subject to final ratification at the federal
level in the US and at the European Commission level in the EEC.

Cross-market supply, where Japanese assembly plants in the US supply
EEC needs and, if the dollar value rises, Japanese assembly plants based in
the EEC meet US demand, is a potential problem requiring a proactive
response. The US and the EEC need to bury their long-standing trade
differences and reach agreement on a common definition of local content
levels for third-country inward investors *and* their component suppliers to
ensure that both parties can identify who really is 'us' and who are 'them'.
This will help to avoid investors playing off one host against another and
creating potentially explosive trade conflicts where the sole beneficiary is
the third country investor.

Unless *backdoor access* is firmly closed, Japanese firms, already adept at
globally networking supplies, will be able to continue to circumvent trade
barriers with little or no inconvenience. The end result will be little added
value to their manufacturing investments in the West and a further
deterioration of the infrastructure and employment.

239

28

BURNING THE PAPER TIGER

Japanese companies see Western governments as paper tigers when it comes to enforcing inward investment agreements. There are no cases on record in the West where a government has enforced local content agreements with Japanese companies who have been unwilling or unable to meet their local content commitments. In practice, once agreements are negotiated they are regarded as the definitive statement and no policing of the letter or the spirit of the agreement takes place. As a result inward investors are free to interpret local content agreements as, when and how they like with little fear of retribution.

Besides the lack of policing inward investments there is no mechanism to punish non-compliance. Even if Western governments did wish to punish Japanese companies for not living up to their commitments they would be hard pressed to do so.

The only legislation in the West specifically designed to control the impact of inward investments in assembly operations is an EEC regulation in 1987 which amends a series of anti-dumping regulations stretching back to 1979[365]. While this is widely accepted as draconian legislation by GATT and a blunt instrument by Japanese inward investors, it is possibly the most effective single piece of Community industrial policy to date. However, it falls short of developing a comprehensive framework to deal effectively with the complex issues involved. For example:

- The community can investigate only if a complaint is lodged that is backed up by sufficient evidence of cause (dumping with component imports) and effect (injury). Given the speed at which an assembly plant can become operational (in contrast to a fully-integrated operation) and the sharp rise in the number of assembly plants in specific industries, irreparable damage can be done before corrective action comes into effect.

- Assembly or production is carried out by any party which is related or associated with the manufacturer whose exports of the like product are subject to a definitive anti-dumping duty and applies only if assembly of a product began or was stepped up after the launching of an anti-dumping investigation. This effectively gives immunity to products assembled by firms not the subject of any anti-dumping action, with the net effect that the vast bulk of assembly operations using high levels of offshore components would go unchallenged.

- The value of the components used in the assembly originating in the country of exportation of the product subject to the anti-dumping duty exceeds the value of all other parts used by at least 50 per cent with the balance from any other source. This has limited utility. Definition of content is a key problem; however, the main issue is the global supply networking which is already a significant feature of Japanese business. Most major Japanese firms already have extensive networks of low-cost, fully and partially owned component facilities throughout the Asian NICs. These could be used to source the bulk of component supplies outside Japan, which would enable Japanese firms to maximize the value-added and skills content offshore and avoid Japan as the key component source.

Several opportunities exist to improve enforcement. The most effective would be to develop blanket legislation with defined local content levels and origin and commitments together with specific achievement dates for all foreign manufacturing operations backed up by a set of prescribed penalties for non-compliance. These penalties could take a number of forms:

- The imposition of special anti-dumping duties to bring the cost of the assembled product up to the cost of imported finished products *plus* the addition of anti-dumping duties.

- Punitive taxes which must be transferred through to the end user to bring the cost of the assembled product up to the average market price of domestic competitors' products to wipe out gains obtained by circumventing trade barriers.

- A disproportionate reduction in existing import quotas by applying a multiple of the low content achieved against the prevailing quota.

- The repayment of all incentives and subsidies with interest, the cancellation of all future incentives and the reimbursement of the imputed value of the profits derived by the investor through non-compliance plus the imposition of corporate taxes on these unreported profits.

With the exception of repaying government incentives all other revenues received through penalty payments could be channelled in part to support restructuring of domestic competitors, with the bulk going to offset taxation to compensate consumers for paying higher prices.

To block loopholes the legislation needs to be retroactive as well as proactive and should shift the onus firmly on to the inward investor to prove compliance by detailing achievements at fixed intervals.

. . . The Inevitable Response

Naturally the Japanese are used to having their cake and eating it and will not take kindly to any moves which limit their investment freedom. Predictably the response from Japan to protect its investments will be strong.

The Japanese government and companies have already developed the capability to influence the way in which they are viewed in the West and have used this to shape a more favourable environment. For several years on both sides of the Atlantic the Japanese have used an extensive public relations programme which plays down the trade imbalance, extols the virtues of Japanese direct investments, promotes the mutuality of economic interests between Japan and its trade partners and, in the US, reinforces the notion that America's competitiveness problems are of its own making. In 1988 alone the Japanese are expected to have paid upwards of $300 million to win the 'hearts and minds' of Americans by funding education, museums, universities, public television as well as public relations and lobbying[366].

The skilful use of lobbying, backed up by sophisticated long-term opinion moulding, has enabled the Japanese to focus effectively on potentially devastating pieces of legislation and diffuse their effects. Toshiba, for example, was able to deflect Congressional efforts in the US to impose harsh sanctions on its annual US sales of $10 billion for illegally selling restricted technology to the USSR. Toshiba embarked on an aggressive lobbying campaign in 1987 and 1988 in Washington and in the media costing an estimated $9 million. Instead of banning all Toshiba sales, Congress finally imposed a three-year restriction on US government purchases of Toshiba products, amounting to about $100 million a year. Since the legislation contained a number of exceptions Toshiba will probably keep most of its government business[367]. Other corporate lobbying successfully stalled and altered the focus of major trade bills and stopped legislation on unitary taxation in 12 states in 1988.

When the EEC began to probe the issue of Japanese assembly plants during the second half of 1986 the *Keidanren*, the Confederation of Japanese Business, delivered a strong public letter to the European Commission protesting any change in existing agreements. When it became obvious in the spring of 1988 that the EEC was going to continue its policy of imposing anti-dumping duties on Japanese assembly plants with less than 40 per cent local content, MITI took the issue to GATT[368]. This was an aggressive move since Japan, for the first time, asked GATT to adjudicate in a trade dispute – despite the fact that challenges by Japanese typewriter assemblers to the EEC's method of calculating anti-dumping duties collapsed at the European Court of Justice in early October 1988[369]. These moves were backed by veiled threats that proposals to extend anti-dumping duties to components could close existing plants and slow and even reverse the flow of Japanese manufacturing investments in Europe. At the same time Epson, to head off provisional anti-dumping duties of up to 33 per cent imposed on $1.8 billion worth of dot-matrix computer printers[370], made a public attack on the EEC, highlighting the risks to employment which these policies created with an estimated £250,000 advertising campaign in the *Financial Times*. These sabre-rattling tactics were designed to sidetrack the European Commission from taking decisive action and to help prevent the issue from spreading to the US, where the level of Japanese investment exposure is far greater.

Japan is a highly successful exponent of brinkmanship which, coupled to procrastination, vague promises, professed anger and the extensive use of opinion moulding and the creation of a measure of influence over political decision making – particularly in the US – has enabled Japan to deflect or halt most Western initiatives to change trade conditions. In the case of moves to improve the quality of inward investment the West has little to lose – small numbers of low-skilled jobs – and everything to gain by pursuing tough policies. Conversely, Japan has everything to gain – continued access to the large wealthy markets of the US and the EEC – while its loss is limited to the transfer of a fairer share of the added-value content to those countries providing market access.

Western measures to control inward investments are simply moves to adjust Western economies to the competitive conditions and interventionist industrial policies which have provided Japan with much of its industrial strength and success over the last four decades. Japan is a pragmatic nation and while changes in the rules of the game would generate hostility Japan has little option but to go along with reasoned and fair changes to the current one-sided flow of trade. Japan's post-war trade history demonstrates clearly that Japan will only respond to tough measures and will respect only those who act forcefully. Strong measures by the US and the EEC to control inward manufacturing investments, to enforce their compliance and to plug loopholes are likely to result in a substantial increase in the quality of investment. Japan has limited manoeuvrability as a result of its dependence on Western markets for its increasingly higher value-added production.

To improve investment quality the only option for the West is to burn its paper tiger image with tough, pragmatic approaches backed up by adequate policing and suitable penalties.

SUMMARY

Many of the beliefs that the West holds dear about its industrial prowess and technological superiority, the values of opening up the Japanese market, increasing protectionism and of Japan's problems with the high yen and in globalizing its business are based on faulty perceptions of the real world.

Japan's second wave of competition – globalizing its business – is spearheaded by aggressive inward manufacturing investments in assembly plants designed to operate within the increasingly protected markets of the West. These plants have the potential to alter radically the competitive balance by mounting a low-cost publicly subsidized challenge to an already battered manufacturing sector in the West.

The key to limiting the impact of these investments is to change the existing rules of the game to provide a situation more advantageous to the West. These changes need to be driven by modifications of the West's behaviour. Japan's move up the value-added chain, its mounting cash surpluses and its lack of credibility as a responsible participant in the international trade system make Japan very vulnerable to a change in the West's attitudes towards market access.

By using market access as the pivotal factor in the approval process the West can dramatically improve the benefits of inward manufacturing investments. However, this needs a more rational understanding of competitive dynamics and of industrial strategy by government to make the approval process more effective. This in turn requires a move away from approving inward investments based on narrow, parochial self-interests to those which provide positive net benefits meeting broader needs on national and, in the case of the EEC, trade bloc needs.

By adopting significant changes in the way in which local content is

245

defined and the levels incorporated in final products, coupling incentives firmly to benefits, closing the backdoor to avoid circumvention by indirect methods and adding a mechanism to enforce compliance the West can achieve a radical shift in the quality of Japanese inward investments.

Although the object of these changes is to create a fair exchange of the value-added benefits of these investments and a level playing field for Western competitors in return for the ability to enter protected markets, Japan's reaction will be predictably hostile. While Japan will be strongly opposed to any change in the status quo, which is now heavily in favour of Japanese investors, Japan will have little option but to comply with forceful measures from a united West. Japan's high value-added industrial policy and its need to sustain economic momentum force Japan to maintain access to the large number of sophisticated and wealthy consumers in the West.

Conversely, the West has no option but to impose controls over heavily subsidized screwdriver plants. These import high levels of components which get around conventional trade barriers and employ inexpensive low-skilled labour, providing a low-cost challenge to domestic industry. Without substantive controls these assembly plants will not reduce the trade surplus or unemployment or contribute to improving the West's manufacturing infrastructure. They also raise the possibility of long-term erosion of the skills base of the West and the continued hollowing out of the manufacturing sector, feeding deindustrialization, reducing competitiveness and causing long-term structural unemployment.

Given Japan's reluctance to meet Western demands to open up its domestic market and restrain exports – which stretches back three decades – there is little guarantee that self-regulated Japanese manufacturing investments will not wreak havoc in the West. On past experience with Japanese promises it is unlikely that Hitachi or Nissan, for example, will feel the need to build large-scale research facilities or adopt fully-integrated manufacturing like IBM, or even develop a full line of products like Ford, in Europe. Similarly, it is difficult to imagine Matsushita or Sumitomo Chemicals developing the scale and breadth of commitment of a Philips or an ICI in the US – whatever the time frame.

Uncontrolled Japanese assembly plants operating inside the protective walls thrown up by the US and the EEC represent the ultimate competitive challenge to the West. Unless the governments of the

West can develop an effective response relatively quickly Japanese assembly plants are likely to become powerful Trojan Horses undermining the competitiveness of the West's manufacturing sector. If Japanese assembly plants in their present form continue to go unchallenged the probability of a decline in manufacturing capability will increase, bringing long-term structural unemployment and declining standards of living.

If the West cannot or will not act decisively and quickly to contain the threat of Japanese Trojan Horse assembly plants the stage will be set for a fundamental shift in the already fragile competitive balance that it will be difficult, if not impossible, to change.

PART 7

ENDGAME

29

PREVENTING AN END RUN

At first glance the growth of Japanese assembly plants in the West offers an attractive, disarmingly simple and easily grasped set of solutions for both parties.

For the West it promises to provide new jobs, access to Japan's legendary management skills, a chance to upgrade the quality of its industrial infrastructure and a decrease in the unfavourable trade balances with Japan. For Japan it offers the opportunity to continue to access the markets of the West and escape the constraining pressures of increasing protectionism and the high yen value.

The growth in Japanese manufacturing investments in the West has considerable merit and a great deal of circumstantial evidence to support the benefits. It also falls on sympathetic ears and is sufficiently remote for its backers in government, industry and labour in both the US and the EEC to be safe for generalizations. Best of all it leaves a warm feeling that something positive is finally happening to the West's often unhappy relationship with Japan.

All this helps to deflect attention away from a real analysis of the potential effects of these transplanted low value-added assembly plants in the West.

Japanese assembly plants in their current forms have the potential to inflict significant competitive pressure on Western manufacturers, induce long-term structural unemployment, escalate deindustrialization and circumvent the traditional apparatus of trade regulation.

However, nobody is paying much attention. The reasons are simple:

- Relatively small investments are involved. So far more than one third of the Japanese manufacturing investments in the West

251

have capital outlays under $5 million and about one third have annual sales of less than $5 million[371].

- Statistics do not reflect the gravity of the problem. There are major difficulties in identifying and defining the amount of Japanese investment in manufacturing in the West. Have you captured it all and do you use book value, original costs or market values?

- Although Japanese manufacturing investments are increasing rapidly they are still small in comparison to the international investments of the major Western trading nations like the US, the UK and the Netherlands.

- Most of the investments have been in greenfield sites and there have been few hostile takeovers of Western firms which generate adverse public opinion.

- These investments are seen largely as creators of new employment in areas of high unemployment and they are perceived as having a local rather than a national impact.

- Although much of this new employment is in low-skilled assembly work, the immediate effect of these gains is positive in the eyes of politicians and organized labour in the West who see *any* new employment as a positive force.

- Many Western companies are deeply involved with Japanese firms and act as their surrogates, allowing them access to the US and the EEC through licensing, imported components and OEM products and joint ventures, dual marketing, toll manufacturing and distribution sharing agreements. It is hardly surprising that few Western companies will 'whistle-blow' on Japanese competitors who are central to their own survival.

- The mid to long-term effects of these new investments on competition, the infrastructure and society are obscure, the consequences hard to pin down and difficult to quantify.

- The Japanese have developed a strong capability to shape public opinion and to diffuse legislation in the West, which has helped to deflect attention away from the potential negative effects of Japanese assembly plants on Western industry.

As a result, the threats posed by Japanese assembly plants have received little recognition and have been accorded a low priority in both the US and the EEC. The US has been relatively impervious to the whole issue of Japanese assembly investments – the 1988 Omnibus Trade and Competitiveness Act contains no legislation on inward investments – and has welcomed their advent. While Europe has been a little more perceptive than the US and is in the painful process of trying to get a consensus to toughen existing legislation, the lure of new jobs – at almost any price – has been too seductive for politicians on both sides of the Atlantic to ignore.

While there is no hard evidence to support the contention that *all* Japanese manufacturing investments in the West are purpose-built assembly plants designed solely to circumvent the twin pressures of protectionism and the high yen value, or that Japanese companies have *no* intention of integrating these assembly plants more fully into the domestic infrastructures of the West, two key facts suggest a need for concern:

- Japanese overseas direct investments have grown spectacularly following the rapid appreciation of the yen against the dollar in late 1985 and surged again in 1986 and 1987 in response to the development of the US Omnibus Trade and Competitiveness Act and the move to develop a uniform internal EEC market by 1992. For example, Japanese overseas direct investments almost doubled in the one year between fiscal years 1985 and 1986 (Figure 29.1).

- Few of the assembly plants of high-technology Japanese firms which have existed in the US and the EEC since the early 1970s have moved backward into fully-intergrated manufacturing sourcing the majority of components locally and none have created substantial R&D capabilities in the West or developed high levels of exports to countries outside the major trade blocs in which they located.

The speed of investment and the momentum created by production units assembling components sourced offshore, neatly outflanking quotas and tariffs, will ensure that the threats posed by these Trojan Horses will become reality before the West can mount an effective response. Japan could well win this new war before the West has even been able to identify the battlefield.

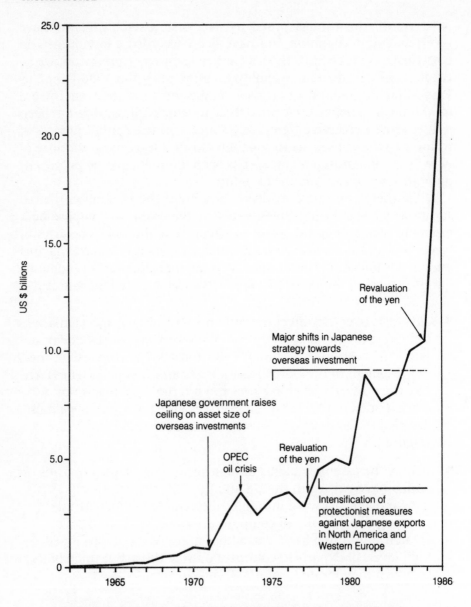

Figure 29.1. The big growth in Japanese overseas direct investment came from increased Western protection in the late 1970s and surged again following the yen revaluation in late 1985.

Source: 'The changing geography of Japanese foreign direct investment in manufacturing industry: A global perspective', P. Dicken, *Environment and Planning*, A, Volume 20, 1988, and Jetro, London, 1988.

Politicians in the West are mesmerized by the need to compete for internationally mobile investments which create new jobs and build industrial strength. This myopia has led to overbidding and a lack of focus on the number and the quality of the jobs being created and the effect on Western competitors operating with higher structural costs. Literally the West has been taxing itself to give Japanese assembly plants advantages over domestic competitors. The short-term benefits bring long-term costs which have a more significant impact than politicians are willing to realize. It also misses the point that industrial strength is built only on a sustained inward flow of value-added skills and technology. However, the issue goes far beyond investments, employment, industrial capacity and skills: it is about industrial power and how a decline will affect Western society in the long term.

The West has reached an industrial watershed. Its historic competitive advantages, built around producing innovative products at high volumes and at low prices, have passed to others. Japan, and to a lesser extent the newly industrialized Asian countries, are able to emulate rapidly and even improve on the West's basic creativity and can manufacture at lower costs and higher quality. The economies of the West are being transformed from producer to service-driven industries and as a result the manufacturing base is decaying. Unfettered Japanese Trojan Horse assembly plants will help to escalate the deindustrialization process if their lower structural costs replace fully-integrated domestic production and displace valuable skills with component imports.

Compounding the problem is the fact that Japanese assembly investments in the West are being copied by the Koreans and Taiwanese. Like the Japanese they see their long-term survival linked to sustained access and use assembly operations as a means to 'domesticate' their exports. Western companies are very likely to find themselves in the near future sandwiched between high-priced Japanese products with established quality images and new low-priced, high-quality competition from the Koreans and Taiwanese – all with a domestic status in the West. With the high and low ends of the market occupied, many Western firms are going to find themselves in a no-man's-land on a road to nowhere as their volume dries up.

Omhae's *triad* concept of three great market regions – the US, the EEC and Japan dominating world trade, industrial production and innovation as equal partners[372] – is already reality and the orthodoxies of 'one world' and 'national economies' are largely redundant.

255

However, the long-term effect may be totally different from Ohmae's prediction. While the Japanese realized that they must become significant world-class players the West is only beginning to grasp the new realities and is way behind in trying to emulate Japan. The reality is that the equal partnership is barely in equilibrium now and will be tilted firmly, and maybe irreversibly, in Japan's favour if Japanese assembly plants, rather than fully integrated manufacturing operations, are allowed to become a significant industrial force inside the markets of the West.

In many respects this is not a purely industrial problem although industrial responses are essential. Rather it is a public policy issue which must be dealt with by governments since the implications are far broader than the problems of one industry – and in the case of Europe – one country. Japan *and* the West are in the process of an inevitable adjustment of their economies and their industries to meet changing comparative advantage. Japan's rapid move into assembly plants largely supplied by components sourced in Japan or from Japanese facilities in the lower-cost Asian NICs has the potential to alter significantly the balance of industrial competition and the content and flow of global trade patterns. In their present uncontrolled form Japanese assembly plants will force the West to bear the brunt of Japan's metamorphosis from an export-driven to a globalized manufacturing economy. While the West will secure short-term gains this will be at the expense of an atrophy in its long run strengths. Doing nothing now about Japan's Trojan Horse investments, and the follow-the-leader responses from Korea and Taiwan will ensure that they become the burning competitive issues of tomorrow as they will set the stage for future industrial problems for the West which could well be unmanageable.

How alarmist are these scenarios? Since the investment cycle is in its early stages there will be arguments that in time Japanese companies will integrate their plants into the infrastructure of the West. Japanese industrialists suggest that assembly plants are the first phase and will be followed in time by fully integrated operations and exports in the second phase and by R&D capabilities in the third phase[373]. Time is one thing in short supply in the West. If the quality of these investments is not increased rapidly by forceful integration they may never become part of the value-added process in the West and make a significant contribution to Western reindustrialization. On past experience over the last 15 years with assembly plants of high-technology Japanese firms which have rarely moved into the second phase and never into the final phase, it is unlikely that Japanese firms without a strong push in the right direction will voluntarily integrate assembly plants with Western suppliers or be careful not to destroy Western competitors. 'We were invited into America. They will have to adjust input and output themselves. It's up to them.'[374] If this blunt statement by Akira Soejima, Senior Managing Director of Fuji Heavy Industries, is representative of the attitudes of Japanese investors in assembly plants the West has need for concern.

Others contend that the decline in the value of the dollar and the integration of the EEC into a unified market at the end of 1992 will have a positive effect on Western competitiveness. US companies have not yet made broad-based gains in export markets as a result of their new-found cost advantage and there are concerns whether internal trade barriers can be removed throughout the Community in so short a time. A single market is unlikely to be completed by 1992. Although the implementation has advanced a long way, the political and social complexities of integrating 12 countries and more than 20 cultural groups are not merely a mechanistic process dealing only with economic issues: A truly integrated market will take considerably more time to achieve. In the meantime the EEC is likely to demand reciprocity from its trade partners and transitional protection for its industries during the critical shift from a collection of single markets to an integrated market – none of which will aid the competitiveness of EEC industries. Ironically, these two great hopes for Western competitiveness have *increased* the flow of inward investments in assembly plants as Japanese companies move to ensure that their operations are firmly inside the protectionist fortresses being thrown up by the US and the EEC.

Compounding the overall problem for the West at government level are two factors. First, neither trade bloc or their constituent states have clear industrial policies which identify the role inward manufacturing investments should play or have proactive legislation to channel investments into desired activities. Second, since economic policies, industrial structures, government, industrial and labour relationships vary significantly between the US and between the individual EEC states the Trojan Horse phenomenon will have a differential effect. With no industrial objectives for inward investment and large differences in motivation, together with limited ability to take action, there is little or no government-to-government solidarity on either the

257

effects of Japanese Trojan Horse assembly plant investments or what to do about them.

Japan's Trojan Horse investments cannot be dealt with simplistically. The West would be naive to believe that by talking a lot and doing nothing things will turn out as well as they did to a lack of response to the challenge faced by Europe from American industry in the 1960s. This is *not* the 1960s and there is no reason to believe on past trade behaviour that Japanese industry will respond in the West as favourably as did the US multinationals in Europe who, with virtually no pressure, rapidly transformed their assembly plants into fully integrated operations, transferred technology and skills, created R&D capabilities and exported European-produced products. Europe survived and prospered under the American invasion of the 1960s largely by not following Servan-Schreiber's call to action because it turned out to be unnecessary[375]. However, there is no guarantee that Europe – or for that matter the US – will be able to provide the steady increases in standards of living that they have begun to expect as a right if they follow the same relaxed policies under the onslaught of the second wave of Japanese competition spearheaded by Japanese assembly plants.

What to do? It is easy to single out foreign investment as the villain and some have already suggested that foreign investment saps economic vitality and erodes political independence[376]. This is a dangerous course to take. Open investment policies are essential to the success of a global economy at the heart of which is interdependence. It also misses the points that some foreign investments are better than others and it is not where the money comes from but what it does to improve national value-added contributions that count. The real need for the West is to develop and implement mechanisms that channel foreign investments into patterns which maximize contributions, particularly in the manufacturing sector. All countries need genuine investors but none can afford a large number of foreign investors with questionable motives who prefer only to take and give little in return.

Others suggest that increased protection is the only way to save Western markets from Japanese domination. Again this is a dangerous game to play. The world has benefited greatly from free trade and more protection would only stifle economic development. No one, with the exception of Japan, has been able to build competitive industries behind protective walls and no one, including Japan, has been willing to sell at competitive world prices behind protective barriers. Protection is bad for competition and consumers. More protection will make the West less competitive at the expense of consumers.

The West *does* need new investments which create new jobs, new skills, new technologies and new abilities to turn knowledge into new products to increase its competitiveness. But it needs equal, not junior, partnership with Japan as the price of access to its most valuable asset – its consumers. The transfer of investments without the transfer of skills and technology deprives the West of its full economic potential. Investment is a two-way street and transplanting a small number of low-skilled jobs largely funded by Western taxpayers' money to get around trade and cost barriers is a very poor exchange for access to the West's mother lode of consumers.

However, the centripetal pull of the West's markets on Japanese industry exposes Japan's 'Achilles heel'. Japan's industrial policy of relentlessly moving up the value-added chain has increased its reliance on access to the large and wealthy markets of the US and Western Europe. These are the only markets able to absorb high value-added products in quantity. Japan is now being sandwiched simultaneously between limits on its access to these key markets and by the cost advantages of manufacturers from the Asian NICs in other markets. Japan needs access to Western markets *more* than the limited access that the West has to Japan's market. Japan is clearly vulnerable to any moves in the West which endanger market access. By clearly signalling that the *price* of access is conditioned by the *quality* of manufacturing investment the West is likely to achieve a significant change in the added-value content in Japanese manufacturing investments in the West. Both the West and Japan have still to learn the fundamental rules that there are no 'free lunches' in international trade and all give and no take (in the West) and all take and no give (by Japan) are no longer acceptable forms of behaviour.

Japan's hostility is guaranteed to any change in the status quo. Provided that the West seeks only to secure a more equitable share of the value-added benefits and to provide a level playing field for its industries in return for access to its most valuable asset – its consumers – Japan will have little room to manoeuvre. The initiatives suggested in this book to control inward investments are attempts to adjust Western economies to the competitive conditions and the interventionist industrial policies which have provided Japan with much of its industrial strength and success over the last four decades. The timing for a strong Western response to Japanese Trojan Horse investments is

259

right. Japan's attitude to world trade has now become politically unsustainable and there is rising concern even within Japan itself that if Japan continues to ignore Western trade concerns a protectionist backlash would cause major industrial, and ultimately economic and social, problems in Japan itself[377].

There is no room for the ambivalence and illusion which has characterized much of the West's past response to Japanese competition. Western industry can no longer export, innovate or manage its way out of its competitive failures. The threats posed by Japanese Trojan Horse investments are not going to go away . . . and there is every indication that they will make the West's competitive problems worse.

The message is simple. Unless the West comes to grips with the complex problems posed by Trojan Horse investments and adopts a game plan which, while welcoming Japanese investments, ensures that they make strong value-added contributions through tough co-ordinated inward investment policies backed up by effective legislation there is a strong probability that the West's competitiveness will erode further. This will have a major impact on Western society and its economic and political structures as standards of living begin to fall.

The solution lies in changing political attitudes in the West by getting governments first to understand that Japanese direct investments in assembly plants are not panaceas for solving long-term national unemployment and second to develop the political will to set their own national industrial agendas rather than allowing the Japanese companies the freedom to set agendas to suit the needs of Japanese firms. If Japanese companies are able to avoid integrating their assembly plants fully and rapidly into the industrial infrastructures of the West and are allowed to manipulate their environments to replicate Japanese social and material conditions this will create fundamental industrial, social and political problems for the West.

If the West does not move forcefully and quickly to contain Japan's new initiative this could be the *ultimate challenge* to Western industrial competitiveness. The Japanese will win this last industrial confrontation if they can keep obscuring the fact that at best their assembly plants are substitutes for exports. In most respects Japanese assembly plants in their current form are the biggest 'snow-job' since the Trojan Horse. Doing nothing is no longer an option. Plants subsidized with Western taxpayers' money using Japanese-made equipment to assemble components created, designed and developed in Japan using low-skilled, low-cost Western labour make no value-added contribution to

260

the West. With lower structural costs they have the potential to decimate Western companies and turn the industrial landscape of the US and Europe into modern wastelands. If the decisions on creating new ideas, developing skills and processes, on employment and financing begin to shift from Washington and Brussels to Tokyo and Osaka how long will it take for economic and ultimately political sovereignty to follow?

The West does have options. Doing something about the problem depends largely on the courage and conviction of governments in the West. If they continue to ignore the challenge of uncontrolled Japanese investments in assembly plants and do not work together to develop effective policies on inward investments they will not be able to stop Japan making an end run on Western industry.

Japan's Trojan Horse assembly plant investments in their present low value-added uncontrolled state are a timebomb ticking away at the heart of the West's industrial competitiveness . . . and time is running out.

REFERENCES

Chapter 1
[1] See, for example, *America Versus Japan*, T.K. McCraw (ed.), Harvard Business School Press, Boston, 1986
[2] *Forbes*, 27 April 1987
[3] *Flexible Rigidities: Industrial Policy and Structural Adjustment in the Japanese Economy*, R. Dore, Stanford University Press, Stanford, 1986

Chapter 2
[4] See, for example, *A Comparative Investigation of Japanese Marketing Strategies in the British Market*, P. Doyle, J. Saunders and L. Wright, University of Warwick, 1987, and *The New Competitors*, P. Kotler, L. Fahey and S. Jatusripak, Prentice-Hall, Englewood Cliffs, 1985
[5] *The Economist*, 16 May 1987
[6] 'Japan's Drive for the European Car Market – Lessons from US Experience,' M. Wray and D. Norburn, *Long Range Planning*, Vol. 20, No. 4, August 1987
[7] *International Management*, December 1983
[8] *Japanese Manufacturing Companies Operating in Europe*, Jetro, Tokyo, 1986
[9] *Fortune*, 20 February 1984
[10] *Industrial Collaboration with Japan*, L. Turner, Routledge & Kegan Paul, London, 1987
[11] *The Financial Times*, 16 January 1984
[12] *Business Week*, 19 March 1984
[13] 'Beware Japanese Bearing Gifts', C. Lorenz, *The Financial Times*, 16 January 1984

Chapter 3
[14] *Statistical Summary of Japan's Economy 1983*, Ministry of Foreign Affairs, Tokyo, 1983

Chapter 4
[15] *Japan Versus Europe: A History of Misunderstandings*, E. Wilkinson, Penguin, London, 1983
[16] *International Herald Tribune*, 8 June 1987
[17] *The Economist*, 2 May 1987

18   *Fortune*, 24 November 1986
19   'Market Entry in Japan: Barriers, Problems & Strategies', H. Simon,
     International Journal of Research in Marketing, No. 3, 1986
20   'Who Says You Can't Crack the Japanese Market?', V.R. Alden, *Harvard Business Review*, January–February 1987
21   *Second to None: American Companies in Japan*, R.C. Christopher, Crown, New York, 1986
22   'Direct Investment in Japan as a Means of Market Entry', P.B. Buckley, H. Mirta and J.R. Sparkes, *Journal of Marketing Management*, No. 3, 1987
23   'Beyond the Japanese Export Boom', P. Drucker, *Wall Street Journal*, 8 January, 1987
24   *The Financial Times*, 17 June 1986
25   Cross-Investment: A Second Front of Economic Rivalry, D. J. Encarnation, *California Management Review*, Vol. 24, No. 2, Winter 1987
26   *The Economist*, 13 September 1986
27   *Business Week*, 18 March 1986
28   *International Herald Tribune*, 1 April 1987
29   *The Financial Times*, 22 February 1987
30   *The Financial Times*, 4 February 1987
31   *Forbes*, 29 June 1987
32   *Forbes, op. cit.*
33   *Fortune*, 25 April 1988

Chapter 5
34   *The Financial Times*, 20 May 1987
35   *The Economist*, 28 March 1987
36   *Wall Street Journal*, 16 April 1987
37   *The Financial Times*, 17 July 1987
38   *International Herald Tribune*, 21 April 1987, and *The Financial Times*, 13 May 1987
39   *The Financial Times*, 26 May 1987
40   *International Herald Tribune*, 23/24 May 1987
41   *The Financial Times*, 16 June 1987
42   *The Economist*, 11 July 1987
43   *Newsweek*, 30 March 1987

Chapter 6
44   *Business Week*, 11 May 1987
45   *White Paper on World and Japanese Overseas Direct Investment*, Jetro, Tokyo, 1987
46   *International Herald Tribune*, 6 April 1987

Chapter 7
47   *International Herald Tribune*, 16 October 1986
48   *Business Week*, 23 February 1987
49   *The Financial Times*, 2 March 1987
50   *The Financial Times*, 21 November 1986
51   *The Financial Times*, 13 April 1987
52   *The Economist*, 4 April 1987
53   *The Economist, op. cit.*

54   *Asian Wall Street Journal*, 11 December 1986
55   *Newsweek*, 13 April 1987
56   *The Economist*, 11 April 1987

Chapter 8

57   *The Financial Times*, 7 November 1986
58   *The Financial Times*, 2 September 1986
59   *Asian Wall Street Journal*, 11 December 1986
60   *Forbes*, 1 December 1986
61   *International Management*, December 1986
62   *Time*, 29 December 1986
63   *The Financial Times*, 17 July 1986
64   *Business Week*, 17 November 1986
65   *The Financial Times*, 30 October 1986, *Business Week*, 17 November 1986 and *Wall Street Journal*, 12 November 1986
66   *Time*, 29 December 1986
67   *Fortune*, 2 February 1987
68   *The Economist*, 30 August 1986
69   *The Financial Times*, 28 February 1987
70   *Business Week*, 13 July 1987, and *The Financial Times*, 31 May 1988
71   *The Financial Times*, 27 July 1987
72   *International Management*, December 1986, and *Business Week*, 23 February 1987
73   *The World in 1987*, Economist Intelligence Unit, December 1986
74   *The Financial Times*, 3 March 1987, and *Fortune*, 30 March 1987
75   *Wall Street Journal*, 7 October 1986
76   *Wall Street Journal*, 4 February 1987
77   *The Financial Times*, 4 March 1987
78   *International Herald Tribune*, 14 August 1987
79   *The Financial Times*, 27 July 1987

Chapter 9

80   *Business Week*, 11 August 1986
81   *International Herald Tribune*, 29–30 November 1986
82   *Fortune*, 16 March 1987
83   *The Financial Times*, 9 January 1987
84   *Wall Street Journal*, 11 August 1986, and *Forbes*, 29 December 1986
85   *Business Week*, 19 January 1987
86   *Business Week*, 11 August 1986
87   *International Herald Tribune*, 19 March 1987
88   *Fortune*, 2 March 1987
89   *Fortune*, op. cit.

Chapter 10

90   *Business*, April 1986
91   *The Financial Times*, 8 June 1987
92   *The Financial Times*, 10 June 1987
93   *The Economist*, 19 July 1986

94   *Asian Wall Street Journal*, 13–14 March 1987
95   *Business*, April 1986
96   *Asian Wall Street Journal*, 13–14 March 1987
97   *International Herald Tribune*, 19 March 1987 and 7 December 1988
98   *The Economist*, 30 June 1984
99   *The Financial Times*, 28 February 1987, and *Business Week*, 7 March 1988
100   *The Financial Times*, 4 March 1986
101   *Business Week*, 9 June 1986
102   *The Financial Times*, 30 August 1986
103   *The Economist*, 30 August 1986
104   *Fortune*, 30 March 1987

Chapter 11
105   *The Financial Times*, 30 July 1986
106   *The Financial Times*, 7 July 1986
107   *The Financial Times*, 9 August 1986
108   *The Financial Times*, 12 July 1986
109   *Japanese Manufacturing Companies Operating in Europe*, Jetro, Tokyo, 1986
110   *Wall Street Journal*, 19 August 1986
111   *Wall Street Journal*, 11 August 1986, and *Asian Wall Street Journal*, 14 November 1988
112   *Business Week*, 5 August 1987
113   *International Management*, March 1985
114   *The Economist*, 16 August 1986
115   *Fortune*, 1 September 1986
116   *The Financial Times*, 1 July 1986
117   *Business Week*, 14 July 1986, and *Wall Street Journal*, 24 October 1986
118   *Japanese Manufacturing Companies Operating in Europe*, op. cit.

Chapter 12
119   *OECD Science and Technology Indicators*, No. 2 – R&D, Invention and Competitiveness', Paris, 1986
120   *Wall Street Journal*, 4 March 1986
121   'Comparing R&D Strategies of Japanese and US Firms', S.B. Johnson, *Management Review*, Vol. 25, No. 3, Spring 1984
122   *International Herald Tribune*, 14 July 1984
123   *The Financial Times*, 25 July 1986
124   'Competing with the Japanese Approach to Technology', J. Prentice, *Long Range Planning*, Vol. 17, No. 2, 1984
125   'Japanese Manufacturing Techniques: Their Importance to US Manufacturers', K. Suzuki, *Journal of Business Strategy*, Vol. 5, No. 3, 1985
126   *Fortune*, 13 October 1986, and *Business Week*, 11 July 1988
127   *International Management*, October 1984
128   *The Economist*, 23 August 1986
129   *The Economist*, op. cit.
130   *Wall Street Journal*, 28 August 1986
131   *The Economist*, 23 August 1986

132 *Community Competitiveness in High Technology: The United States, the European Community and Japan – Trade and the World Economy*, B. Cardiff, Reading University, 22–23 September 1986
133 *Wall Street Journal*, 1 February 1985

Chapter 13
134 *Competition in Global Industries*, M.E. Porter (ed.), Harvard Business School Press, Boston, 1986
135 *European Management Journal*, Vol. 4, No. 1, 1986

Chapter 14
136 *Wall Street Journal*, 18 May 1983
137 'Lifetime Employment in Japan: Exploiting the Myth', T.E. Mather, *Business Horizons*, November–December 1985
138 *Wall Street Journal*, 18 May 1983
139 'Alliance: The New Strategic Focus', B.G. James, *Long Range Planning*, Vol. 18, No. 3, 1985
140 *Time*, 16 July 1986
141 *Wall Street Journal*, 11 August 1986
142 *Fortune*, 13 October 1986
143 *The Financial Times*, 22 July 1986
144 *The Financial Times*, 14 August 1986
145 *The Financial Times*, 16 February 1987
146 *The Financial Times*, 5 August 1986
147 *Business Week*, 5 August 1987
148 *The Financial Times*, 22 July 1988

Chapter 15
149 *The Financial Times*, 19 August 1986

Chapter 16
150 *Wall Street Journal*, 21 September 1987

Chapter 17
151 *Buying into America*, M. and S. Tolchin, Times Books, New York, 1988
152 'The Changing Geography of Japanese Foreign Direct Investment in Manufacturing Industry: A Global Perspective', P. Dicken, *Environment and Planning*, Volume 20, 1988

Chapter 18
153 *Wall Street Journal*, 15 September 1986
154 *Wall Street Journal*, 9 September 1986
155 'Market Research the Japanese Way', J.K. Johansson and I. Nonaka, *Harvard Business Review*, May–June 1987
156 *The Financial Times*, 30 July 1986
157 *Business Week*, 26 August 1985
158 *Business Week*, 20 August 1984
159 *Business Week*, 14 July 1986
160 *Business Week, op. cit.*
161 *Wall Street Journal*, 8 January 1987, and *Forbes*, 24 August 1987

162   *The Financial Times*, 3 October 1986
163   Council Regulation (EEC) No. 1022/188 of 18 April 1988
164   *Business Week*, 9 June 1986
165   *Business Week, op. cit.*
166   *Business Week*, 14 July 1986
167   *Business Week*, 9 June 1986
168   *Wall Street Journal*, 17 December 1986

Chapter 19
169   *The Financial Times*, 24 September 1986
170   *Business Week*, 14 July 1986
171   *The Economist*, 13 December 1986
172   *Business Week*, 14 July 1986, and *International Management*, July–August 1987
173   *Business Week, op. cit.*
174   *Time*, 23 May 1986
175   *The Financial Times*, 27 August 1986
176   'Japanese Transplants: A New Model for Detroit', R.R. Rehdner, *Business Horizons*, January–February 1988
177   See, for example, *Japanese Participation in British Industry*, J.H. Dunning, Croom-Helm, London 1986, and *The Threat of Japanese Multinationals*, L.G. Franko, Wiley, New York, 1983
178   *Direct Foreign Investments*, K. Kojina, Croom-Helm, London, 1978
179   'The Japanese at Work: Illusions of the Ideal', P. Briggs, *Industrial Relations Journal*, Volume 19, No. 1, 1988
180   'Japanese Manufacturing Techniques and Personnel and Industrial Relations Practice in Britain: Evidence and Implications', N. Oliver and B. Wilkinson, *Industrial Relations Journal* (forthcoming)
181   *Los Angeles Times*, 10 and 12 July 1988
182   *Under Japanese Management: The Experience of British Workers*, M. White and M. Trevor, Heinemann, London, 1983, and 'The Japanisation of Production and Industrial Relations at Lucas Electrical', P. Turnbull, *Industrial Relations Journal*, Volume 17, No. 3, 1986
183   *The Financial Times*, 28 January 1988
184   *Japanese Direct Investments in the EEC: Effects of Integration*, J.L. Morris, 1987 (Background Report to DGI/EEC, Brussels)
185   White Paper on World Direct Investment, Jetro, Tokyo, 1988
186   'The Who, Why and Where of Japanese Manufacturing Investments in the UK', J. Morris, *Industrial Relations Journal*, Volume 19, No. 1, 1988
187   *Wall Street Journal*, 31 March 1987
188   'Japan's Drive for the European Car Market: Lessons from US Experience', M. Wray and D. Norburn, *Long Range Planning*, Vol. 20, No. 4, August 1987
189   *Wall Street Journal*, 28 August 1986 and 13 September 1986
190   *The Financial Times*, 28 January 1988
191   *The Financial Times*, 30 June 1987
192   *The Economist*, 28 May 1988
193   *Business Week*, 14 July 1986
194   *Wall Street Journal*, 7 October 1986

[195]   *The Financial Times*, 1 July 1986
[196]   *The Financial Times*, 10 January 1987
[197]   *The Economist*, 27 October 1984
[198]   *The Financial Times*, 30 July 1986
[199]   *The Financial Times*, 28 January 1988
[200]   *The Financial Times*, 27 August 1986
[201]   *The Financial Times, op. cit.*
[202]   *Wall Street Journal*, 25 March 1984
[203]   *The Financial Times*, 1 July 1986
[204]   Jetro 1988, *op. cit.*, and *Forbes* 25 August 1986
[205]   *Fortune*, 1 September 1986
[206]   *The Economist*, 23 May 1987
[207]   EEC 1022/88, *op. cit.*
[208]   J.L. Morris, *op. cit.*
[209]   *Business Week*, 9 June 1986
[210]   *Time*, 26 March 1986
[211]   *The Financial Times*, 10 January 1987
[212]   *Newsweek*, 30 May 1988
[213]   *The Financial Times*, 9 October 1987
[214]   *Business Week*, 28 July 1986, and *International Herald Tribune*, 28 March 1988
[215]   'Japanese Overseas Investment: The New Challenge', F.E. Marsh, EIU, No. 142, 1985, and *Fortune*, 22 December 1986
[216]   *The Financial Times*, 5 August 1987
[217]   *The Financial Times*, 1 July 1986

Chapter 20

[218]   *The Economist*, 27 April 1985
[219]   *Business Week*, 26 August 1985
[220]   'The Japanese are here – For better or worse?', J.L. Morris, *Welsh Economic Review*, Volume 1, No. 1, 1988
[221]   Wray and Norburn, *op. cit.*
[222]   *The Financial Times*, 14 August 1986
[223]   *Time*, 24 November 1986
[224]   *Wall Street Journal*, 17 December 1986
[225]   *The Financial Times*, 2 July 1986
[226]   *The Financial Times*, 12 June 1986 and 5 February 1987
[227]   *Business Week*, 9 June 1986
[228]   *Wall Street Journal*, 26 June 1986
[229]   'The Japanisation of British Industry', S. Ackroyd, G. Burrell, M. Hughes & A. Whitacker, *Industrial Relations Journal*, Vol. 19, No. 1, 1988
[230]   Ackroyd *et al., op. cit.*
[231]   'Invitation to Sunderland: Corporate Power and the Local Economy', S. Crowther and P. Garrahan, *Industrial Relations Journal*, Vol. 19, No. 1, 1988
[232]   EEC 1022/88, *op. cit.*

Summary

[233]   *South*, February 1987, and *The Economist*, 26 March 1988

Chapter 21

[234] *The Financial Times*, 13 May 1987
[235] *The Economist*, 21 February 1987
[236] *Business Week*, 3 March 1986
[237] *The Economist*, 20 December 1986
[238] *Business Week*, 27 April 1987
[239] *Business Week*, 3 March 1986

Chapter 22

[240] 'An Industrial Policy of the Right', R.B. Reich, *McKinsey Quarterly*, Spring 1984
[241] *The Financial Times*, 26 June 1987
[242] *The Management Challenge: Japanese Views*, L.C. Thurow (ed.), MIT Press, Cambridge, 1985
[243] 'Industrial Policy: The Case for National Strategies for World Markets', R.P. Nielsen, *Long Range Planning*, Vol. 17, No. 5, October 1984
[244] *The Management Challenge: Japanese Views, op. cit.*
[245] *America v Japan*, T.K. McCraw (ed.), Harvard Business School Press, Boston, 1986
[246] *Business Week*, 1 June 1987
[247] *The Financial Times*, 11 May 1987
[248] *The Financial Times*, 10 February 1987
[249] *The Financial Times*, 26 February 1987
[250] See, for example, *The Japanese School: Lessons for Industrial America*, B. Duke, Preager, New York, 1986
[251] *Economic Prospects: East and West*, J. Winiecki, CRCE, London, 1987
[252] *The Economist*, 20 December 1986
[253] *International Management*, October 1987
[254] 'Competing with Japan's Approach to Technology', J. Prentice, *Long Range Planning*, Vol. 17, No. 2, February 1984

Chapter 23

[255] 'Managing our way to Economic Decline', R.H. Hayes and W.J. Abernathy, *Harvard Business Review*, July–August 1980
[256] *Running America's Business: Top CEO's Rethink Their Major Decisions*, R.B. Lamb, Basic Books, New York, 1986
[257] 'Do You Really Have a Global Strategy?', G. Hamel and C.K. Prahalad, *Harvard Business Review*, July–August 1985
[258] *Business Week*, 18 May 1987
[259] *Business Week*, 3 March 1986
[260] *Business Week*, 3 December 1984
[261] *The Financial Times*, 2 June 1986
[262] *The Financial Times*, 16 January 1984
[263] *Business Week*, 3 December 1984
[264] 'Joint Ventures with Japan Give Away Our Future', R.B. Reich and E.D. Mankin, *Harvard Business Review*, March–April 1986
[265] 'Has Marketing Failed or was it Never Really Tried?', S. King, *Journal of Marketing Management*, Vol. 2, No. 1, Summer 1985

266 'The Misuse of Marketing', R.C. Bennet and R.G. Cooper, *McKinsey Quarterly*, Autumn 1982

267 *Mobilizing Invisible Assets*, H. Itami with T.W. Roehl, Harvard University Press, Cambridge, 1987

268 'Another Hidden Edge: Japanese Management Accounting', T. Hiromoto, *Harvard Business Review*, July–August 1988

269 *Business Week*, 21 September 1987

270 *International Herald Tribune*, 2–3 April 1988

271 *Manufacturing Matters: The Myth of the Post-Industrial Society*, S.S. Cohen and J. Zysman, Basic Books, New York, 1987

272 *The American Samurai*, J.P. Alston, W. de Gruyter, New York, 1986

273 *A Comparative Study of US and Japanese Marketing Strategies in the British Market*, P. Doyle, J. Saunders and L. Wright, University of Warwick, July 1987

274 *Business Week*, 17 August 1987 and *Wall Street Journal*, 20 April 1988

275 *The Economist*, 4 July 1987

276 'From Competitive Advantage to Competitive Strategy', M.E. Porter, *Harvard Business Review*, May–June 1987

277 *The Financial Times*, 24 July 1986

278 *Business Week*, 18 May 1987

279 *Business Week*, 3 March 1986

280 *Business Week, op. cit.*

281 *Wall Street Journal*, 3 August 1987

282 *Wall Street Journal*, 29 September 1987

283 *The Economist*, 14 March 1987

284 *Management Today*, September 1987

285 *The Financial Times*, 27 December 1986

286 *International Herald Tribune*, 3–4 December 1988

287 'Competitiveness Survey', *Harvard Business Review*, September–October, 1987

288 'The Enemy Within', G. de Jonquieres & A. Kaletsky, *The Financial Times*, 11 May 1987

Summary

289 'The Enemy Within', *op. cit.*

Chapter 24

290 *The Economist*, 14 March 1987

291 *The Economist*, 17 October 1987

292 *International Herald Tribune*, 1 August 1988

293 *White Paper on World Direct Investment*, Jetro, Tokyo, 1988

294 *The Economist*, 17 October 1987

295 *The United States–Japan Economic Problem*, F. Bergsten and W. Cline, Institute for International Economics, Washington, D.C., 1987

296 *Business Week*, 16 November 1987

297 *The Financial Times*, 26 August 1987

298 *The Financial Times*, 31 May 1988, and *Forbes*, 22 August 1988

299 *The Economist*, 9 August 1986

300 *Forbes*, 27 April 1987

[301]   *The Economist*, 13 September 1986
[302]   *Trade Policy for Troubled Industries*, G.C. Hofbauer and H.E. Rosen, Institute for International Economics, Washington, D.C., 1986
[303]   *Hard Heads, Soft Hearts*, A.S. Blinder, Addison-Wesley, Connecticut, 1987
[304]   *World Bank Development Report 1986*, Washington, D.C., 1986
[305]   *Forbes*, 27 April 1987
[306]   *The Economist*, 13 September 1986
[307]   'Why Protectionism Doesn't Pay', R.Z. Lawrence and R.E. Litan, *Harvard Business Review*, May–June 1987
[308]   *Business Week*, 18 September 1987
[309]   *The Economist*, 31 January 1987
[310]   *Business Week*, 22 June 1987 and 20 June 1988
[311]   *Wall Street Journal*, 26 March 1987
[312]   *Wall Street Journal*, 16 June 1987
[313]   *The Financial Times*, 6 July 1987
[314]   *The Financial Times*, 12 July 1987, and *Business Week*, 11 July 1988
[315]   *International Herald Tribune*, 13 November 1987
[316]   'From Trade To Global Investment', P. Drucker, *Wall Street Journal*, 26 May 1987
[317]   *Wall Street Journal*, 27 August 1987
[318]   'The Changing World Economy', P. Drucker, *McKinsey Quarterly*, Autumn 1986
[319]   'From Trade To Global Investment', *op. cit.*
[320]   'Do You Really Have A Global Strategy?' G. Hamel and C.K. Prahalad, *Harvard Business Review*, July–August 1985
[321]   'How the Japanese Write Their Own Rules of the Game', C. Lorenz, *The Financial Times*, 11 October 1985
[322]   'The State of Strategic Thinking', M.E. Porter, *The Economist*, 23 May 1987
[323]   'Do You Really Have A Global Strategy?', *op. cit.*
[324]   *Mobilizing Invisible Assets*, H. Itami with T.W. Roehl, Harvard University Press, Cambridge, 1987
[325]   *The Financial Times*, 24 November 1987
[326]   *International Management*, March 1987
[327]   *The Financial Times*, 7 December 1987

Chapter 25
[328]   'Only Retaliation Will Open Up Japan', R.T. Green and T.L. Larsen, *Harvard Business Review*, November–December 1987
[329]   *International Herald Tribune*, 21 January 1988
[330]   *Frontiers of Management*, P. Drucker, Harper & Row, New York, 1986

Chapter 26
[331]   *Fortune*, 9 November 1987
[332]   *Asian Wall Street Journal*, 7–8 November 1986
[333]   *The Economist*, 15 and 20 October 1988
[334]   *The Financial Times*, 28 January 1988
[335]   *The Financial Times, op. cit.*

336 *The Financial Times*, 3 December 1988
337 *The Economist*, 24 October 1987
338 *The Financial Times*, 29 September and 13 October 1988
339 *The Financial Times*, 22 October 1987
340 *Los Angeles Times*, 12 July 1988
341 *The Financial Times*, 7 December 1987
342 *The Economist*, 14 November 1987
343 *The Economist*, 19 September 1987
344 *The Financial Times*, 14 October 1986
345 *The Financial Times*, 15 December 1987
346 Council Regulation (EEC) No. 1022/88, 18 April 1988
347 1022/88 and 1021/88, *op. cit.*
348 *Business Week*, 9 February 1987
349 *The Economist*, 24 October 1987 and 8 October 1988
350 *Business Week, op. cit.*
351 *The Financial Times*, 16 December 1987
352 *The Financial Times*, 5 March 1987
353 *The Financial Times, op. cit.*
354 *The Economist*, 12 March 1988
355 *Business Week*, 5 October 1987
356 *The Financial Times*, 13 November 1987
357 See 'Japan's Global Challenge in Electronics; The Philips Response', C.J. Van der Klugt, *European Management Journal*, Vol. 4, No. 1, 1986
358 *International Herald Tribune*, 28 March 1988

Chapter 27

359 *The Financial Times*, 16 February 1987
360 *Business Week*, 11 January 1988
361 *The Financial Times*, 4 November 1987
362 *Business Week*, 27 April 1987
363 See, for example, 'Cooperating to Compete Globally', M.V. Perlmutter and D.A. Heenan, *Harvard Business Review*, March–April 1986, and *Triad Power*, K. Ohmae, The Free Press, New York, 1985
364 For example, 'Joint Ventures with Japan Give Away Our Future', R.E. Reich and E.D. Mankin, *Harvard Business Review*, March–April 1987, and 'Japanese Alliances: In Search of Reality', C. Lorenz, *The Financial Times*, 21 November 1986

Chapter 28

365 Council Regulation (EEC) NO. 1761/87, 22 June 1987
366 *Business Week*, 11 July 1988
367 *International Herald Tribune*, 14 October 1988
368 *The Financial Times*, 16 February 1987
369 *The Financial Times*, 6 October 1988
370 *The Financial Times*, 22 July 1988

Chapter 29

[371] *The Financial Times*, 27 August 1986

[372] K. Ohmae, *Triad Power*, The Free Press, New York 1985

[373] *Western Mail*, 27 January 1988

[374] C. Rapoport and K. Done, 'On the Way to a Glut', *The Financial Times*, 17 March 1988

[375] *The Financial Times*, 3 March 1987

[376] M. and S. Tolchin, *Buying into America*, Times Books, New York, 1988

[377] *International Herald Tribune*, 29 September 1987

BIBLIOGRAPHY

Abegglen, J.C., *The Strategy of Japanese Business*, ABT Books, Cambridge, 1984

Abegglen, J.C. and Stalk, G. *Kaisha: The Japanese Corporation*, Basic Books, New York, 1985

Alston, J.P., *The American Samurai*, W. de Gruyter, New York, 1986

Bergsten, F. and Cline, W. *The United States–Japan Economic Problem*, Institute for International Economics, Washington, D.C., 1987

Blinder, A.S., *Hard Heads, Soft Hearts*, Addison-Wesley, Connecticut, 1987

Booz, Allen & Hamilton, *Direct Foreign Investment in Japan: The Challenge for Foreign Firms*, Tokyo, 1987

Boranson, J., *The Japanese Challenge to US Industry*, Lexington Books/D.C. Heath, Massachusetts, 1981

Braddon, R., *The Other 100 Years' War: Japan's Bid for Supremacy – 1941–2041*, Collins, London, 1983

Christopher, R.C., *Second to None: American Companies in Japan*, Crown, New York, 1986

Cohen, S.D., *Uneasy Partnership: Competition & Conflict in US–Japan Trade Relations*, Ballinger, Cambridge, 1986

Cohen, S.S. and Zysman, J., *Manufacturing Matters: The Myth of the Post-Industrial Society*, Basic Books, New York, 1987

Davidson, W.H., *The Amazing Race*, John Wiley, New York, 1984

Dore, R.F., *Flexible Rigidities: Industrial Policy and Structural Adjustment in the Japanese Economy*, Stanford University Press, Stanford, 1986

Doyle, P., Saunders, J. and Wright, L., *A Comparison of Japanese Marketing Strategies in the British Market*, University of Warwick, 1987

Drucker, P., *The Frontiers of Management*, Harper & Row, New York, 1986

Dunning, J.H., *Japanese Participation in British Industry*, Croom-Helm, London, 1986

The Economist Intelligence Unit, *The World in 1987*, EIU, London, 1986; *The World in 1988*, EIU, London, 1987

Fields, G., *From Bonsai to Levis*, Macmillan, New York, 1983

Finn, R.B. (Ed.), *US–Japan Relations: Learning from Competition – Annual Review 1985*, Transaction Books, New York, 1986

Franko, L.G., *The Threat of Japanese Multinationals; How the West can Respond*, Wiley, New York, 1983

Hofbauer, G.C. and Rosen, H.E., *Trade Policy for Troubled Industries*, Institute for International Economics, Washington, D.C., 1986

Hofheinz, R. and Calder, K.E., *The Eastasia Edge*, Basic Books, New York, 1982

Hunt, V.D., *Mechatronics: Japan's Newest Threat*, Methuen, New York, 1988

Itami, H. with Roehl, T.W., *Mobilizing Invisible Assets*, Harvard University Press, Cambridge, 1987

Jetro, *Japanese Manufacturing Companies Operating in Europe*, Jetro, Tokyo, 1986

Kojina, K., *Direct Foreign Investment*, Croom-Helm, London, 1978

Kotler, P., Fahey, L. and Jatusripak, S., *The New Competitors*, Prentice-Hall, Englewood Cliffs, 1985

Kujawa, D., *Japanese Multinationals in the US: Case Studies*, Praeger, New York, 1986

Lamb, R.B., *Running America's Business*, Basic Books, New York, 1986

Marsh, F.E., *Japanese Overseas Investment: The New Challenge*, Economist Intelligence Unit, No. 142, London, 1985

McCraw, T.K. (Ed.), *America versus Japan*, Harvard Business School Press, Boston, 1986

Morishima, M., *Why Japan Succeeded*, Cambridge University Press, Cambridge, 1982

Morris, J., *Japanese Investment in the EEC: The Effects of Integration*, Background Report to DG1, EEC, Brussels, 1987

OECD, *OECD Science and Technology Indicators: No. 2 R&D Invention and Competitiveness*, OECD, Paris, 1986

Ohmae, K. *Beyond National Borders: Reflections on Japan and the World*, Dow Jones-Irwin, Homewood, 1987

Ohmae, K. *Triad Power*, The Free Press, New York, 1985

Pascale, R.T. and Athos, A.G., *The Art of Japanese Management*, Warner Books, New York, 1981

Pepper, T., Janow, M.E. and Wheeler, J.W., *The Competition: Dealing with Japan*, Praeger, New York, 1985

Porter, M.E. (Ed.), *Competition in Global Industries*, Harvard Business School Press, Boston, 1986

Prestowitz, C., *Trading Places: How We Allowed Japan to Take the Lead*, Basic Books, New York, 1988

Sakiya, T., *Honda Motor*, Kodensha, New York, 1982

Sasa, M. and Kirby, S., *Japanese Industrial Competition to 1990*, ABT Books/EIU, Cambridge, 1984

Servan-Schreiber, J.J., *The American Challenge*, Atheneum, New York, 1968

Sethi, S.P., Namiki, N. and Swanson, C.L., *The False Promise of the Japanese Miracle*, Marshfield, 1984

Schlossstein, S. *Trade War*, Congdon & Weed, New York, 1984

Shimizu, R., *The Growth in Firms in Japan*, Keio Tsushin, Tokyo, 1980

Takamiya, S. and Thurley, K., *Japan's Emerging Multinationals*, University of Tokyo Press, Tokyo, 1985

Tolchin, M. and S., *Buying into America*, Times Books, New York, 1988

Tung, R.L. (Ed.), *Strategic Management in the US and Japan: A Comparative Analysis*, Ballinger, Cambridge, 1986

Trevor, M., *The Internationalization of Japanese Business*, Campus/Westview, Frankfurt, 1987

Turner, L., *Industrial Collaboration with Japan*, Chatham House Papers 34, Royal Institute of International Affairs, Routledge & Kegan Paul, London, 1987

Wilkinson, E., *Japan versus Europe*, Penguin, London, 1983

Winieck, J., *Economic Prospects: East and West*, CRCE, London, 1987

Wolf, M.J., *The Japanese Conspiracy*, Empire Books, New York, 1983

World Bank, *Development Report 1986*, Washington, D.C., 1986

White, M. and Trevor, M., *Under Japanese Management: The Experience of British Workers*, Policy Studies Institute, London, 1983

Yoshino, M.Y., *The Japanese Marketing System: Adaptations & Innovations*, MIT Press, Cambridge, 1979

Yoshino, M.Y., *Japanese Direct Investments in the United States*, Praeger, New York, 1987

Yoshino, M.Y. and Lifson, T.B., *The Invisible Link: Japan's Sogo Shosha & The Organization of Trade*, MIT Press, Cambridge, 1986

INDEX

The Mercury titles on the pages that follow may also be of interest. All Mercury books are available from booksellers or, in case of difficulty, from:

Mercury Books
W.H. Allen & Co. Plc
Sekforde House
175/9 St John Street
London EC1V 4LL

Further details and the complete catalogue of Mercury business books are also available from the above address.

THE DECLINE AND RISE OF BRITISH INDUSTRY

By David Clutterbuck and Stuart Crainer

Britain's lengthy industrial decline . . .

'The prime reason for decline, no question about it, has been the anti-industry bias of the past 100 years.' – *Lord Young, Secretary of State for Trade and Industry*

Britain's recent dramatic rise . . .

'In a turnaround barely imaginable a decade ago, the 20th century's archetype of unstoppable industrial decline has suddenly stopped declining and come roaring back.' – *Fortune magazine*

Has Britain *really* recovered from its decades-long industrial decline? What has to be done to maintain the recovery? And how did our industry become so uncompetitive in the first place?

Here are the facts and the statistics behind the collapse of British industrial power and influence between the end of the Second World War and the late 1970s, and the subsequent return to apparent health in the Thatcherite years.

The authors have interviewed people from all sides of industry – the chief executives of many of Britain's largest companies, trade union leaders, politicians of all major parties and prominent academics.

Views vary widely on the causes of the decline; yet there is a remarkable degree of agreement as to what needs to be done to continue the recovery. *Continue* is the key word, for though the patient is off the critical list, he is far from dancing with rude health.

'*The Decline and Rise of British Industry* is an important book. It makes an important contribution to our understanding of what has happened and what is happening to our industry – and thus to the courage and conviction which business leaders must show in the coming years.' – *Sir John Hoskyns, Director General, Institute of Directors.*

ISBN 1–85251–030–7

£15.00

TURNAROUND

How twenty well-known companies came back from the brink

Edited by Rebecca Nelson with David Clutterbuck

Turnaround brings together 20 companies from Britain, Italy, Holland, Eire, Scandinavia, France and West Germany, all of which have one thing in common. All have either been brought to the brink or have stagnated rapidly to an extent where crisis action was essential. Most of these companies have undergone a radical change in circumstances; some are still in the throes of a long and painful recovery.

The studies cover a wide spectrum of manufacturing and service industries. They are presented in an anecdotal, accessible style, in most cases from the perspective of the executive responsible for turning the heavy economic losses into healthy profits. They demonstrate clearly the dilemma facing the crisis chief executive who must learn to act quickly, decisively, accurately, and often ruthlessly, because he does not have the margin for error which usually accompanies comfortable profit.

This book will provide valuable insights to other managers who may have the responsibility of crisis leadership thrust upon them.

ISBN 1–85251–090–1

£12.95

WHO CARES WINS

How to unlock the hidden potential in people at work . . . and turn ordinary companies into winners.

By Peter Savage, with foreword by Sir John Egan,
Chairman of Jaguar Cars

Today's winner is without question the company that shows how to utilise the men and women at its disposal more effectively than its competitors can utilise theirs. In *Who Cares Wins*, a practical guidebook to modern management, Peter Savage draws on his own extensive experience to explain how anyone can master the art of group motivation. His step-by-step outline of the key to effective man-management looks at the problems and challenges confronting modern managers and supervisors at every level from the chief executive down, and considers how recent theories of 'excellence' can be transformed into practical and profitable reality.

Savage looks in detail at the right ways and wrong ways of approaching personal relationships at work. He explains how to create a platform for change, then looks at how it can be used, with spectacular results, to unlock unexpected extra energy from colleagues and employees. He identifies this crucial hidden energy as 'discretionary potential' – that piece of ourselves we all take to work but more often than not don't bother to apply. We all know already there are more effective ways of working within organisations large and small: *Who Cares Wins* is the story of how to achieve them.

ISBN 1–85251–070–6   **£12.95**